BK 174.4 S532
STUDIES IN FAIR COMPETITION
/SHARP, FRA
D0886818

BUSINESS ETHICS

The Century Studies in Economics
WILLIAM H. KIEKHOFER, EDITOR

BUSINESS ETHICS

STUDIES IN FAIR COMPETITION

BY

FRANK CHAPMAN SHARP
EMERITUS PROFESSOR OF PHILOSOPHY
UNIVERSITY OF WISCONSIN

AND

PHILIP G. FOX
ASSOCIATE PROFESSOR OF BUSINESS ADMINISTRATION
UNIVERSITY OF WISCONSIN

APPLETON-CENTURY-CROFTS, INC.
NEW YORK

681-10

PRINTED IN THE UNITED STATES OF AMERICA

PREFACE

This book deals with the right and wrong of the transactions that take place in the competitive business world. It inquires what the honorable business man will do and will refuse to do from moral considerations in the course of the day's work. A complete study of this subject would require a far larger volume than it has seemed desirable to prepare. The authors have therefore deliberately confined themselves to a small group of intimately related problems. The basis for inclusion in this group has been the fundamental character of the principles involved, the closeness of the connection between them, the importance of their application to present-day business life, and also the amount of the existing literature on the subject. These considerations, particularly the last, account for the exclusion of the monopoly problem, of any direct and systematic treatment of the conflict between labor and capital, and of the more general problems concerning the relations between employer and employee.

These same considerations, together with the fact that we are dealing with moral principles, not social machinery, explain the absence of any treatment of the varied proposals that are being made in the interest of economic and social reform, particularly those which depend upon the intervention of government in business affairs. These include alike the experiments of the "New Deal" and the speculations of Socialism, with whatever lies between. Whether the competitive system is destined to persist or is in the process of decay, it is, at any rate, still with us; and for the present, at least, we must all meet the situations which it creates. A study of these situations will serve not merely to prepare us for action today; it is essential for the guidance of our thought in shaping the world of tomorrow. Those who believe it possible and desirable to create a new economic society need to understand the existing system in all its aspects, including the ethical, as completely as do those who expect to dwell in it permanently.

At first glance the reader may be disposed to think that, notwithstanding the promise contained in the title, the authors have laid more stress upon unfair methods of competition than on the determination of what constitutes fairness. It is true that the descriptions of the former bulk larger in our text than does our account of the latter. This, however, is due in part to the fact that while normally there is but one way, or at most a limited number of ways, of directly reaching a destination, there are many ways of missing it; one right course and many possible wrong ones. In addition, we are moved by the conviction that nothing in the world can be really understood except as seen in the light of what it excludes. Our aim throughout has been constructive. It has sought as its ultimate goal the discovery of what modes of positive action the spirit of fairness requires in its application to business life.

We have made it a practice throughout this study to compare our conclusions with the opinions of the courts. Law and ethics are not identical; but they are very intimately related and cover to a large extent the same ground, inasmuch as law is, or aims to be, the administration of justice. Judges, to be sure, must base their decisions on precedents. But every precedent was once a new case. It attained the authority which makes it a precedent, and in the long run it retains this authority, because it has commended itself to the reason and conscience of succeeding generations of judges and, in addition, enjoys at least the tacit support of the public, which possesses the power through legislation to annul old precedents or create new ones. Hence we have thought it might prove both useful and interesting to the reader to compare our findings with the decisions of judicial tribunals. In the preparation of this part of our work we have received very valuable assistance from Professor Malcolm P. Sharp, of the University of Chicago Law School, for which we here express our grateful acknowledgment. At the same time it must be understood that we take upon ourselves the full responsibility for every statement which we make on this subject.

Our book is the outgrowth of a course in business ethics which the senior author started in the year 1913–14. From 1926 the junior author has been associated with him in the work of teaching, as well as in the determination of the form and content of the material taught. In our class-room exercises we have employed throughout either the case method or some allied device which has elicited the opinions of our students, with the reasons therefor, on most of the topics considered in this book. The value to us of their vigorous and often penetrating discussions has been quite beyond computation. They have frequently suggested aspects of our problems which had escaped our attention; they have raised problems which might not otherwise have occurred to us; and they have supplied us with a criterion by which to select for treatment those subjects which, at least to college men and women, seem most important, interesting, and otherwise best worth examining.

Some twenty-five business and professional men, engaged in various occupations, and living in widely different parts of the United States, have read the first draft of this book, which was prepared for them in photolithographic form. We have profited greatly by their suggestions and criticisms, and take this opportunity to express our thanks for their disinterested labors and our appreciation of the interest which they have shown in our aims and the confidence in us which led them to undertake the task.

The following pages presuppose no initial acquaintance with the literature of ethical theory. The reader who is interested in the theoretical point of view which underlies our study will find it presented in the senior author's *Ethics,* particularly in the first nine chapters.

Articles by the authors appearing in Volumes XXX, XXXI, XLV, and XLVI of the *International Journal of Ethics* have dealt with a number of the subjects treated in this book.

FRANK CHAPMAN SHARP
PHILIP G. FOX

CONTENTS

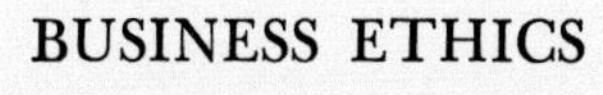

BUSINESS ETHICS

Here, then, business ethics finds a place for itself in the practical affairs of everyday life. It starts from the demonstrable fact that in business as everywhere else there are decent men who do care whether their conduct measures up to the best moral standards or not. And it believes it can be of some use to such men because all of us repeatedly do wrong when we suppose that what we are doing is perfectly right. If ethics can not make us completely objective, it can at least show us what objectivity means; it can wake us up if we have been walking in our sleep; it can show us how to go about to resolve the difficulties of a complicated situation. This does not mean that ethics can supply us with a pass-key which will enable its possessor to open all doors by a turn of the hand. What it can do, however, is—if the metaphor may be changed—to supply the captain of the ship with chart and compass. And this, it may turn out, is a great deal.

That the consequent penetration of business life by intelligence vill not be without its practical results in the end, is shown by the istory of past changes in moral standards. One of the oldest of eco-omic institutions is slavery. We find it in full operation at the awn of history, particularly in highly developed civilizations like hose of Egypt and Babylonia. It continued—wherever it paid—al-ost unquestioned for generation after generation. Finally in the ighteenth Century a few "cranks" began not merely to question its ghtness but actually to agitate against its continued existence. All ensible" people, of course, either laughed at them for their pains, , if their financial interests were affected, wished them in an insane ylum or tried to lodge them in jail. As late as the year 1800 the stitution was in full vigor—wherever it was profitable—and prom-d to live forever despite the ranting of the "cranks". Before the r 1900 it had been swept out of existence in every part of the ilized world. The causes which led to this astounding revolution re very complex. Nevertheless the application of intelligence to problem was one of them. We therefore have reason to hope t intelligent reflection may not be without its effects upon the ral standards of Twentieth Century economic life.

CHAPTER 1

IS FAIR COMPETITION POSSIBLE?

Have Business Men No Moral Standards?

The purpose of business ethics is to help us determine what business practices are right and what wrong.

It is sometimes said that business men care nothing whatever about right and wrong; all they are interested in is making money. Therefore all talk about the ethics of business is wasted breath. This characterization is a libel. There are, indeed, business men who are perfectly willing to make money through racketeering, that is, through the employment of hoodlums to murder, intimidate, and rob. But we venture to believe that they are a very small minority. And in our opinion, not one in a thousand would be willing to make even a large fortune by distributing opium and cocaine to seventh and eighth grade school children (as was done once in a certain midwest city), in order to develop a habit which would drive them into the arms of a drug store conveniently situated in the vicinity of the school. In other words, in the business world as everywhere else, everyone draws the line somewhere.

So far are business men from being without moral standards that the majority of them, like the majority of other people, have three. There is first the standard which John Smith applies to his treatment of other people—his competitors, his customers, his employees, and those from whom he purchases his supplies. There is, second, the standard which he expects them to apply to him. Finally there is the standard which he applies to other people's treatment of each other.

For example, a certain coal dealer, having made a great deal of money by selling coal in the conventional way, decided to branch out. The method he pursued was to go to small towns and propose to the sole or leading retailer to buy him out. The price offered was uniformly 50% of the value of the plant. If the unfortunate victim of this program refused the offer, he was informed that the person in question would establish a business in the same town and would match every price set by the local dealer with one 20% lower. The result was that our predatory adventurer accumulated by this and similar practices a large fortune. Instead of resting on his laurels he decided to become a national figure and invested most of his capital in an allied line. As soon as he was well under way the "big business" organization dominating the industry made essentially the same proposition to him that he had made to scores of smaller dealers. He decided to fight rather than to surrender and finally retired from the field bereft of a large part of his wealth. Thereupon he called upon High Heaven to witness the injustice with which he had been treated. The men who had robbed him of his money were no better than common thieves and ought to be behind the bars.

Now when we stop to think about it we can not fail to recognize that this sort of thing is absurd. Every child knows that what is right or wrong for one person to do is right or wrong for everyone else under the same circumstances. It was a seven year old boy who once in an old-fashioned horse car startled the other passengers by saying to his father in a loud and complaining voice: "You licked me the other day for lying to you, and you just lied to the conductor when he asked you how old I was". We all know now as well as we did when we were children that if an act is wrong for other people it is wrong for us. But we are continually forgetting this simple fact.

Thus it appears that much of the wrong-doing in the business world—as elsewhere—is done not because the doer means to do wrong, but because he believes it is "all right" *for him.* It is one of the aims of business ethics to help men free themselves from the bias of self-interest and thus to measure their own actions and the actions of other people *objectively,* that is to say, by the same standards.

A good share of the wrong acts not covered by this explanation is due to sheer thoughtlessness. In a lively book entitled *Astir,* Mr. J. A. Thayer, at one time owner of *Everybody's Magazine,* tells how

he induced *Collier's Weekly* to drive fraudulent advertisement
its columns. As advertising manager, first of the *Ladies' Hom*
nal, and then of the *Delineator,* he himself had served as a
in this movement. During his connection with the *Deline*
wrote, under the name of a friend, the following letter
Collier: "I see *Collier's* every week, and I find in it patent n
and other advertisements which the *Ladies' Home Journal*
Delineator do not insert. Why do you accept such advertisi
sure you do not need the money."

In a very short time he received the following reply
Collier himself: "Upon receipt of your letter I called our
ing staff together and we have decided, as soon as certain
are completed, to discontinue the insertion of such adv
Needless to say the promise was kept. Not merely this,
tion thus dropped led to one of the most vigorous and
campaigns against the patent medicine evil ever underta
country.

Mr. Collier was a man of the highest character and
telligence and yet he was actually serving as an agent
crooks. This case is quite typical in its way. Wrong i
being committed in perfect good faith because the pers
given serious consideration to the matter one way or
has merely conformed without question to the customs
There are thus many essentially honest business men
morals are concerned, are walking in their sleep. It
functions of business ethics to wake them up.

There is still another type of wrong-doing in the
which business ethics can perhaps do something to les
often arise which are so complex as to make it impo
the most objective, thoughtful and intelligent man
In every department of life we are compelled to
sometimes in the twilight, sometimes in the dark. C
presses in one direction, another in the other. Ir
often choose one alternative merely because to put
decision is to decide; and perhaps as often as not w

[1] J. A. Thayer, *Astir, A Publisher's Life Story* (Boston, Sma
1910), p. 205.

Does Our Competitive System Make Fair Dealing Impossible?

But the claim that the study of the ethics of business is doomed to futility is sometimes urged on grounds far more radical than blanket assertions that business men are all crooks and brutes who do not care a particle whether their actions are right or wrong. A certain school of writers maintains that all talk about ethics in the business world is useless, not so much because of the kind of men to be found there, but because of the very nature of the business system itself. This makes fair dealing absolutely impossible in the business world, regardless of what the persons concerned would like to do. Business today is conducted for the most part on the competitive basis. But, according to these critics, to talk about the right and wrong of competition is as absurd as to talk about fair kinds of kidnapping or justifiable methods of holding up pedestrians at the point of a revolver. Business, in its fundamental nature, they assert, consists in nothing else than an attempt to annihilate your competitor or to drive him out of the field, to squeeze the last dollar out of your customers, and to grip every cent in a tight fist when you are compelled to buy. But all this, they claim, is in its essential spirit nothing but war. It may be correctly represented by two kings marshalling their forces for the purpose of seizing a slice of each other's territory; or, more simply, by two dogs fighting for a bone. Always and everywhere it is the attempt to gain through the loss of another. To talk about applying the principles of morality to this brutal struggle is to talk nonsense. For morality involves precisely a certain regard for the interests of other human beings, and a consequent willingness to be satisfied with less than one has power to seize.

This description of business competition may seem plausible at first glance. But a square look will show that it distorts fundamental facts. War involves two parties, one of whom can gain, if he succeeds in gaining at all, only at the expense of the other. But business competition can not be represented by less than three parties, two competitors and a prospective purchaser. Business competition is the offering to this third party of goods or services on the part of the competitors, as a result of which the former accepts the offer most favorable to himself and is thereby better served. Business competition is thus competition for the opportunity to serve. This is true whatever may be the motives involved. In fair competition that person gains the opportunity to serve who really makes the better offer. In return he receives the reward. The loss of the second competitor is thus only indirectly due to the action of his rival. It is due primarily to the act of the purchaser in choosing what he regards as the better alternative in preference to the poorer. No wrong is thereby done the rejected competitor unless it is the duty of the purchaser to choose the less advantage rather than the greater. It is impossible to see how this can be the case under any but exceptional circumstances.

In the United States there are some six to ten million business men competing for orders from one hundred and twenty million possible customers. Let us represent the competing business men by *A* and *B*, and any given customer by *C*. Now when *A* competes with *B* for an order from *C* he of course knows perfectly well that his success will mean the loss of that order and of the consequent profits on the part of *B*. This looks like war, where, if France conquers Germany, France gains Alsace-Lorraine and Germany loses it. But in the economic struggle there necessarily enters, as we have just seen, a third factor, namely *C*, a representative of the community of consumers, the satisfaction of whose wants supplies the reason for the existence of the entire system. If *A* gets an order because he offers better goods (or terms) than *B*, then *C* is served by this transaction as well as *A*. It is true that if *A* and *D* and *E* are uniformly successful in their competition with *B*, *B* will be forced out of business. But again, if their success is due to superior service *B's* failure is normally the effect of unfitness for his job, in some sense (perhaps many senses) of the term unfitness. He is the wrong man for the place, and, as such, a burden to society; and the cost of his bungling or idleness or want of enterprise, or whatever it may be, is something which (apart from exceptional circumstances) society ought not to be required to carry. Indeed this outcome is in the interest of the man himself, for he is evidently a square peg in a round hole. If so, the competitive system will force him to look for the square hole and help him to find it, at least in the sense that it will afford a fairly reliable gauge of success in having found it. The basis of business survival should be economic efficiency; and competitive activities, if carried on as just described, derive a large measure of their justification from the fact that they afford an automatic device for determining who are the efficient. Thus whereas war is destructive, the competitive system is fundamentally constructive.

May a Bargain Be Fair to Both Parties?

In asserting that the sale of goods by *A* to *C* profits both *A* and *C*, we are denying a very ancient and still widely held notion that in trade one party necessarily gains at the expense of the other. In primitive forms of barter it is easy to see the absurdity of this opinion. *A* bakes bread, but he can not live on bread alone. If, then, he exchanges some of his bread for shoes, the baker, who needs shoes, will profit, and the shoemaker, who needs bread, will profit also. Now essentially the same thing happens today in every business transaction involving the passing of goods from one person to another. The fact that money is used to replace the exchange of directly utilizable goods makes no difference whatever in the real nature of the transaction.

What seems to have confused the Roman and the Medieval theorists, as well as some of our own contemporaries, is the fact that where money enters, goods are sold at a price greater than that at which the seller purchased them; in other words, they are sold, if possible, at a "profit". But this "profit" includes the cost of maintaining a shop or other salesroom, the risks involved in purchasing goods which one may or may not be able to dispose of, the interest on the capital locked up between the time of purchase and sale, and other items of the same kind; most important of all, payment for the time and energy spent in selecting, bringing together, and selling the wares; since the trader, like the baker and the shoemaker, must live by what he gains from his day's work. Allowing for these factors, the exchange of goods for money at a profit to the seller may easily represent a fair exchange.

When, therefore, an intelligent and honorable business man plans his buying or selling policy, he will recognize that the alternatives are not necessarily, either I kill you or you kill me, as in an interview with a tiger. He will realize the possibility of entering into business relations which are mutually advantageous, and, if he chooses, equally profitable.

But, it may be replied, the competitive system necessarily involves the "higgling of the market", the attempt as buyer to push the seller down to the lowest price to which he can be forced, and as seller, to push the buyer up to the highest possible price which can be extracted from him. The answer is that the system necessarily involves nothing of the sort. A business man may have a conception, however vague, of a fair price. He may be content to receive it as seller and to give it as buyer. This is what is sometimes called a "live and let live" policy. In accordance with such a policy he may, if he chooses, reserve the higgling of the market for situations in which he is seeking to protect himself against what he regards as an unfairly low rate of return for his goods or services, or against unfairly high demands on the part of suppliers. He need not be "money mad", but merely resolute to defend his own legitimate interests.

Such self-defense is not merely his right, it is also in a perfectly proper sense of the term, his duty. For one of the fundamental duties of man, as the whole drama of English political history demonstrates, is to stand fast in the defense of one's rights. For it is not true, as an occasional moral philosopher has apparently supposed, that it is morally praiseworthy, in determining what should be one's relations with one's fellow-men, to leave one's own interests entirely out of account. A certain amount of self-regard is a moral requirement, an asset on the balance-sheet of conscience and not a liability. To deny this is to run into the absurdities illustrated by Lecky's story of the hermit and the cake.

A certain Christian hermit was so holy as to raise the enthusiasm of an admirer to such a pitch that he presented the hermit with a magnificent cake. But the good man was far too holy to eat the cake himself, so he presented it to a rival hermit, living a mile or two away. But this hermit, unfortunately, was just as holy as the would-be benefactor, so he presented the cake to a third competitor in well-doing, who in turn presented it to a fourth, who, on his part, returned it to the first. Caught in this whirlpool of self-abnegation, the cake might have been circulating to this day had not the stern hand of death long since struck down these misguided contestants for the crown of righteousness. Obviously the moral ideal requires not the annihilation of egoism, but the setting of such limits to its expansion as are required by the rights of others. This is precisely what the racketeer and the hold-up man refuse to do.

Our conclusion is that a business man can, if he so wills, be a man of honor; that is to say, one who respects the rights and has an interest in the good of others. There may be business men who would not hesitate to rifle peoples' pockets at the point of a revolver or kidnap children if they thought they could make a dollar by the operation. The point is that there is room in the business world for an entirely different type of man. A physician is engaged in a highly competitive profession. Most physicians must live by their fees, and they do not forget to send in their bills. But the great majority of physicians, we venture to believe, fight disease and rejoice in victory not merely for the sake of their own profit but for the sake of their patients also. A business man may, if he will, take precisely the same attitude toward his customers. In fact a pretty good summary of business ethics might be formulated in the words: Treat your customers and your fellow business men as you expect your physician to treat you.

Furthermore, as a matter of fact, there are many such men, as any-one may assure himself who will pass in review those business men whom he knows personally. One of this kind,

> "the president of an old and large plant near New York City, stated with high dignity the ideals under which he and his partner managed their business:
>
> " 'We are not money mad. We strive to be worthy sons of the worthy fathers who started this manufacturing business two generations ago. We wish to see our employees prosperous, well paid, not overworked; we wish to surpass the world in the excellence of our products.' " [2]

[2] Harrington Emerson, "Twelve Principles of Efficiency", *Engineering Magazine,* XXXIX (1910), 690.

Our conclusion is that the competitive system is not inherently immoral, and therefore that it affords room for fair business practices as well as unfair ones. This conclusion, we believe, stands, regardless of whether or not some better economic system may be conceivable and attainable.

What Is Fair Competition?

What then is fair competition? The tree is known by its fruits. And the competitive system can be defended only in so far as it is an effective instrument for supplying the economic wants of human beings. But an intelligent believer in this system does not necessarily approve everything that goes on in the competitive world, any more than his preference for democracy over dictatorships necessitates his approval of every device which democracy adopts or every trick of a ward politician. His standard of judgment will be very simple in principle, however difficult many times to apply in practice. As he approves of economic competition in so far as he believes it to be, on the whole, the most effective practicable method of supplying man's economic wants, so he will approve of those particular competitive practices which most effectively supply such wants, and will condemn all those which run counter to this end. This means that he will distinguish between fair and unfair competition.

For him fair competition will consist in seeking success solely by offering better services (including terms) than his competitors. In competition conducted on this basis he will consider a man justified in injuring his competitor where this injury is an inevitable incident in the most effective service of the community; otherwise, he will not. And this "injury" will consist simply in the seller's inducing a prospective buyer to do what the buyer himself is entirely justified in doing (indeed what in a very real sense he ought to do), namely, to buy from him rather than from his rival because he is offering a superior service. *Fair business competition,* therefore, *is that form of competition in which success is sought solely on the merits of one's goods or services.*[3]

[3] Fair business activities must be fair to all concerned and therefore to one's employees. Competition which seeks to gain the favor of prospective customers by offering goods whose price is made possible by oppression of employees, whether by

The Program of the Following Study

With this standard as our clue we shall attempt to thread our way through certain portions of the labyrinth of business affairs. By "business" is here meant those activities of human beings which are employed in the production of goods destined for exchange, together with those activities involved directly in the process of exchange itself. Under "goods" are of course included services, as those of the factory worker, the clerk, or the domestic servant. An American farmer of one hundred years ago who lived in almost complete economic independence, consuming only those things which his fields and animals produced, and consuming practically all they produced, could not be considered, in so far as he neither bought nor sold, as forming a part of the business system of his day. On the other hand, the modern farmer, who sends most of his wheat or potatoes to the market, is in so far a business man.

What features of this great field we intend to examine will appear from the following considerations. Right and wrong in conduct turn on the way in which human beings treat each other. The actions in which we treat our neighbor fairly or unfairly derive their character from the relationship in which we stand to him. The most fundamental relationship in the business world is that between buyer and seller. Where competition exists another relationship at once makes its appearance, namely, that between competitor and competitor.

The usual situation which obtains in modern business life may accordingly be represented thus:

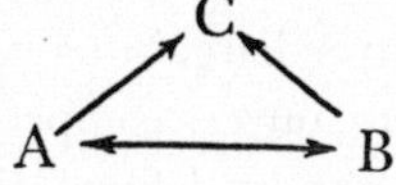

Here *A* and *B* are each offering goods or services to *C*. *A*, let us suppose, makes a sale to *C*; and thereupon *C* pays *A*. *B* seeks to sell

low wages or similar economies, is not fair competition. We shall deal with wages in the latter part of this book. In the meantime our discussion of what constitutes fair competition assumes the existence of a fair wage, and whatever else may be included in fair treatment of employees.

to *C* but fails. This relationship between *A* and *C* creates a relationship between *A* and *B*, the relationship, namely, of competitors for the favor of *C*. Thus arise the fundamental, though by no means the only problems of business ethics: What constitutes fair service, fair price and fair treatment of competitors? These problems will form the core of the following study.

We shall begin our survey with the relationship between buyer and seller. Each of these parties is morally bound to observe certain rules in the process of reaching an agreement. For example, the seller ought not to lie about the character of his goods, and the buyer ought not to lie about the prices offered him by other dealers. In this situation and many others the principles underlying fair treatment are essentially the same for both buyer and seller. On the other hand, each has certain special obligations to the other. It turns out, however, that those of the seller are more varied, more complicated, and on the whole more difficult to analyze than those of the buyer. In the interests of brevity and simplicity of presentation, therefore, we shall take the point of view of the seller throughout our discussion of this topic, and ask, What constitutes fair treatment of the prospective or actual purchaser by the supplier; or more briefly, What constitutes fair service?

The agreement to sell means, of course, the agreement to transfer goods or supply personal services in return for a specified sum of money. The second topic called for in our program would accordingly seem to be that of fair price. In the business world about us, however, outside, at least, of the field of monopoly, the amount of money actually received is determined—whether rightly or wrongly—by the play of forces which we call market conditions. But a market means not a single buyer bargaining with a single seller, but a group of buyers and sellers, buyers competing with buyers and sellers with sellers. Fair price can be defined, therefore, only in relation to the prices which are created in the market. For this reason, as will appear in its place, the problem of what constitutes fair price, as distinguished from actual price, cannot profitably be studied until we have examined not merely the relations between buyer and seller, but also those between competitor and competitor. Accordingly our second group of problems will be: What constitutes fair treatment of one competitor by another?

As was suggested above these two sets of problems cannot be kept entirely distinct. After the American Waltham Watch Company had gained a national reputation by fifty years of the highest kind of service another organization settled in the city of Waltham and sold its inferior products as Waltham Watches. Obviously it thereby swindled its customers and at the same time stole the good will of the older company, whose products had always been put on the market simply as Waltham Watches. Whether an incident like this should be treated as unfair service or unfair competition is a mere matter of convenience.

After studying the relations of the seller to his customers and his competitors we shall be prepared to deal with what is at the same time one of the most perplexing and important problems which face our world today, namely: What is a fair price? Intimately associated with this topic, as we shall see, is the problem of fair wage.

Business ethics raises many other problems besides these three. But these are the most fundamental. They will accordingly supply the subject matter of the following inquiry.

FAIR SERVICE

CHAPTER II

COMMERCIAL COERCION: YOUR CUSTOM OR BANKRUPTCY

Service in the form of supplying the economic wants of human beings involves two distinct processes. The first is production. The production of material goods includes the obtaining of raw materials; the working of them over into useful forms; transportation of the completed commodities to places where they are needed; and often storage until the time when they will be used. The second process may be called salesmanship. This consists of information and sometimes persuasion—making people aware of the existence of the goods and the nature of their uses, and awakening the desire to possess them. The first process deals primarily with material objects which are later to be sold; the second deals with human beings. The one seeks to control physical nature; the other to influence human nature.

Both production and salesmanship have their own ethical problems. The former resolve themselves in large part, as far as the producer's relations to his customers are concerned, into the duty of aiming at economy and efficiency. Any other obligations to customers that may arise during this process will come to light in the course of our examination of the duties of salesmanship. For *completely* honorable methods of selling goods will necessitate honorable practices throughout the production process, because shoddy materials and bad workmanship must be misrepresented if they are to hold their own in the competitive field. Thus it will be possible for us to reduce our study of fair service to a survey of the principles of fair salesmanship.

Before we begin our examination of selling practices, however, we shall have to give some attention to a method of disposing of goods which involves neither informing nor persuading—which indeed one hardly knows whether to call selling in any real sense of the term. It consists in forcing one's goods on those who do not wish to buy them by threatening them with ruin or something near ruin in the event of refusal. "Give me your trade and give me all of it, or I will put you out of business", is its war cry. This of course means the attempt to succeed through coercion. We shall devote the present chapter to this subject.

Murder as a Method of Competition

We begin with an incident which gave rise to a famous law suit in Eighteenth Century England, and we quote the official record of it as follows.

"Certain ship owners sent a vessel called the Bannister, with a crew on board, under the command of one Thomas Smith, and loaded with goods proper for trading with the natives, to a part of the coast of Africa called Cameroon, to trade with the natives there. While this ship was lying off Cameroon, a canoe with some natives on board came to the same for the purpose of establishing a trade, and went back to the shore. Thereupon the commander of a certain ship called the Othello, with the intention to hinder and deter the natives from trading with the said Thomas Smith for his own benefit and that of his employers, with force and arms fired from his ship a certain cannon loaded with gun powder and shot at the said canoe, and killed one of the natives on board the same. Whereby the natives of the said coast were deterred and hindered from trading with the said T. Smith, and the owners of the Bannister lost their trade." [1]

Nowadays—unless we are racketeers—we do these things in a less "messy" manner, and the hints we throw out are more delicate. One variety of the Twentieth Century up to date fashion in this kind of business activity is represented by the following incident.

The Crystal Oil Company was engaged in selling oil at retail to the citizens of Des Moines, Iowa. It delivered its goods to the homes of its customers in tank wagons. It must have given satisfactory service, for its business grew rapidly and steadily. During the first five years of its existence it obtained its oil exclusively from the Standard Oil Company, but in 1898 it decided to purchase in part from another wholesaler. At once the Standard began a campaign with the purpose of either destroying it or compelling it to give the Standard its entire trade. In the pursuit of this end it entered the retail field,

[1] Tarleton *v.* McGawley, 170 *English Reports: Full Reprint* 153.

and conducted systematic warfare against the company that dared to patronize a rival. The devices employed are thus described in the decision of the court which was called upon to pass judgment upon this method of grappling your customers to your soul with hoops of steel.

"In the prosecution of its business, the Crystal Company was accustomed to supply its customers with cards to be displayed from a window or other conspicuous place, indicating a desire to purchase oil and inviting the distributor to stop and furnish the needed supply. When the Standard entered the field its drivers were directed to give special attention to the Crystal Company's 'green cards,' and, at the outset at least, there was little or no attempt to build up a retail trade with the public generally, but to take away or destroy the trade of the Crystal Company. The Standard's drivers would make it a point to get in advance of the Crystal's wagons and wherever a green card was displayed would stop and make the sale if possible, sometimes permitting the buyer to suppose that he or she was dealing with a Crystal agent, and in other cases appropriating or carrying away the Crystal's cards. The Standard's hand in these efforts was not disclosed to the public. The drivers were instructed to do business ostensibly as independent dealers, driving their own wagons, none of which were marked with the Standard's name, though in fact the outfits were furnished and all expenses paid by it, and the entire business was carried on under the secret management of its agent, who held frequent meetings with the drivers, urging them to 'go after the green cards,' to 'hustle the green cards,' to 'go after the Crystal Oil Company', and at the same time cautioned them to 'keep quiet' about the real ownership and management. When the Crystal Company had been eliminated the manager in charge had a final meeting of the drivers at his residence, where he said, 'The fight is over and we have bought them out.' "

The fight *was* over, for having bought the material equipment of the rebellious customer for fifteen cents on the dollar the Standard at once retired from the retail trade.[2]

[2] Dunshee *v.* The Standard Oil Co., 152 Iowa 618 (1911).

The customary method of referring to the opinions of American courts is as follows. The reports of the decisions of the highest state court are referred to by citing the name of the state in question. The number of the volume precedes the name of the state, and the number of the page follows it. After this may come the date of the decision in brackets. Thus: 152 Iowa 618 (1911) means: Reports of the opinions of the Supreme Court of Iowa, Vol. 152, page 618, a decision of 1911. The reports of the cases decided by the Federal District Courts and Circuit Courts of Appeals are referred to as Fed. ("Federal Reporter") with volume and page as indicated above. The reports of case adjudged by the Supreme Court of the United States are now referred to as U.S.

References to the law journals are to be interpreted in the same manner. Thus 32 *Harv. L. Rev.* 516 means Vol. 32 of the *Harvard Law Review*, page 516.

We are not here concerned with the deception employed in this brutal campaign. We are concerned with the campaign itself. We can see little difference in principle between this high-handed demand: "Buy from me or I will ruin your business", and the action of the thug who points a revolver at your head and says, "Your money or your life".

To this statement some people will reply that a wholesaler can not be denied the right to go into the retail business if he so desires. The answer is, it makes all the difference in the world with what intent he does it.

The Place of Intent in Morality

The word intent, as here used, refers to the total foreseen or expected consequences of an act. Thus if *A* murders and robs *B*, his intent may include the following elements: (1) The enrichment of himself; (2) the destruction of *B's* life; (3) sorrow and financial loss for the family, in case *B* has a family, and *A* is aware of this fact; (4) the murderer's remaining in hiding for a period of time; (5) the risk of discovery, of a trial for murder, and consequent electrocution. That part of the intent for the sake of which the action was performed, that is to say the motive, is here represented by (1). As to (2) and (3), *A*, as we may suppose, is entirely indifferent or at most mildly regretful. (4) he doubtless dislikes, but accepts as the price of (1). The possibility represented by (5) we may be sure he decidedly dislikes, but accepts as he does (4). In this illustration the intent covers certain consequences which the actor desires, others which he dislikes, and still others to which he is indifferent. But in so far as they are foreseen, whether as certain, probable, or possible, they form part of the intent.

To discover whether a given act is right or wrong we must first ask, With what intent was it done; what consequences did the actor believe would follow his act? This method of discovering innocence or guilt we understood perfectly well even as young children; especially its corollary, namely, that consequences which we did not foresee—as when we threw a stone at a cat and broke a window instead—we ought not to be thrashed for. It is true that where failure to foresee consequences is due to carelessness or indifference on our part this failure to look before we leap may itself be morally blameworthy. But this indubitable and important fact does not concern us in this connection.[3]

May a Banker Operate a Barber Shop?

As an illustration of the fundamental role of intent in our moral judgments take the case of Tuttle *v.* Buck.[4] Here a small town banker, angered because a barber had refused to rent a shop from him, started another barber in business in the rejected premises, hired his men away from him, and "by personally soliciting and urging the [barber's] patrons no longer to employ [him], by threats of his personal displeasure and by other means", succeeded in ruining the object of his childish wrath. Upon the accomplishment of his purpose he at once closed up his own establishment. May not a banker go into the barber business? Under ordinary circumstances, certainly. But not when the intent includes the ruin of a man who had done him no wrong, and is carried through simply for the sake of ruining him. The fundamental moral question always is, not what are you doing, but what are you driving at? What are you up to?

The application of this principle to the destruction of the unfortunate Crystal Oil Company is obvious. Fair competition, as we have seen, is the attempt—or intent—to win success solely by giving better goods or service or terms than your competitor. If the Standard Oil Company had been able and willing to meet these conditions they could probably have retained their customer and need not have feared the defection of others. As it was they chose rather to follow what they probably regarded as the more profitable course and commit commercial murder.

[3] The word "intent" is here used in its exact signification—as in the language of the law. Like many other words it has more than one meaning. Thus when I say: "I intend to go to the theater this evening", I mean that I have decided to go. These two significations of the word must not be confused.

[4] 107 Minn. 145 (1909).

"Merely Crippling"

Just as I have no right to ruin a man because he refuses to adopt a policy which brings his money into my pocket, so I have no right to harm his business in any degree for the same reason. No one could excuse himself for throwing acid into a man's face or crippling him for life by saying: "I did not kill him, I merely crippled him". What is true of physical violence is true, in principle, of commercial violence of whatever kind and amount.

A threat to cripple which might or might not have led to bankruptcy is represented by the following incident in the history of the Eastman Kodak Company. At a time when this company was manufacturing and selling most of the photographic films in the United States, they found foreign manufacturers were making inroads on their market. Thereupon they acquired the Paragon, G. M. and San Jacq Laboratories, all fully equipped for film-printing and developing, the combined capacity of which was equal to that of all existing laboratories east of Chicago. Then they let it be known that they would refrain from operating these laboratories if the film printing companies would agree to use Eastman products exclusively. The presence of these huge plants, ready to go into operation at a moment's notice, induced practically all the printers of films in the country to sign the agreement.[5]

As before, the condemnation of all policies of this kind lies in the fact that they involve an attempt to succeed through other means than the intrinsic merit of the service.

The Relation of Law to Ethics

The most authoritative code of morals which we possess in the United States today is incorporated in that body of judicial opinions which constitute the common law. This code represents the carefully considered judgments of men who are not indeed experts in the theory of ethics, but who are in most instances men of ability and character who have devoted no small portion of their professional careers to determining what is right and what wrong in con-

[5] *Federal Trade Commission Decisions,* VII (1926), 434.

crete situations. Thousands of their conclusions, alike on matters moral and non-moral, have indeed been ignored until they have been forgotten; but the "leading cases"—those which are appealed to in contemporary controversies,—are those which have survived, in the main, because they have commended themselves to the critical common sense of succeeding generations. In so far as these deal with moral issues, therefore, they are to be regarded not indeed as infallible, but as worthy of high respect and careful study on the part of those who are interested in ethics.

This view of the relation of the common law to ethics may appear novel to some. We are often told that a judge does not make law but simply declares it. If so, who made the first decisions? If law is the administration of justice these original decisions represented the court's opinion as to what had been just or unjust in the conduct of the parties then at the bar, and what, if anything, ought to be done about it. Furthermore the dead man's hand does not destroy all spontaneity in later occupants of the bench. "Cases without precedent", writes Professor Gray, "are more frequent than persons not lawyers generally suppose".[6]

When such situations arise routine minds will grasp the nearest support they can find in the records of the past; in other words they will play safe at all costs. But a court composed of vigorous and courageous men, possessed of intelligence and initiative, will not hesitate to strike out on new lines and decide the issue on its merits. Examples of both kinds of decisions will be found below, in the present and in later chapters. Thus Tarleton *v.* McGawley, Tuttle *v.* Buck, and Dunshee *v.* The Standard Oil Company, all belong essentially to the latter type.[7]

It is true that the decisions of a judge can never represent his personal moral convictions with entire accuracy and completeness. In the first place there are certain precedents which he can not ignore, and whose authority he can not evade. For example, he can not enforce a promise made without "consideration", *i. e.* without a counterpromise of a return service of some sort; and this, notwithstand-

[6] John C. Gray, *Nature and Sources of Law* (New York, The Macmillan Company, 2nd ed., 1921), p. 100.

[7] See below, p. 27.

ing the fact that he himself may regard a promise as equally binding with a contract. In the second place certain actions and failures to act ("forbearances") of which he may vigorously disapprove are necessarily excluded from the purview of the law because of the impossibility of enforcement, such as respectful and affectionate care of aged parents; or because of indefiniteness of obligation, as contributions to charity, and indeed most forms of positive assistance to others. Again, judges have always to bear in mind that while they are dealing with an individual concrete situation their decision may be used as a precedent for other cases which for all their apparent similarity really call for different treatment; or it may afford a basis for future extortionate or malicious demands or threats on the part of other persons; or it may offer an opening to petty and frivolous complaints.[8]

For this and other reasons equally decisive the spheres of law and morals are not completely coterminous; but they have a common center and to a large extent the same area. In view of these facts it seems worth while to examine the opinions of the courts on the ethical problems raised in this study. Accordingly, as far as judicial decisions can be found that deal with the same situations, we shall make a practice of citing them. The reader will thus have an opportunity to compare the conclusions of the authors with those of the eminent men who have examined the situations in question from a nearly related and yet not quite identical point of view.

In accordance with this policy we turn to the attitude of the courts to the preceding forms of coercion.

Coercion and the Law

The decision of the United States Supreme Court with regard to the agreement entered into between the Eastman Kodak Company and the printers of films turned on the extent of the powers granted to the Federal Trade Commission by Congress. The court decided unanimously to uphold the order of the Commission dissolving the agreement as being in restraint of trade. But the ma-

[8] For further discussion of this subject see below, p. 78.

jority held that the Commission had exceeded its powers in ordering the Eastman Company to divest itself of its film printing laboratories. The minority, however, looking beneath the surface to the purpose for which the laboratories were acquired, namely to gain a monopoly, upheld the decision of the Commission throughout as consonant with the intention of Congress in creating it. The opinions of both majority and minority turned, in any event, upon the interpretation of a statute and throw little or no light upon the attitude of the judges toward the ethical problem involved.[9]

On the other hand in the remaining cases described above ethical considerations are the determining factors.

The earliest decision, we believe, that deals with actual murder and the threat of murder as a means of directing the streams of commerce toward oneself is that of Tarleton *v.* McGawley. The court found shooting at your competitor's customers a highly unfair method of conducting a business.

Even more fundamental in certain respects is Tuttle *v.* Buck. In this case the majority of the judges made the following declaration.

"When a man starts an opposition place of business, not for the sake of profit to himself, but regardless of loss to himself and for the sole purpose of driving his competitor out of business, and with the intention of himself retiring upon the accomplishment of his malevolent purpose, he is guilty of a wanton wrong and an actionable tort. . . . To call such conduct competition is a perversion of terms. It is simply the application of force without legal justification which in its moral quality may be no better than highway robbery."

In Dunshee *v.* The Standard Oil Company (the Crystal Oil Company case) the opinion of the Minnesota court in Tuttle *v.* Buck is quoted with approval and applied as follows.

"As we understand appellants' contention, it is that their conduct did not transgress the bounds of legitimate competition, and that so long as they kept within this limitation the question of the alleged malice or motive inspiring their acts is wholly immaterial. . . . If this be the correct view of the law, a man may excavate the earth near the boundary of his

[9] Federal Trade Commission *v.* Eastman Kodak Co. *et al.* 274 U.S. 619 (1927). Reprinted in *Federal Trade Commission Decisions,* XI (1930), 669. For the case itself, see above, p. 24.

own land for the mere purpose of seeing the foundation of the house of his neighbor slide into the pit thus prepared for it; he may dig through his own soil to the subterranean sources of his neighbor's spring or well and divert the water into a ditch, where it will serve no purpose of use or profit to himself or anyone else; if a banker or merchant, he may punish the blacksmith who refuses to patronize him by temporarily establishing a shop on the next lot and hiring men to shoe horses without money and without price, until he has driven the offending smith to come to his terms or to go out of business; and if a farmer, dependent upon a subterranean supply of water for the irrigation of his soil or watering of his live stock, he may contrive to ruin his competing neighbor by wasting the surplus not reasonably required for his own use. The laws of competition in business are harsh enough at best; but if the rule here suggested were to be carried to its logical and seemingly unavoidable extreme, there is no practical limit to the wrongs which may be justified upon the theory that 'it is business'. Fortunately, we think, there has for many years been a distinct and growing tendency of the courts to look beneath the letter of the law and give some effect to its beneficent spirit, thereby preventing the perversion of the rules intended for the protection of human rights into engines of oppression and wrong.

"Coming to the case in hand, we may concede to the appellants the undoubted right to establish a retail oil business in Des Moines, to employ agents and drivers, and send them out over the same routes and make sales to the same people with whom the Crystal Oil Company was dealing; but in so doing it was bound to conduct such business with reasonable regard and consideration for the equal right of the Crystal Company to continue its business and to continue supplying oil to such of its customers as desired to remain with it. If, however, there was no real purpose or desire to establish a competing business, but under the guise or pretense of competition, to accomplish a malicious purpose to ruin the Crystal Company or drive it out of business, intending themselves to retire therefrom when their end had been secured, then they can claim no immunity under the rules of law which recognize and protect competition between dealers in the same line of business seeking in good faith the patronage of the same people. And if, under such pretense of competition, defendants maliciously interfered with the business of the Crystal Oil Company in the manner charged, and injury to the latter was thereby inflicted, a right of action exists for the recovery of damages. [There are indeed legal precedents for the contrary position.] But we think such precedents are out of harmony with fundamental principles of justice, which, as we have said, underlie the law, as well as out of harmony with the later and better considered cases.

"No man entering or carrying on business has any right to demand protection against fair competition, and if he can not meet it and succeed he must expect to fail, and for losses and injuries resulting the law affords him no remedy. But if competition be 'war', in which 'everything is fair,' or if it be so regarded by those who participate therein, certainly the law will not give that doctrine its sanction."

Tying Contracts

The practice of threatening with ruin business organizations which refuse to respond to the crack of the whip blossomed out some fifty years ago into a regular system. This assumed several forms, the most important of which were called "tying contracts", and "full line forcing". Both depended for their effectiveness upon the possession of an actual or virtual monopoly, such as a patent, or some very popular specialty for which there was a very large and insistent demand, so that if the producer or dealer was to remain in business he must sell it, or if it was a mechanical device, use it. The tying contract required that he who purchased the indispensable commodity must buy a certain other article or other articles also; or, at all events, must refrain from buying the "tied" article or articles from any competing producer. Thus the General Electric Company, having purchased the German patents on the tungsten and tantalum electric lamps, refused to sell them to retailers who carried the older carbon filament lamps manufactured by any other electrical supply company. Similarly the Eastman Kodak Company refused to allow a retailer to handle their cameras if he sold what was at that time the far superior photographic paper produced by a competing factory.[10]

The nature of the pressure thus brought to bear upon the retailer will be realized if we remember that it is one thing to lose a sale and quite a different thing to lose a customer. Thirty years ago ten million householders were rushing to the electrical supply shops for the purpose of buying the new and economical electric lamps. Suppose an average would-be purchaser asked a dealer for tungsten lamps and was informed that he did not sell them. What would he do? Would he stop to inquire for the reasons of this apparently eccentric or—worse still—unenterprising policy? He would do nothing of the sort. He would walk out of the shop in disgust and confine his trading thereafter to the rival shop across the street.

[10] *Cf. Federal Trade Commission Decisions* XIV (1931), 527, for action against a company holding a patent on a machine for banding cigars which compelled all renters to use the bands of an affiliated organization.

But why, it may be asked, should not the dealer be glad to stock up with General Electric carbon filament lamps? The obvious answer is that his unwillingness to do so shows that either in price or quality or in some other respect the General Electric product was, in his judgment, inferior to the output of its competitors. The fundamental wrong of this practice, then, is that it consists in selling goods not on their individual merits but on the merit of some specialty which the dealer can not refuse to carry, and which is used to force upon him things he does not want to buy.

The results of this practice are bad in whichever direction you turn, except, of course, for the party that swings the whip. It destroys the chances of producers who, apart from the control of the specialty, may be as efficient as, or more efficient than those who thus seize their business; it prevents retailers who wish to select what they regard as, on the whole, the best products on the market for their customers, from doing so except under conditions which are practically prohibitive; most serious of all, it limits the field of choice for the ultimate consumer and thus directly destroys the open market. Thus goods are driven from the market not because of their inferiority, but because of some specialty by means of which the producer screens the inferiority of his other products, the unreasonableness of his prices, or whatever other characteristics prevent them from gaining favor with the public on their merits alone.

Full Line Forcing

The Hold-up. If a "tying contract", where, ordinarily, only one type of commodity is tied to the other, is morally illegitimate, still more reprehensible is the parallel practice called "full line forcing". Here the producer who happens to be in a favored position refuses to sell any of his products except as the dealer agrees to refrain absolutely from purchasing from his competitors. Thus, before the courts put a stop to the practice, the Continental Tobacco Company compelled dealers who carried any of their cigarettes to agree to handle no other brands than theirs.

It has been frequently maintained that all devices designed to force the retailer to confine his purchases to one manufacturer are not essentially methods of excluding other manufacturers from the market, but are merely methods of leading the retailer to increase the size of his orders by becoming the exclusive agent of the manufacturer; and that they are therefore not to be judged differently from exclusive agencies, which are usually held in high repute. But full line forcing differs fundamentally from the exclusive agency in purpose, method, and results. The exclusive agency grants to a selected retailer the exclusive right to handle the product in his territory. It thus protects the dealer against the competition of other retailers in connection with this one brand. For this and other reasons it is often eagerly sought by the retailer and is invariably a matter of willing agreement between the two parties. But it does not deny other manufacturers access to the territory. They have only to select another dealer to represent them, and the competition between the various brands, both as regards the manufacturers and the retailers, goes on as strenuously as before. Full line forcing, on the other hand, does not make the retailer the exclusive representative of the manufacturer, nor does it protect him in the possession of his territory. The manufacturer forces his conditions upon all of the retailers in a city, or at least upon as many of them as can be prevailed upon to accept them. Success in this endeavor accordingly means that all other manufacturers are driven out of the territory. The only competition remaining is then the competition of the dealers in attempting to outdo each other in disposing of this one brand of goods. Thus where exclusive agencies are common, the public is, for the most part, still able to obtain the offerings of various agencies; whereas under a system of full line forcing it is shut up to the use of a single line. The purpose of the one arrangement is thus to confine the local market for a single brand to one retailer; the purpose of the other is to confine the general market for a whole class of goods to one manufacturer.

The exclusive agency, moreover, is economically practicable for only a few lines; and in most of those lines it is a necessity. These include certain style products, in connection with which it would be uneconomical for a community to have many large stocks in retailers' hands, with the result of prohibitive losses due to goods going out of fashion. It is useful in the sale of many mechanical products which require technical demonstration and expert technical service, as in the case of radio, mimeographs, typewriters, automobiles, high grade lenses and the like. Where proper distribution of products requires the dealer to maintain an expert repair and demonstration service which is outside the reach of the casual dealer, the agency becomes practically necessary. Where a local territory can be adequately covered by a single firm, as in the sale of automobiles, the agency is the most economical form of distribution, and, as such, is desirable.

The Bribe. A flat refusal to sell anything except to purchasers who agree to buy everything is apt to produce dissatisfaction and give offense. Accordingly, a second and apparently less violent method was contrived for getting precisely the same results. Here the producer of the patented article or indispensable brand, instead of refusing to sell, offers a rebate upon the dealer's agreement to make no purchases from a competitor. The rebate may be payable at the time of the purchase, or it may be and usually is "deferred", that is to say, paid at intervals of six months or a year on presentation of evidence that during this period there has been no straying into forbidden pastures. Obviously this arrangement might just as well be described by saying that the retailer is charged a higher price than his competitors if he refuses to sign the agreement. Faced with a proposition of this type, he knows that if he is to remain in business his prices must be approximately those of his competitors. He knows, too, that if he elects to accept the higher price in buying, he cannot long remain in competition with a neighbor who chooses the lower prices and then cuts the prices at which he sells. It is a simple matter for the manufacturer to place the standard price at such a point that the dealer who pays it cannot hope to compete with the dealer who accepts the rebate.

This in fact is exactly what has happened again and again. Thus the Supreme Court of Massachusetts, in its decision in the well known case of Commonwealth *v.* Straus,[11] made the following statement.

"There was evidence from which the jury might find that the price named and the rebate offered (here 6%) were such as were intended by the de-

[11] 191 Mass. 549 (1906).

fendant as a practical refusal to sell any goods except upon a condition which would entitle the purchaser to the rebate and were understood by the purchaser to be so intended. Witnesses testified that it would be impossible for the purchasers to carry on business successfully on the offered terms except upon compliance with the condition which would bring the rebate."

In other words, this device was merely another form of full line forcing. Accordingly if we ask the ethical question: "What were these people up to?" the answer is simply they were pursuing a policy like that of the Standard Oil Company in the Crystal Oil Company incident—a policy of rule or ruin.

Parallels with acceptable practices are usually called upon to do service in the defense of unfair devices. In this case it has often been said that the practice in question is merely a system of getting the dealer to increase the size of his orders by confining them to one firm, thus entitling him to quantity discounts. But there is no real similarity between the two methods. In full line forcing the dealer does not receive a rebate because his purchases are so large that he is entitled to them. He receives it whether his purchases are large or small, but only on condition that he has not purchased from competing manufacturers. Thus prices are determined, *not* by the amount bought from one party but upon the amount not bought from others.

Discounts for quantity purchases have indeed been objected to by small dealers who feel called upon to defend themselves against the great buying power of large stores and chain organizations, but in general they must be regarded as quite justifiable. It is well known that it costs proportionately less to sell goods in large amounts than in small amounts. As far as packing expenses, shipping expenses, administrative and bookkeeping labor are concerned, it ordinarily costs nearly as much to sell a $50 bill of goods as a $1,000 bill. Certainly it costs far less than 10 times as much to sell a $10,000 order than to sell one for $1,000. The quantity discount is merely a means of recognizing these savings and of passing a portion of them on to the dealer who gives the orders on which the savings have been made.

When Full Line Forcing May Be Justifiable. While in principle all forms of full line forcing must be condemned, it is possible that in consequence of exceptional conditions a few of them may have a certain justification. The United Shoe Machinery Company, for example, long refused to lease its machines to anyone who in the complicated process of manufacturing shoes made use of a rival machine. The A. B. Dick Company at one time sold its mimeographing machines only to those who agreed to purchase the necessary supplies from them. The Gratz Company were manufacturers of jute and agents for the sale of steel ties, both of which were used in baling cotton. Early in 1916, and again in 1917, it refused to sell the ties without an order for the corresponding amount of jute. This it was able to do because it held a virtual monopoly of the former. The Shoe Machinery Company defended its policy by claiming that the use of the entire set of machines which it made was requisite for obtaining the best results; and that it might be held responsible for the consequent impairment of the product if the machines of its rivals were introduced at any point in the process. The Dick Company urged similar considerations. The Gratz Company attempted to justify itself by asserting that because of the scarcity of ties and the prospect of a large cotton crop at the time, it feared the marketing of the crop might be endangered if the ties should fall into the hands of speculators. It is not our province to determine the truth of these allegations. We can only say that if well founded, they might constitute the basis of a valid defense of the sales policies in question. This defense, however, would have to show that the policies were necessary, in the last resort, for the protection of the ultimate consumers.

The Law of Tying Contracts and Full Line Forcing

Both tying contracts and full line forcing were outlawed by many of the state courts in the first decade of the present century, when the practice became most common and also most flagrant in character. It was supposed by many persons, including members of the Federal Trade Commission, that they were forbidden explicitly by the Clayton Act, which was enacted by Congress in 1914. The pertinent section (III) of the latter reads as follows

"It shall be unlawful for any person engaged in commerce, in the course of such commerce, to lease or make a sale or contract for sale of goods, wares, merchandise, machinery, supplies or other commodities, whether patented or unpatented . . . or fix a price charged therefor, or discount from, or rebate upon, such price, on the condition, agreement or understanding that the lessee or purchaser thereof shall not use or deal in the goods, wares, merchandise, machinery, supplies or other commodities of a competitor or competitors of the lessor or seller, where the effect of such lease, sale, or contract for sale or such condition, agreement or understanding may be to substantially lessen competition or tend to create a monopoly in any line of commerce."

This expectation, however, was doomed to disappointment. For the Federal Courts have ruled that tying contracts "are not unlawful as opposed to public policy *per se,* but only when insisted upon in a sale by a corporation which has a monopoly".[12] On this ground the case against the Gratz Company was dismissed by the United States Supreme Court.[13] On the other hand, the tying clauses of the Dick Company and the United Shoe Machinery Corporation were declared by the same Court to be contrary to the Clayton Act because they were being used by organizations which dominated their respective fields.[14] As far as interstate commerce is concerned here is where the matter now rests. We regard this situation as unfortunate, though we realize the difficulties that might arise from a stricter interpretation of the law. However, this form of unfair competition is far less common than it was twenty years ago when the Clayton Act was passed, and as compared with many other unfair business practices is today a somewhat sporadic phenomenon.

[12] See Federal Trade Commission *v.* Paramount Famous-Lasky Corporation *et al,* 57 Fed., 2nd series, 158 (1932); reprinted in *Federal Trade Commission Decisions,* XVI (1933), 660.

[13] Gratz *v.* F.T.C. 253 U.S. 421 (1919). Reprinted in *Federal Trade Commission Decisions* II (1920), 564.

[14] For the former case see the opinion expressed in Motion Picture Patents Company *v.* Universal Film Mfg. Co., *et al.,* 243 U.S. 517 (1917). For the latter case see 258 U.S. 451 (1922).

CHAPTER III

INTENTIONAL MISREPRESENTATION

The practices described in the preceding chapter are so far outside the field of fair service that, as far as the immediate victim is concerned, the more flagrant among them do not differ greatly from a holdup at the point of a revolver. We now pass to agreements of purchase and sale which, whatever their character in other respects, at least are made without compulsion.

The Place of Information in the Sale of Goods

Economic service in the field of material goods consists, as we have seen, in the preparation of articles of merchandise for the market, and in salesmanship. Salesmanship is divisible into information and persuasion. Ignoring the latter for the present, we shall confine our attention in this and the three following chapters to the ethics of information.

The informational feature of salesmanship plays a very important role in educating us in the uses of economic goods. For most people formal education in childhood and youth is largely controlled by the state. But education in consumption, accomplished through the informational efforts of advertising and other agencies, has been allowed to pass entirely into the hands of private business men. The responsibility for education in effective purchasing accordingly rests upon them just as inescapably as does responsibility for education in its traditional sense upon the teachers in our schools and colleges. Since the manner in which we live our lives depends so largely upon the material things with which we surround ourselves, it is of the utmost importance that this education at the hands of the business men be kept as truthful and as unbiased and as progressive as the education we receive in our public schools.

The current methods of informing the public about the nature and quality of one's goods, whether through the clerk behind the counter, the radio "barker", or the advertisement in the newspaper or on the billboard accomplish the following purposes. They acquaint people with products available for their consumption and show how to procure them. They teach the public new uses to which commodities may be put which they may not have discovered through their own experience, and thus make possible a more comfortable, a more attractive, and it may be a higher type of life. By increasing consumption they make possible our present large scale production, upon which the cheapness and plenty of our material equipment largely depend. By suggesting the adoption of new articles into our standard of living they encourage originality in productive effort and thus contribute greatly to the material progress of the world. By smoothing the path of commodities through our complicated system of distribution they eliminate delays and wastes. Finally, by instituting honest comparisons between competing products they may assist the public in making advantageous choices and thus in getting the most out of their opportunities.

It is obvious that an agency so powerful, when placed in the hands of the expert, is capable of terrible misuse, so that it may become a veritable curse to the community. That is to say information may become misinformation; and thus instead of being one of the pillars of fair competition it may become the very foundation of unfair competition.

Misrepresentation may be of two kinds, intentional and unintentional. We shall begin with a study of the former. The lawyers call it "wilful misrepresentation"; the rest of us call it lying.

What Is a Lie?

A lie is an attempt to make someone else believe what I myself do not believe. But since some people, otherwise intelligent, seem to have very vague notions as to what this term actually involves, we shall make a short survey of some frequently unrecognized forms of lying. These are perhaps reducible to four in number. We shall begin with illustrations taken from outside the business world.

(1) A young woman was permitted by her old-fashioned father to

go to a dance only on condition that she be "in" not later than twelve o'clock. As a matter of fact she reached home about three. Asked by her father the next morning at what time she came in, she answered promptly "a quarter of twelve", and considered she had told the truth, since three *is* a quarter of twelve. Here the lie turns on the use of an ambiguous term.

(2) At a grade crossing one night a train struck an automobile and killed its five occupants. The railroad maintained a watchman at this crossing, and at the inquest he testified that he swung his lantern as he saw the car approach the track. But he omitted to state that owing to his negligence the lantern was not lighted. The distinguishing feature of this exhibit is that a statement is made which is true in itself but from which it is expected a false inference will be drawn.

(3) A boy with an excellent record for good behavior was reading a "yellow covered" novel during school hours when he was supposed to be studying. Suddenly the teacher announced that she was going to institute a search for contraband literature and immediately began to translate words into deeds. Our youth, fearing that his hitherto unsullied record as a model pupil was about to be smirched, hastily slipped the book into the desk drawer of the boy sitting next to him. He did this well knowing that the latter had so bad a reputation that the teacher would pay no attention to his loud and voluble protestations of innocence. This is the lie through action.

(4) One day Mrs. *A* told Mrs. *B* a very uncomplimentary tale about their neighbor Mrs. *C*. She told it in good faith, though not without some malicious pleasure arising from the fact that she did not like the lady concerned. Later, however, she learned that her story was entirely without foundation. Nevertheless under the influence of her dislike for Mrs. *C* she failed to report her discovery to her auditor, who continued to believe the story as it was told. This variety of unveracity may be called the lie of suppression.

Now we have already remarked that morality is a matter of intent; the rightness or wrongness of an act turns on the answer to the question: What are you up to? and if your intent is unjustified the means you use make no difference in its character. Thus it is obvious that whether a woman murders her husband by shooting him with a revolver, putting arsenic into his soup, or locking him up in a cellar closet and letting him starve to death, murder is murder. Similarly whether you lead a person to believe what you don't believe by a clean-cut misstatement, or by using ambiguous terms, half truths, actions, silence, or what not, a lie's a lie for a' that.

Illustrations from the Business World

The above simple definition will make quick work of a great variety of business lies, in which the liar piles one lie upon another in the attempt to hoodwink himself into the belief that after all he is really telling the truth. Parallels to the above types are unfortunately all too easy to find in certain everyday selling practices.

(1) A manufacturer of soap powder recently advertised his product as "THE BIGGEST BOX OF SOAP ON THE MARKET FOR 10¢". Investigation proved that it was his *box* that was the biggest, and this happened to be the case merely because his soap chips were "fluffy". Moreover, there was no other direct competitor in the local market for 10¢, his chief competition coming from a manufacturer selling 10 ounces of soap for 9 cents, whereas the manufacturer advertising "The Biggest Box of Soap on the Market for 10¢" sold only 9 ounces for 10¢.

(2) a. In a contract for the sale of land the owner informed the purchaser that there was one lien on the property. He was abundantly right; there were sixteen. His manner of handling the English language was like that of the real estate dealer who notified his client in a distant city that he had been offered $1,800 for a piece of land belonging to the latter. As a matter of fact he had been offered $2,100, and intended to pocket the unreported $300, plus, of course, his regular fee.

b. Another variety of this species must have attracted the attention of every smoker. The manufacturers of the Lucky Strike cigarette plastered the bill boards and all other available advertising spaces with the words: "It's toasted". What they did not say is that almost all cigarette tobacco is subjected to the heating treatment which they chose to call "toasting". A half truth was employed to serve as a springboard for a complete lie, namely, that this particular brand of cigarettes had the advantage of a certain process in its preparation which competing cigarettes did not enjoy. In the presence of this brand of smug mendacity one feels like saying with Sir Leslie Stephen: "If you are going to lie, lie like a man".

(3) A manufacturer of macaroni conceived and acted upon the bright idea of packing sixteen ounces of his product in a package large enough to hold twenty ounces. As required by law he marked his cartons plainly with the legend, "Net contents one pound", which he knew not one out of ten purchasers would ever stop to read. The price was the normal market price for this amount. The bright idea worked to perfection. His competitors discovered this fact and began to enlarge the boundaries of their packages. Thereupon he increased the size of his carton to a twenty-four ounce capacity, the amount of macaroni still remaining the same as before.

The whole long and dreary tale of simulation of other peoples' goods belongs here. A single example will suffice. In the city of Washington, stores of a particular color, with signs of a certain design and size, and arranged and furnished in a specific manner, were opened for the sale of orangeade. They were very successful. Thereupon a competitor appeared upon the scene who established a series of stores of his own, identical, as far as appearance was concerned, in every minutest detail with those of his predecessor.[1]

(4) A farm owner told a prospective purchaser in good faith that his farm contained 120 acres and negotiated the sale on this basis. Later he discovered its area was only 108 acres. This interesting fact, however, he kept to himself.

A lie of suppression, on a far larger scale but in essentially the same manner, is the following. The Royal Baking Powder Company, manufacturer of a cream of tartar powder, had for many years directed its advertising policy toward disparaging powders containing phosphate and alum. One of its chief competitors was Price's Baking Powder, also made with cream of tartar. The Royal Baking Powder Company finally purchased Price's business and for some time continued to manufacture the powder as a cream of tartar powder. In September of 1919, however, for a variety of

[1] *Federal Trade Commission Decisions*, VII (1926), 279.

reasons, the Royal Company changed the formula and began to manufacture Price's with a phosphate content instead of cream of tartar. Its advertisements and its salesmen stated that the new product would be offered at about half of the price at which Dr. Price's powder had been sold formerly. The Price name and style of can were retained practically unchanged. The new price was sufficiently low, considering the prices of competing phosphate powders of similar quality. But nothing was said about the change from cream of tartar to phosphate.[2]

After these disgusting exhibitions of oily dishonesty it will be refreshing to turn to a picture of an entirely different kind, if for no other reason than to take the bad taste out of our mouths. After Lee's surrender to Grant at Appomattox he found himself in a very serious economic situation. Up to that time he had enjoyed wealth all his life; this was now gone. He had himself been an army officer from his youth; this occupation was now gone. He had a family to support. Whither should he turn? An opportunity soon presented itself. A group of business men organized a life insurance company to operate in the South with the intention of capitalizing the prestige of his great name. In pursuance of this plan they offered him the presidency. But he flatly refused to take it on the ground that he knew nothing of the life insurance business. To this objection they replied: "That makes no difference; what we want is the use of your name". His answer was: "There is not money enough in the country to buy my name".

A genuine difficulty arises when lying is continued for so long a time that words have literally changed their meaning and no longer deceive. We begin a letter:—"My dear Mr. Smith", and may not know Mr. Smith, or if we do, may hate him. "I am very glad to meet you" has practically passed into the same category.

If the old term with a new meaning really deceived no one the subject would not be worth discussing. But even if everyone in the "trade" understands it, and four-fifths of the ultimate consumers do also, there is the odd fifth. Most people know that "Hudson Seal" is dyed muskrat; many people know that practically all "Castile soap" on the American market is made of something other than olive oil;

[2] *Federal Trade Commission Decisions,* IV (1923), 1.

a few people know that wood which comes from Africa or the Philippines can never be mahogany, however closely it may resemble in appearance the famous product of the Central American forests. There are all kinds and degrees of ignorance in these matters, and no one to blame. In this situation there are two things to be done, and both of them are being done to a very encouraging degree. A considerable number of business men's associations, such as the Manufacturers of Sheffield Silver Plated Hollow Ware, the Retail Furniture Dealers of New York City, the members of the rebuilt typewriter industry, either on the invitation of the Federal Trade Commission or on their own initiative, have met with representatives of the Commission in "trade practice conferences", and adopted a standard system of classification and naming. The same thing has been done by other business organizations acting independently of the Commission. This work should be supplemented, and in part is being supplemented, by standardized and yet flexible systems of grading for quality and other characteristics. And names should be chosen for the different grades of quality which will not mislead the customer. This last precaution is unfortunately not always observed. Thus A-1 may mean third quality, and "best extra" the fifth; and the United States Department of Agriculture actually sanctions this procedure in many cases. The movement for standardization, if carried through to the end with proper care and with complete honesty and frankness, would settle the terminology for the "trade" and for all intelligent consumers. What then remained to be done could easily be taken care of in the retail stores by using accurate labels and by giving proper directions to the sales force.

Mr. Isaac Liberman, the president of Arnold Constable of New York, writes in the *Magazine of Business* [3] as follows:

"Whatever the article may be every customer has a different view point, and a bad point which may lose one sale will make another where this particular factor is not important, although its frank admission wins complete confidence in the merchandise. In our fur department every coat or fur piece carries a tag telling what kind of fur it is and what its wearing qualities are. Quite often expensive furs—squirrel for example—do not

[3] April, 1928, p. 453.

wear well, and so we say on the tag: The skins are small and are reputed for their flattering beauty. The hairs are tender and silky, accordingly they may not wear well."

Another kind of problem, which may at first sight seem to present some difficulties is represented by selling commodities under blanket guarantees, which, from the very nature of the situation, can not be made good. Thus for a long time R. H. Macy and Company, operating one of the largest department stores in New York City, regularly advertised to this effect: "Lowest in the city prices", and at prices "6% less than elsewhere". One advertisement explained the phrase as follows:

"Lowest in the city prices—means that Macy's prices are at least 6% less every day of the year, on every article of merchandise. This applies not only to regular stocks, but to the special items offered in competitive sales as well. Our customers may read the advertisements of other stores with the knowledge that they can make their purchases at Macy's and, as usual, save at least 6%."

This guarantee was unquestionably offered in good faith, and Macy and Company doubtless made every effort to live up to it. But stated in these sweeping terms its untruthfulness could have been easily demonstrated at any time by an examination of the extremely wide and complex marketing system of New York. It may have been true of the great majority of Macy's sales, but it obviously could not be true of all, and therefore the claim should never have been made in this form. Through the influence of the Better Business Bureau of New York City this particular store has been led to change the form of this statement in its more recent advertising.

A man may lie about his own state of mind just as he may lie about anything else. "The state of a man's mind", said Lord Justice Bowen, "is just as much a fact as the state of his digestion." To represent myself as certain about that which I think to be at best probable, or as thinking that probable which I believe is merely possible, with the odds against it, or to make any statement confidently when I really know nothing about the matter one way or the other —all this is lying. Of this sort was the promise which gave rise to the case of Langley *v.* Rodriguez.[4] Rodriguez agreed to sell to a

[4] 122 Calif. 580.

packing company his crop of raisins, then growing, for two cents per pound delivered at the packing house. In order to induce him to sign this agreement Bates, representing the company, promised on its behalf that when the grapes were ready to be gathered it would advance to him $350 on the price to enable him to pick and cure his crop. Rodriguez testified that without such a promise he would not have signed the contract. It appeared from the evidence that when Bates made this oral promise he did not know and was without reasonable ground for believing that the packing company would advance any money on the contract price. As a matter of fact it refused to do so. Rodriguez, therefore, properly refused to deliver the raisins, and the court decided that he could not be compelled to do so.

The Consequences of a Lie

Some people seem to be able to do a good deal of lying without any appreciable pangs of conscience—although it must be noted that if such a person is called a liar he will ordinarily feel deeply insulted. In his own picture of himself he has merely been "bluffing", or "playing the game", just as professional thieves—except the most abandoned—never "steal". But even among those who are most careful about telling the truth there not infrequently arises the question: May I not lie in such and such circumstances? and the answers of different people to this question fall out quite differently. In view of this situation it may not be unprofitable to examine the consequences of lies. This will throw much light on the problem; and our experience in the class room and observation of the life about us alike show that it is one concerning which most people have very sketchy ideas.

The effects of a lie may be divided into two classes, the primary and the secondary. Thus if I buy worthless bonds on the misrepresentation of a salesman, the primary effects are the loss of my money and the ensuing consequences to myself and my family and perhaps my creditors. These consequences are the same, of course, whether the salesman's statements were made in good faith or were known by him to be false. The secondary effects of a lie are those arising from the fact that the cause of the incorrect belief was a lie. The illustrations of the following paragraphs will make clear the meaning of this definition. Our discussion will be confined to these secondary effects. They may be due to the fact of detection or they may be due to other causes. We begin with the former.

Consequences that Depend upon Detection. The most obvious secondary effect of a detected lie is distrust of the liar. We infer, quite properly, that if he will lie once he will do it again, at least under similar circumstances. This distrust will not readily disappear except in the face of much evidence of the adoption of better principles, evidence based upon the exhibition of veracity under strong temptation to the contrary.

What is far more serious than the fact that the liar becomes an object of suspicion is the fact that each detected lie tends to weaken our confidence in other persons besides the liar. There is a certain tendency for this suspicion to spread first to what we may call adjacent territories, and from these to the next until, if we are very unfortunate in our surroundings, we may be ready to say, not merely in our haste but at our leisure, All men are liars. On August 1, 1914, most of the South American trade was in the hands of the British and the Germans. Within twenty-four hours the German trade had disappeared like April snows. Thereupon our fellow-countrymen rushed in to fill the void. In a certain city one American jobber swindled everyone with whom he had any business dealings. When this fact came out the business of every American in that city was practically ruined: "All American business men are thieves". The worst harm done by such men as Kreuger and Stavisky is the destruction of confidence in human nature as such for which they are responsible. The liar thus debases the coinage upon which human intercourse depends for its existence. In this respect he is like the counterfeiter, who of course is himself one kind of a liar.

It is thus the nature of a lie to breed suspicion. In addition, every lie tends to breed more lies. This tendency works itself out in a number of ways. For instance a single lie may start a series of lies, or what may be called a lie-feud, through the determination of the victim to protect himself by counter-lies. Again it may awaken the retaliatory desire to pay back the liar in his own coin. Curiously enough this desire may extend its range to cover all persons in the same class. Thus many an exemplary individual, when a counterfeit coin has been passed off on him on a street car, will consider himself justified in passing it back to another conductor, whereas he would never think of using it to pay for a cigar. Some time ago a man signing himself "A Victim" wrote the following letter to the *Chicago Tribune.*

> "I wish to take this means of warning all cashiers who deal with the public to beware of an elderly man with gray hair, about 5 feet 6 inches tall and of stocky build, who may want you to change a $20 bill for him and then decides he wants his $20 bill back again later. He has a clever way of cheating you out of several days' pay. Should you encounter this dirty crook, grab him and hold him till I get there. What I would do to him wouldn't look good in print. I have always tried to be especially courteous and respectful toward old people, but after my experience with this crook they will all look alike to me."

Childish and absurd as such an attitude is, it represents a spirit which in one form or another will show itself on occasion in a very large number of human beings.

A far more serious consequence, however, than either of the preceding is the lowering of the morale of an entire community through the influence of example. Curiously enough this is a fact of which apparently few people ever think. In our course in business ethics we have for many years conducted an exercise to bring out the students' views of the consequences of lying. They are able to work out for themselves most of the effects which we have been enumerating. But the effects of example do not appear in more than 10% of the papers. Yet what could be more obvious? Everyone knows that human beings are more or less like sheep. They do things in many cases for no other reason than that others are doing them. But in morals there enters a far more significant factor.

Many people who are willing to do their full share in a coöperative enterprise provided the other participants do the same, lose heart or interest when they find those equally responsible for the success of the common enterprise are shirking, to say nothing of "lying down on the job". Their zeal cools, they gradually slacken their pace, and in the end they may become slackers themselves. It was precisely in this way that a great and famous business organization, created and maintained by several brothers for many years with distinguished success, fell to pieces within a comparatively short time after control passed into the hands of the second generation. "In the end," said an observer, "it became a race as to which of the partners should arrive at the office latest in the morning."

What is true of participation in the management of a business organization holds for the maintenance of confidence in the spoken or written word. This is emphatically a coöperative enterprise, the most important in the world since it is the foundation of everything else. Every act of shirking tends to infect the whole group. "I will never again declare my cigars when I cross the frontier", said an honorable German business man once. "I am not going to be better than other people" ("Ich will nicht besser als die anderen sein"). At the Austrian custom house at the German-Austrian boundary, he had been the only man to admit the possession of cigars, though he was absolutely certain that ten or twelve of his fellow-travelers had them in their baggage or on their person.

Consequences Which Are Independent of Detection. Such are the consequences which flow from the detection of a lie. But a lie has another series of consequences which follow whether it is detected or not. The first is, in many instances, the loss of the confidence of others. This statement no doubt sounds paradoxical; for how, it will be asked, can a man lose confidence when others know nothing of the lie and do not even suspect the liar? The answer is that there are two ways to lose anything. The first is to have it in one's possession and to allow it to pass out of one's possession. The other is to lose the opportunity to gain possession. A young lawyer might be paid his fee in cash and lose it through the professional activity of a pickpocket. Or he might lose an equal sum by being away from his office for a day's hunting; the would-be client who finds the door locked going across the hall to the office of a rival. The same is true of confidence. Have we not all seen someone tell the truth under great temptation to lie? When he has told the truth to his own hurt we have said to ourselves: "There is a man who can be depended upon in any circumstances; we can believe him even where the appearances are all against him". Of this accession of confidence everyone robs himself who tells the easy lie in order to get out of a tight place, or in order to gain any other end at the expense of the truth.

Every lie, furthermore, diminishes the amount of confidence that would otherwise exist in the world in still another way. It makes it difficult, if not impossible, for the liar to believe in the truthfulness of others. "You can not believe in honor", writes Bernard Shaw, "until you have achieved it. Better keep yourself clean and bright; you are the window through which you must see the world." A childlike confidence in the complete goodness of every human being is not a desirable equipment for the conduct of life. But the cynical belief that everyone is a liar or a thief is likely to have equally mischievous consequences. For excessive suspicion creates no inconsiderable proportion of the treachery and deceit which it fears. Sooner or later it shows itself; and then is fulfilled that ancient and well-attested maxim:—"Call a man a dog and hang him". Thus the prophet helps to bring his own prophecies to pass.

The detected lie tends to make other people lie. The lie, whether detected or not, tends to make the liar himself tell ever more lies. This may be due to a variety of causes. There is of course the necessity of covering up the first lie with a second. Even more important are the workings of the law of habit. Again even a lie told with the best of motives may end by dragging a whole chain of lies behind it. For when we have justified to ourselves one lie on the ground of its good effects another situation will presently turn up just a little farther removed from the line, and it will be difficult to see why we should not justify a lie in this case also. This will in due time be followed by another situation differing only slightly and just a bit farther from the line, and so on, until the boundaries between truth and falsehood have ceased to have any definite location for our eyes. It is for these reasons that "while it is easy to tell one lie it is difficult to tell only one".

We may summarize the results of our—by no means exhaustive—survey of the secondary effects of lying as follows: Every lie breeds or tends to breed more lies; every lie breeds or tends to breed suspicion. While it is true that certain of these effects may be due in part to the weakness of will or want of principle of him to whom the lie is addressed or who otherwise knows of it, nevertheless they are all such, human nature being what it is, as could have been foreseen by anyone seriously intent on using his eyes. The liar, therefore, cannot dodge the responsibility of his share in bringing them into existence. And the responsibility is tremendous because the consequences are tremendous. In Europe today no government believes even the most solemn assurances of any other government; and with good reason. In the same way a community of individuals, if such there were, in which no one could depend upon the word of anyone else, would be headed, like Europe, straight for the abyss. And every serious lie is a move in this direction.

There is, however, light as well as shadow in this somber picture. For just as every liar is a force making for destruction, so is every honorable man a constructive force in his community. The man who tells the truth is a creator alike of confidence and of morale. He renews our faith in human nature; some of his strength passes over into us; our eyes, which had perhaps become dulled, see in him our deepest admirations incorporated in a living person, and what we admire in him we can not help wishing to possess ourselves; as we tend to pass our resentment at individual ill treatment on to the world about us, so we tend to pass on to others our personal gratitude for his fair treatment of us; as we see him shoulder his share of the burden we become more willing to shoulder our share too; as he makes it easier for those about him to play a straight game he makes it easier for us to play a straight game.

CHAPTER IV

"INNOCENT" LIES

Some Alleged Justifications for Lying

The Lie with Good Effects. Some acts of fraud are justified by many persons on the ground that after all they were either quite harmless or perhaps actually beneficial in their effects. Let us test this theory of beneficent lies by a brief examination of a certain sales campaign which at first glance, at any rate, would seem to meet this specification.

A good many years ago there was placed on the American market, amidst much beating of drums, a "nerve food" for tired people called Sanatogen. "Sanatogen", it was claimed, "is a scientific compound, every particle of which represents the finest concentrated tissue-constructing nutriment, endowed with unique revitalizing and rejuvenating powers." The product was advertised in the highest class periodicals, and testimonials from prominent people were freely used.

The senior author of this book participated in the rush for this life-giving substance and is therefore in a position to supply the reader with "inside information" as to its effects. After partaking of the contents of two cans and a part of a third (at one dollar per can) he found himself greatly invigorated and strengthened and consequently much better able to perform his duties to the youth of the nation. In fact everything was going beautifully when one day he unfortunately met his family physician who told him he could buy his cottage cheese more cheaply at the grocer's. Thereupon the spell vanished as by a magician's wand. However he has always felt that on the whole he got his money's worth. There must have been thousands of other such innocent lambs who were greatly helped by this wonderful compound of milk and mind. In view of these facts could there have been any moral turpitude in this particular lapse from truth? Nay, was it not rather positively laudable?

In attempting to answer this question we shall ignore the effects upon numberless people who were really ill and whose delay in repairing to a physician may have had very serious consequences. We shall, instead, confine ourselves to the issues raised by its effects upon the author on the one hand, and upon the trade on the other.

These effects, as far as the author was concerned, included the following. (1) The destruction of whatever confidence he may have had in the German manufacturers and their American agents; (2) the strengthening of his suspicion of proprietary drugs as such; (3) an increased skepticism concerning the claims of advertising in general and of mass advertising in particular, especially when backed by testimonials. These effects must have been multiplied thousands of times as one addict after another awoke from his dream of "revitalized and rejuvenated powers" as a result of eating three cans of disguised cottage cheese.

This campaign had another set of effects, however, which may well have been even more serious than those just enumerated. The owners and promoters of Sanatogen must have left the field gorged with gold. Now there are a great many men who have excellent intentions and who, if left to themselves, would be sufficiently honest and respectable for the ordinary exigencies of life, but who cannot bear to see the wicked prosper when they themselves have no share in the plunder. And some of these, it is to be feared, may not have confined themselves to such a comparatively innocuous method of parting the fool from his money as did the makers and marketers of our "tissue constructing nutriment". In other words every highly successful fraud necessarily does its part to lower the morale of business men in general, and thus the whole tone of business life.

This, then, is an example of the workings of a "harmless" or perhaps even "beneficent" swindle.

The plain fact is that when a man lies—certainly about serious matters, we are not talking about fish stories—he is striking a blow not merely at some individual, but at the community as a whole. He is sowing lies; he is sowing distrust. The distrust will bear fruit in the form of more lies; and the new lies will create more distrust. Therefore the obligations to veracity are not merely obligations to the person addressed, but to society as such. The liar is exploiting the confidence which other people have created, often at great sacrifice to themselves. He is thus evading the fundamental obligation of self-respect, which is to refuse to play the part of a parasite or a sponge.

If I Don't Lie, My Competitor Will. A justification for fraud that is sometimes offered is: "If I don't swindle him, my competitor will". This suggests a sign said to have hung outside a certain clothing store: "Why go elsewhere and be cheated? Come in here". If a man really wishes to see what is right, and is not merely trying to throw dust into his own eyes, he will do well to turn whatever problem he may be facing into a murder case. Thereupon the scales will suddenly fall from his eyes, and he will behold things as they are. Applying this method of procedure to the situation under discussion, does anyone suppose that if a man offered to pay you for killing a business rival of his you could justify yourself in a court of law or morals by saying: "I knew that if I didn't accept this offer someone else would"?

We have been talking about crooked drug manufacturers. For the sake of a change let us take an illustration of the opposite policy from the same field. About 1921 and 1922, when the vitamin craze swept over the United States, an old and reputable concern manufacturing pharmaceutical products, E. R. Squibb and Son, was approached by many sales companies who wished to have so-called "vitamin" tablets prepared for them. These companies brought their formulae to the House of Squibb and requested bids on lots as large as 5,000,000, 10,000,000 and 20,000,000 tablets. The laboratories of the latter company investigated the formulae, found that they were frauds, as far as their vitamin qualities were concerned, and announced this fact to the board of directors. Although the manufacture of these pills would have been an exceedingly profitable venture, and although the packages would have contained no indication of who had manufactured them, the board of directors turned down the requests for bids, announcing that they would have nothing to do with such business. These men evidently regarded it as their duty to keep themselves clean, whatever some of their less scrupulous competitors might choose to do.

"All That Blockheads Have Is Mine". The last justification offered

for fraud which we shall consider is the following. The fact of my success in deceiving the "sucker" whom I "took in" demonstrates that I am more clever than he. But the clever man is justly entitled to the fruits of his cleverness. Therefore—. In other words, the superior mind is under no obligations of good faith to his inferiors. There can be no doubt that this view of human relations, whether definitely formulated or not, is held by a great number of persons.

In our business ethics course at the University of Wisconsin we begin our work with a series of "cases", one of which is the following.

> "Some years ago Adolph Segal began the construction of a sugar refinery in the city of Philadelphia. During the process of construction, and while Mr. Segal was hard pressed for cash, he was offered a loan by one Gustav E. Kissel, a broker for an undisclosed principal. The offer was accepted, and in return for the loan a majority of the stock of the refinery company and all its bonds were deposited with Kissel. At the same time written authority was given him to exercise the voting power of the stock. The undisclosed principal was in fact the American Sugar Refining Company, and a few days after these arrangements were completed Kissel attended a meeting of the board of directors of the Pennsylvania Refining Company, causing four of the seven directors to resign and himself and three others subject to his control to be elected to fill the vacancies. The majority of the board then adopted and spread upon the minutes of the company the following declaration: 'Resolved, that the Refinery do not run and that no proceedings looking to the beginning of operation be taken until further order of the board.' "[1]

About two per cent of the undergraduates entering the course in business ethics in the University of Wisconsin answer this question as follows: "When a man is such a fool as Segal, anyone has the right to 'do' him". About twice this number believe he was not wronged because he ought to have been looking out for a trap; which comes to about the same thing.[2]

So much for the principle itself. Where it lands us if it is carried through consistently is shown very well by the following conversation

[1] W. H. S. Stevens, *Unfair Competition* (Chicago, University of Chicago Press, 1917), p. 215.

[2] Apparently Segal was acting in collusion with the American Sugar Refining Company, but the situation is almost invariably interpreted by the students as an instance of extreme folly in allowing the control of one's property to pass out of one's hands to an unknown party in return for a loan, even though it was contracted to meet a pressing necessity. Hence their answers to our question represent with a fair degree of accuracy undergraduate opinion at the University of Wisconsin on this point.

between Mr. Samuel Crothers and an ex-forger, described by the former in his delightful essay "As He Sees Himself", in *The Pardoner's Wallet*.[3] The former forger had decided to abandon his profession, as on the whole not a paying proposition. He had, of course, called upon Mr. Crothers to borrow money.

"At last I said, 'You have told me what you did before you concluded to reform. I am curious to know how, in those days, you looked at things. Was there anything which you wouldn't have done, not because you were afraid of the law, but because you felt it would be wrong?'

" 'Yes,' he said, 'there is one thing I never would do, because it always seemed low down. I never would steal.'

"It was evident that further discussion would be unprofitable without definition of terms. I found that by stealing he meant petty larceny, which he abhorred. In our condemnation of the sneak-thief and the pickpocket we were on common ground. His feeling of reprobation was, if anything, more intense than that which I felt at the time. He alluded to the umbrellas and other portable articles he had noticed in the hallway. Anyone who would take advantage of an unsuspecting householder by purloining such things was a degenerate. He had no dealings with such moral imbeciles.

"It seemed to me that I might press the analogy which instantly occurred to me between 'stealing' and forgery.

" 'Do they not', I said, 'seem to you to amount to very much the same thing?'

"I had struck a wrong note. Analogies are ticklish things to handle, for things which are alike in certain respects are apt to be quite different in other respects. His mind was intent on the differences. The sneak-thief, he told me, is a vulgar fellow of no education. The forger and the check-raiser are experts. They are playing a game. Their wits are pitted against the wits of the men who are paid high salaries for detecting them. They belong to quite different spheres."

The point of view of Mr. Crother's caller is that the superior mind has superior rights as against its inferiors. "All that cowards have is mine" (*i. e.,* what I have a right to) was the motto of one of the famous English buccaneering families of the Middle Ages. Similarly our forger might have said, with a consciousness of complete rectitude: "All that blockheads have is mine".

If this principle holds true it of course makes an end of practically all morality, from short-changing to safe blowing, and from this to murdering your rival. For no one knowingly allows himself to be robbed, to say nothing of killed. Consequently success, whether

[3] Boston and New York, Houghton Mifflin Co., 1905.

in theft or murder, provided it is not due to superior physical force, means that the swindler or the murderer is at least for the moment the superior to his victim in knowledge if not in intelligence. Most human beings, we may remember, have three codes.[4] It may be suspected that this particular code is one of those which we reserve for application to our treatment of our neighbor, but which we should consider it outrageous for him to presume to apply to his treatment of us.

May It Be My Duty to Lie?

Is it, then, our conclusion that a man ought never to lie? This does not follow from anything we have said. The first obligation of an accountant is to treat the affairs of his clients as absolutely confidential. Suppose such a man is asked a leading question about the business condition of a client by one of the latter's competitors. To refuse to answer may under certain circumstances be to answer, or at least to suggest an answer. The only way in which he can be loyal to the trust imposed upon him may be to lie. Here there is a conflict of claims. There is a general obligation to veracity on the one side; on the other a business rival is asking for information to which he has no right. As between two evils the accountant must choose the less. In this instance the decision seems relatively easy. His obligation to his employer is paramount. But there are others which are not so simple. For such, no universal rule can be laid down. When we are faced with a dilemma of this kind each of us must determine for himself where the less evil lies.

In situations of this sort, we must squarely face the fact that even a lie which in the end we must pronounce justifiable will have many of the bad effects which we traced in the preceding chapter. You can not get something for nothing in this world of ours, squirm and twist as you will. A doctor lies about the condition of his patient to the sick man himself and perhaps to the family. This he does with the best intention in the world. But the ultimate outcome is that the family do not believe him even when he is telling the truth. This does not mean that we must never lie, but that we lie always at the risk of sacrificing important interests. People usually put our ques-

[4] See above, p. 3.

tion in the form, May I lie? They should rather ask, Must I lie? As a final word on the subject we beg leave to quote with approval the suggestion of Mark Twain: "When in doubt, tell the truth".

Partnership in Lying

A manufacturer of desiccated cocoanut was always at some expense in getting rid of the shells. One day he was surprised by an offer of cash for a large supply. He naturally inquired what they were to be used for. In reply he was told they were to be ground up and mixed with pepper, the mixture to be placed on the market as pure pepper. Thereupon he refused to make the sale.

Many excellent persons would apparently regard the manufacturer as overconscientious. But it is easy to show that he took the right course. A man is responsible for all the consequences that he foresees will follow his own action. This is simply another form of the statement that morality is a matter of intent. It makes no difference whether these consequences follow from a man's own act taken by itself, or his own act in conjunction with the acts of others. Intent is everything. Responsibility is not like pie. There is always enough to go around; and the size of each piece is independent of the number of persons involved. Counterfeiting, for example, happens to require the coöperating activities of a considerable number of persons, because each must be an expert in his own line. There is the paper maker, the ink maker, the engraver, the printer, and the man who passes off the finished product on the unsuspecting public. No one can suppose that the government detectives or the courts confine, or ought to confine their attention to any single link in the chain.

Some of the worst offenders in this matter will be found among the publishers of our newspapers and magazines. There are indeed many honorable men in this field who, at a serious loss of income, refuse to have anything to do with this disreputable business.

"A $66,000 schedule was recently offered to a well known publisher. He lost the business because he and the advertiser couldn't agree on the propriety of a single word. The advertiser wanted to say 'No other food is so wholesome'. The publisher said that other foods could be as wholesome as this particular advertiser's was. His stand was: 'You can't go further in our columns than to say "No other food is more wholesome".' A difference of one word; a loss of $66,000 revenue. That's courage." [5]

There is a great deal more of this kind of courage than many cynically minded people suppose. From a detailed study made by the National Better Business Bureau in 1934 it appears that the publishers of this country "sacrifice millions annually to protect their readers". For example, "the Bureau asserted that an analysis of twelve publishers showed that they had rejected more than two and one-quarter millions in advertising revenue during the past seven years." This did not count "the additional copy that might have been offered to them if their standards had not been so well known".[6]

It is probable that there is far more of his kind of honor in the advertising world today than there was a generation ago. But the number of those who give publicity to advertisements which they must know to be fraudulent is still all too large. Without the aid of this type of purveyor many of the vilest swindles ever perpetrated in this country would have been impracticable: some of them huge thefts on a national scale, some of them booming drugs which prey not merely upon the pockets but also the health of the poor and ignorant. A man who is convicted of being a "fence", that is to say, a receiver of stolen goods is promptly sent to the penitentiary, and everyone approves. But the men who, through the publicity which they sell, open the doors to what are nothing but acts of theft seem to think they form an exception to the rule.

Does this mean that a newspaper or a magazine is bound to check every statement made in every advertisement that is brought to its office? Certain publishers employ a special staff for this purpose; but perhaps this practice may be regarded as a counsel of perfection. But whatever may be said of this precaution, one thing is certain. When a man rises to the position of an advertising manager he is supposed to be something better than a fool; furthermore he is supposed to have had some experience in dealing with the world. Accordingly he should be able to distinguish for the most part between honest

[5] S. Ronald Hall, "The Most Deceitful Kind of Advertising". From *Advertising and Selling,* June 17, 1926, p. 30.

[6] *Chicago Journal of Commerce,* Dec. 9, 1935, p. 4.

and fraudulent claims, and that without wearing himself out in the attempt. But where he has any reason for suspicion he should either investigate or refuse publicity. "The true test is to exercise such care as a reasonably prudent man under such circumstances would exercise if his own interests were directly and vitally affected." [7]

Just as a publisher can not escape responsibility for the character of the contents of his advertising columns, so an employer can not evade responsibility for the lies told by his managers or salesmen, if he is aware of them or has any reason for suspecting their existence. In particular no one has a right to tempt people who are dependent upon him for a living, by staging high pressure drives or other similar devices, the slogan of which is, in effect: Make sales anyway you can; only make sales. As a matter of fact these drives, looked at from a long run point of view, are as foolish as prodding the body with alcohol or a market with inflation. But quite apart from this fact, unless it is understood that a salesman who lies to his customers in the race for the pennant will endanger his position, the employer is responsible for the methods that are likely to be used. It is the duty of an employer to know whether his employees are doing what he wants them to do. If his own pocketbook were being endangered he could always discover ways of finding it out. The employer who says, "I ask about nothing but results", testifies thereby that he is entirely indifferent to one very important set of results, in which are included his own reputation for honesty and the character of his salesmen.

The Law of Intentional Misrepresentation

The Legal Conception of a Lie. The conception of intentional misrepresentation held by the common law is essentially identical with that which has been presented in this and the preceding chapter. This fact appears from the definition of fraud offered by Professor Samuel Williston in his work on the law of contracts. "The essential element of fraud . . . is a mistake of one party as to a material

[7] Address of Chairman Humphrey of the Federal Trade Commission, at the trade practice conference for publishers of periodicals, Nov. 12, 1928, *F.T.C. Trade Practice Conferences* (1929), p. 169.

fact, induced by another in order that it might be acted upon, or (in cases where there is a duty of disclosure) at least taken advantage of with knowledge of its falsity, in order to secure action." [8] This means that in the great body of modern legal decisions in the field of misrepresentation, the point on which everything turns is whether there was a mistaken belief intentionally produced by a person who knew it to be mistaken. Whether he has attempted to attain his ends by the use of ambiguous terms, half-truths, or some external act is treated as irrelevant.

For example, the fact that a carefully framed half-truth may amount to fraud has been frequently recognized by the courts; and never more strikingly than in an English case decided since the depression began. Lord Kylsant, of a distinguished English stock, was a director of the Royal Mail Steam Packet Company. In 1928 he was responsible for circulating a prospectus advertising a new issue of debenture stock. It was found that knowing the facts, and with an intention to mislead the public, Lord Kylsant was responsible for so framing the prospectus that it told the exact truth, but only part of it, in such a way that it misled members of the public into buying. Specifically, the prospectus contained true statements about dividend payments made since the war; but did not say that these dividend payments were made possible by non-recurrent sources of income, including repayments of war taxes by revenue authorities and the readjustment of reserve accounts. Lord Kylsant was prosecuted under the English Larceny Act of 1861 which makes it a crime for a director of a corporation to publish or circulate a written statement "which he shall know to be false in any material particular" for the purpose of getting money for his corporation. Though it was strenuously insisted that the prospectus was strictly true; and though it was recognized that one can not be convicted of a crime which is not clearly described by the statute under which a prosecution is conducted, Lord Kylsant was convicted, and his conviction was sustained by the Court of Criminal Appeal.

"The falsehood in this case consisted in putting before intended investors, as material on which they could exercise their judgment as to the

[8] *Contracts,* Vol. III, Section 1487.

position of the company, figures which apparently disclosed the existing condition, but in fact hid it. . . . There was ample evidence that Lord Kylsant knew that the prospectus was false in the sense indicated." [9]

A review of this case in 45 *Harvard Law Review* 1078 points out in some detail the extent to which this view of misrepresentation holds in American law.

Failure to correct a misstatement made in good faith and later discovered to be erroneous, or a misstatement representing what at some time in the past was actually true, is also treated by the courts as deceit. It was in accordance with this principle that the farm owner of page 40 (above) was adjudged to have defrauded the purchaser.[10] On the same grounds a Federal Court held that the failure of the Royal Baking Powder Company to inform the public that it had replaced cream of tartar with phosphate in Price's baking powder was a dishonest practice which justified the order of the Federal Trade Commission directing the company to cease and desist from concealing this fact from the readers of its advertising matter and its labels.[11]

Furthermore the law is clear that "a statement made without positive knowledge and yet in a positive manner as if one had good grounds for his belief is also actionable deceit". In 1827 Chief Justice Best said: "He who affirms either what he does not know to be true, or knows to be false, to another's prejudice and his own gain, is both in morality and law guilty of falsehood and must answer in damages".[12] This is the foundation of the decision in Langley *v.* Rodriguez, referred to above, page 43.

The Legal Rights of the Blockheads and the Careless. The effects of such decisions, however, have been greatly limited by the declaration of many courts to the effect that in the absence of confidential relations between the contractors "the party deceived must have been in a situation such as to have no means of detecting the deceit". The leading case seems to be Slaughter's Administrator *v.* Gerson.

"Where the means of information are at hand and equally open to both parties and no concealment is made or attempted—the misrepresentation

[9] Rex *v.* Kylsant, 1 K.B.D. 442 (1932).
[10] 41 N.H. 95 (1860).
[11] See 281 Fed. 744 (1922).
[12] Williston, *op. cit.* Sec. 1509.

furnishes no ground for a court of equity to refuse to enforce the contract of the parties. The neglect of the purchaser to avail himself, in all such cases, of the means of information, whether attributable to his indolence or credulity, takes from him the just claim for relief." [13]

This position has been reaffirmed recently by a Pennsylvania court. Here deliberate lies had been told by the seller to a person considering the purchase of stock. The latter had the corporation accounts before him, or at all events, readily available, and they indicated the falsity of the statements made. The question thereupon arose whether one who defrauds another will be liable to the latter if he foolishly or carelessly relies on his false statements. In the case before us, it was held, such liability did not exist. In referring to an earlier Pennsylvania decision, the court observed that ". . . this court quoted approvingly the statement of Chancellor Kent . . . that the law does not go to the romantic length of giving indemnity against the consequences of indolence and folly, or a careless indifference to the ordinary and accessible means of information".[14] Volume XIX of the *Virginia Law Review* (1933), page 299, cites a large number of cases agreeing with this decision.

This, however, is not the law in all jurisdictions. In Carpenter *v.* Wright, for example, the Kansas Supreme Court is able to cite a number of precedents from different states for the following declaration: "A fraudulent representation that a tract of land is free and clear of incumbrances and upon which the other relies and is induced to purchase the land when in fact it is subject to a valid mortgage, is sufficient [ground] upon which to base a recovery for the wrong and injury sustained, although the injured party might have discovered the incumbrance by a search of the public records".[15]

This seems to be the position of the *Restatement of the Law of Contracts*. Sec. 476 treats of the "Effect of Fraud or Misrepresentation that Induces Acts Affecting Contractual Relations". It declares that "where a party is induced to enter into a transaction with another party that he was under no duty to enter into by means of the latter's fraud or material misrepresentation the transaction is voidable as against the latter . . . subject to [certain] qualifications",

[13] 13 Wallace (= 80 U.S.) 385 (1871).

[14] Emery *v.* Third National Bank of Pittsburgh, 308 Pa. 504 (1932).

[15] 52 Kan. 221 (1893).

among which those enumerated in Slaughter *v.* Gerson nowhere appear.

How far the common law has traveled in the past three centuries towards the requirement of strict veracity on the part of the seller is shown by an English case reported as of 1625. Here a goldsmith sold a stone which he "affirmed" to be a bezoar-stone when it was not; but because he did not "warrant" that it was a bezoar-stone by using a legal formula which would clearly indicate that he understood his representation or promise might be relied on, he was not liable to the buyer.[16] No such plea would be entertained by any common law court today.

The Legal Consequences of Partnership in Lying

Whatever may be said of the narrow vision of individual courts the general rules of law with regard to "actions contributing to fraud" are based upon a clear and consistent recognition of the fact that he who induces another man to produce certain results or even knowingly makes it possible for him to do so is as truly responsible for such results as the immediate actor.[17] This position has been affirmed time after time by the American as well as the English courts.[18] If this statement holds for those who do no more than place in the hands of others instruments of fraud much more is it true of those who actively induce others to unite with them in fraudulent transactions.

What applies to manufacturers and wholesalers who put into the hands of retailers the means of swindling their customers holds equally for all publishers of fraudulent advertisements. A trade practice conference for publishers of periodicals was held in New York in November 1928, at which the Hon. William E. Humphrey, Chairman of the Federal Trade Commission, presided. In his address he said:

> "How can this gigantic evil of false advertising be suppressed? The Department of Justice, the Post Office Department, and the Federal Trade

[16] Chandelor *v.* Lopus, Cro, Jac. 4.

[17] See H. D. Nims, *The Law of Unfair Business Competition,* 3rd edition (1929), p. 969, Sec. 381. Compare pp. 771; 917; 969 to 974.

[18] See, *e. g.* the U.S. Supreme Court in Federal Trade Commission *v.* Winstead Hosiery Co., 258 U.S. 483 (1922).

Commission have waged war unceasingly against it. But the result has been most unsatisfactory and discouraging. What of the responsibility of the publisher? He becomes part of the plan. Without his assistance the consummation of the scheme would be impossible. Knowingly or unknowingly, the publisher helps rob the unfortunate victim. He brings the victim and the crook together. He shares in the ill-gotten gains. In publishing such advertisement the publisher is violating the law. He is guilty of an unfair practice. In a suit by the Federal Trade Commission to suppress such advertising the publisher is not only a proper party but, under recent decisions, he is a necessary party." [19]

[19] *F.T.C. Trade Practice Conference* (1929), p. 171.

CHAPTER V

"LET THE BUYER BEWARE"

THE OBLIGATION TO TELL THE WHOLE TRUTH

The witness on the witness stand must swear not merely to tell nothing but the truth but also to tell the *whole* truth. Has the purchaser a similar right to the whole truth, *i. e.* so much of the truth as he needs in order to pass an intelligent judgment upon the value of what he is proposing to buy? Or is it enough if the seller neither by word nor deed makes an active attempt to mislead him? This is the problem of the validity of that ancient maxim, *caveat emptor:* Let the buyer beware. This asserts that the seller is under no obligation to reveal any defects in his wares, and has performed his whole duty to his customer if he has refrained from actual misrepresentation.

Caveat emptor does not refer to half truths so manipulated as to create a totally false belief, like the statement of the guard who testified that he swung his lantern, but omitted to say it was not lighted.[1] Here the omission of a detail is intended to color, or rather to discolor, the entire picture. But *caveat emptor* refers rather to cases where the commodity has, let us say, four qualities, a, b, c, d, and the seller dwells upon the good ones, a, b, c, and passes over the defective one, d, in silence. The question is, whether silence under such circumstances is justifiable. The nature of the problem will appear from the examination of a concrete case.

A ranchman sells to a packing firm a herd of cattle infected with Texas fever, a disease not easily detectable in its early stages. In answer to a specific inquiry he informs the prospective purchaser that the cattle are all perfectly sound and healthy. This is of course a lie, and is manifestly wrong. Again he sells a similarly infected herd, and, being asked no questions about their health says nothing about it. Is this wrong also?

[1] See above, Ch. III, p. 38.

Active deception in trading involves a willingness to profit by taking advantage of the ignorance of the buyer. The end in view is that the latter shall get something which either he would not buy, or would not buy at that price if he knew what he was getting. The intention in the second transaction is the same. There is therefore at bottom no difference in the wrong. Passive deception is still deception, and when done with the same intent is of the same nature as a positive lie.

Can a Man Act by Doing Nothing?

The failure of many essentially honest persons to perceive the identity between passive and active deception is due, in part at least, to a failure to note that a man may act by refraining from action just as much as by contracting his muscles. In Dumas' novel, *The Black Tulip,* William of Orange—later King William III of England—watches from his window the mob lynch his chief rival, the great and patriotic Dutch statesman Jean de Witt, when he well knows that a few words from him would calm the crowd, purge them of their unreasoned suspicions and insane rage, and induce them peaceably to disperse. Instead he quietly watches the tragedy through to the end, notwithstanding the entreaties of his secretary. Why does he not intervene to save a man whom he knows to have committed no wrong, but on the contrary to have shown heroic courage, great resourcefulness, and almost superhuman skill in directing the defense of his country against the all but overwhelming forces of that royal robber, Louis XIV? The answer is simple. Jean de Witt, till a few weeks before, had been head of the state; William wants his place and believes he can obtain it if his rival is once out of the way. He has done nothing to spread the false reports which led to the tragedy. But he is willing to profit by them none the less.[2]

Now let us compare this story with a more famous one. Macbeth is the second man in Scotland. He wishes to be the first. So when the "gracious Duncan" comes to visit him in his castle he plunges the dagger into the heart of the sleeping king.

[2] William's part in this affair is a creation of Dumas' imagination. This fact of course does not in any way affect the truth of the ethical conclusions emerging from our analysis of the incident.

Is there any essential difference between Macbeth's decision to act and William's decision not to act? The intent in each case was the same. In each situation a man who was second in the state saw his chance to climb to the highest place over the dead body of one who stood in his way. The latter was able to attain his end by doing nothing; the former had to act. This was the whole difference. The guilt was therefore the same. There was not even a difference in the matter of premeditation. For William had learned the night before of the plans of the leaders of the mob.

What has been asserted is that the action of Macbeth and William's refusal to act are, taken as isolated incidents, identical in moral quality. This does not mean, however, that I should be justified by this event alone in inferring that William was as bad a man as Macbeth. A person who actively murders another has to overcome certain inner inhibitions which might not arise in the mind of one who does no more than allow another person to perish. This difference holds in minor matters as well as in great ones. As far as pure logic is concerned it comes to the same thing whether a man keeps his seat in a street car while a woman is standing, or whether, when a seat is vacated, a man makes a rush and grabs it before the woman can get to it. But in picking a son-in-law, if you had to choose between the two, you would reject the latter as almost certain to be the more selfish.

This distinction between an act and a man is one we make every day. If your errand boy steals a dollar and you are a humane employer you will call him to your office, read him a lecture, and forgive him. But if you catch him stealing the same amount a second time, the affair becomes more serious; and if, after a new forgiveness he falls a third time, you discharge him and perhaps turn him over to the police. Each act is bad by and in itself. But the repetition derives an added seriousness from the fact that it points to some grave and perhaps permanent defect in character.

Whenever a situation involves danger of death we have no difficulty in seeing clearly the fundamental identity between the intent that reaches its goal by inaction and the intent that leads to action. An acquaintance of ours owned a car which had the trick of leaving the road at high speed; in fact it had on occasions turned completely around. No amount of tinkering could correct this bizarre and dangerous habit. Suppose he had sold the car without informing the buyer about this vice; suppose, if you choose, that he had sold it knowingly to an inexperienced driver. Suppose also that the car left the road just once too often with the new owner at the wheel and he had been killed. Anyone can see the responsibility of the vendor in a case like this. But the principle would have been the same if the undisclosed defect had been scored cylinders, which were not dangerous to life but would merely involve additional expense and perhaps much trouble and vexation of spirit.

Ought the Buyer to Discover the Defects for Himself?

If it be objected that the purchaser should have tried out the car for every possible defect before closing the deal, the following reply can be made. In the first place, whatever may be said of automobiles, the fact of the matter is that in 95 cases out of 100 the purchaser has not the ability and knowledge, and cannot be expected to have the ability and knowledge to discover the defects of what he is buying. How many men are aware that "renovated" felt hats, looking exactly like new ones for the first few weeks or until exposed to rain, are sold in many retail stores, along with hats that are really new, without any suggestion from the salesman that there is any difference between the two, except perhaps in the tempting matter of price? [3]

The impossibility of becoming acquainted in detail with all the goods on the market in an age like ours applies to what may be called latent defects. But there are, of course, cases where the purchaser by careful examination might have discovered the defect himself. Here, it may be argued, *caveat emptor* has a very beneficent influence because it produces care and alertness of mind. But if this is a reason for letting the buyer look out for himself it is equally a reason for encouraging lying. For the mendacious salesman might excuse himself just as easily as the silent salesman by urging: "If the purchaser had exercised more care he would have discovered I was lying. He missed a lot of excellent mental training by trusting me in-

[3] See *Federal Trade Commission Decisions*, XVII (1934), 352.

stead of trying to catch me." To all of which we reply: It is far better to help create a society in which men can be trusting and friendly than one in which they are compelled to be mutually suspicious and alert in avoiding traps. Furthermore, while failure to explore every nook and cranny in the anxious search for defects may be due to carelessness or laziness, it may also be due to faith in your honesty. To justify yourself for a breach of confidence under such circumstances is to say: "You have done me the honor to trust me; therefore I am justified in betraying that trust".[4]

Some Concrete Problems and Their Solution

A few illustrations will help to make clear the above conclusions. *A* sold *B* a certain piece of land in Nevada for agricultural purposes, in a region where cultivation of the soil is absolutely impossible without irrigation. *A* expressly reserved the use of the water in the upper reaches of the creek forming the boundary line on one side of the property. But as he wanted it solely for mining purposes, this reservation did not diminish the amount of water flowing farther down the stream, and was therefore not disadvantageous to the purchaser. What the vendor did not say, however, was that he had previously sold the right to use the water of the stream to a third party. Here *A* obtained *B's* money in return for something which was absolutely worthless, and which he would never have bought if he had known what he was getting.[5] The instrument employed to attain this end was silence. By no stretch of the imagination could a transaction of this sort be regarded as selling goods on their merits.

Is it necessary to say that the amount of the loss has nothing to do with the principle? *B* having recently looked over a farm belonging to *A*, offers him a fair sum for it. The amount of his offer is determined in considerable part—as *A* is well aware—by a fine stand of trees which it contains. But between the time that *B* visited the farm and the time he made the offer the trees had all been destroyed by fire. Of this fact *A* is well aware, but not *B*. If *A* accepts *B's* offer without informing him of the change in value he may not be taking money for something completely worthless, but a part of what he

[4] See Cottrell *v.* Krum, 100 Mo. 397.
[5] Adapted from Wilson *v.* Higbee, 62 Fed. 723.

takes he gets for trees which do not exist. And this additional sum slips into his pocket as the result of a misapprehension on the part of *B* of which *A* is aware and for which he is therefore responsible.

Our maxim says: Let the *buyer* beware. But of course it applies equally to the seller. Some fifty years ago, in an Alabama rural community, the real estate market had been experiencing a mild boom for reasons which do not concern us. One day *A*, who lived a hundred miles from this territory and knew nothing whatever about the recent advance in values, wrote to *B*, who lived in the district in question, offering him, if he would effect a sale, whatever sum he could realize on this land over and above $500. Thereupon *B*, not waiting to reply by letter, took the next train to *A's* home and procured an option to purchase at $500, knowing perfectly well that he could immediately sell the property for several times that amount of money.[6] The market price of a piece of land, in so far as it is really capable of determination, is as much a quality of the land, from a business point of view, as its location with reference to a railroad, its freedom from encumbrances, or anything else that affects its attractiveness to a possible purchaser. *B* might as well have told *A* in so many words that the land was worth no more than $500 dollars, but that he would buy it himself at that price and take his chances on a rise. We conclude that *B* through his silence robbed *A* of two-thirds (or thereabouts) of the value of his land; just as the farm owner in the preceding incident robbed the purchaser of the amount which he paid for the non-existent trees. In the one case values had dropped, in the other advanced, without the knowledge of one party to the transaction and with the knowledge of the other. This is the principal difference between the two.

If this view is sound it will hold of chattels as well as of land. In the famous case of Laidlaw *v.* Organ, the defendant, having heard of the signing of the treaty which ended the war of 1812, "purchased a quantity of tobacco of Laidlaw who had not heard of it; and a few moments before the sale was completed being asked whether there was any intelligence calculated to enhance the price of tobacco he remained silent". Laidlaw evidently did not observe the significance of the failure to answer his question and accepted

[6] Byars *v.* Stubbs, 85 Ala. 256.

Organ's offer.[7] The situation here, as far as we are able to see, is different in no essential respect from the preceding one.

These considerations, it seems to us, will enable us to pass upon a problem concerning which there is still much difference of opinion among moralists. A geologist or other expert discovers the existence of iron or oil beneath the soil of John Smith's farm. May he not buy it at ordinary farm prices and pocket the difference? Has he not trained himself to be an expert, and does he not deserve a reward for his diligence? Or, since he may not have worked any harder in life than the farmer—is it not socially expedient that he should be rewarded for the acquisition of this highly specialized and very useful form of knowledge?

To this question we reply that of course he is entitled to a fee for the information he gives the farmer, just as is the lawyer for his services in searching the title. But from this fact it does not follow that he may justly get possession of the underlying store of minerals without the knowledge of the owner. No bargain for purchase or sale is fair where one of the parties does not know what he is getting or receiving. If a man sells a farm which he knows contains exactly 100 acres at an agreed price of $100 per acre, and accepts $11,000 because the purchaser believes it contains 110 acres, he is certainly dishonest, though he did nothing actively to mislead the purchaser. Similarly if the purchaser knows the farm contains 110 acres, but pays on the basis of 100 acres because the owner supposes this represents the area, then he is dishonest. But whether the purchaser gets ten acres of land for which he has not paid, or $100,000 worth of minerals, the principle is the same. And it makes no difference whether the purchaser of the farm is an expert surveyor with special ability to determine the acreage or an ordinary untrained man. The skeptics may be interested to learn that the practice here approved is that which is actually adopted by the great iron and steel companies of the country in acquiring mineral lands.

Summary

Our entire discussion of misrepresentation, whether active or passive, may be summarized in the following proposition; If an agree-

[7] 2 Wheaton (15 U.S.) 178.

ment for purchase and sale is to be fair, the consent of the parties thereto must be based upon a knowledge of all the available essential facts. This means a knowledge of just what they are getting and what they are giving in return.

Limitations to Our Conclusion

No Obligation to Disclose Future Plans. This conclusion, however, must be guarded against a possible misunderstanding. To say that the seller is entitled to know what he is selling is one thing; to say that he is entitled to know what use I am going to make of his property or chattels after they are purchased is quite a different thing. If I see a way to turn what is now almost worthless land into an attractive summer resort, or into a market garden, or into fields for the raising of everbearing strawberries, I am entitled to the profits, since I do the work and must risk the losses of my venture. I ought to be willing to pay the owner the present market value of what is there; and if what I am looking for is minerals and minerals are there, I have no more business to conceal this fact than to deny it. But I am not bound to pay him for future values which will be the creation of my efforts, and hence I am not bound to divulge my purpose in buying. To contend that I ought to be perfectly frank about my plans would be to assert that I am bound to arouse his cupidity and tempt him to hold me up in order that he may share in the fruits of my future labors.

Perhaps this is self-evident, but we venture to add another caution against a possible misapprehension. When the owners of a department store, an office building, or a factory, or the trustees of a hospital or other public institution, wish to enlarge or relocate their plant, or when a capitalist wishes to start a new one, hopeful owners of the desired real estate proceed to boost their terms to a point which amounts to a monopoly price. Here, again, the promoters are under no obligation to reveal the purpose for which they want the land, or to offer the enhanced price which would thereupon ensue.

No Obligations to Disclosure in Speculation. We have written as if qualities and other values of whatever sort were something known or easily discoverable. But frequently this is not the case. In Byars *v.* Stubbs [8] the property of the defendant had a somewhat definite exchange value, knowledge of which, at least within certain limits, could be obtained by various objective methods, such as records of recent sales in the vicinity. But often the value of property is purely a matter of guesswork. Each party is using his judgment and taking the risks of being mistaken. Here, where there is no objective standard of value, each party must do his own guessing, and should not expect to get information or advice from another person who is operating in the same market. In other words, neither party is bound to reveal to the other the process of reasoning by which he has come to his decision whether to buy or to sell. This is because both buyer and seller are taking chances; and since each must stand his losses he is entitled to profit when he gains.

The proof of the correctness of this proposition is supplied by noting the limitations within which it holds. *A* was negotiating with *B* for the purchase of land for mining purposes. At the outset neither really knew the extent of the mineral deposit or its quality. Unknown to *B,* however, *A* made a number of preliminary excavations and based his offer on the information thus obtained. After the sale was completed *B* learned of the trick which had been played on him and refused to give title. The case was tried under the rules of equitable jurisdiction, and the court sustained *B*. The judge evidently regarded this transaction as being what it really was—gambling with loaded dice.

When Judge Gary was president of the United States Steel Corporation he introduced the practice of holding directors' meetings after 3:00 o'clock, the hour at which the New York Stock Exchange closed. He did this to prevent the directors from using the information obtained at the meeting to buy or sell to the detriment of their fellow-stockholders who would not receive the information until the next day. Similarly if a man had direct and definite information that a bank was about to fail, it seems to us he would be essentially dishonest in unloading his stock upon some unsuspecting investor; just as was the owner of the disease-stricken cattle. It is only where the data on which he forms his conclusions are equally available to all,

[8] See above, p. 69.

and all parties are really taking a chance, that he has any right to sell for a fall.

The general principle thus is that both buyer and seller have the moral right to all the available data upon which an agreement of purchase and sale is based. Silence on the other hand, is justified (1) in the face of an attempted "holdup", which aims to take advantage of other people's future plans and labors; (2) where the value of the subject of sale is not a "fact" which is capable of somewhat accurate determination, but a mere matter of "opinion", in which, since each party to the transaction is "taking a chance", he who must bear the losses incident to the game is entitled to the gains.[9]

The practice of speculation itself is tolerable, however, under only two conditions. A man may buy for either of two purposes; (1) with a view to his own use, or in order to facilitate a process which will lead ultimately to consumption, as the purchase of commodities by a manufacturer, wholesaler, or retailer; (2) in order to benefit from price fluctuations. Of course both aims may be united in the same transaction, but the distinction between the two remains. Purchases of the latter sort are called speculation. Speculation is morally justified on two conditions. One is that the process has, on the whole, social utility. For the sake of argument we may admit that justification on this ground is possible. The second condition is that the parties engaged in speculation have at least some notion of the amount of risk involved. Here it is the bounden duty of those who make such transactions possible, the brokers, the investment bankers, or whoever they may be, to reduce the risks of participants as far as possible by making the distinction to their customers between investments which are relatively safe and those in which the element of chance is exceptionally large, such, for example, as the bonds of certain Latin American states. And this they can do in many instances, if they will, by the simple expedient of refusing credit for speculation in shaky securities. The failure to do so in the period from 1925 to 1929 has very properly brought a considerable number of banking houses into disrepute, and has unfortunately tended to arouse an unjustified attitude of suspicion towards bankers as such.

[9] For a further discussion of this subject see Notes, p. 295.

We are not thinking of the small minority who deliberately initiated a campaign of outrageous lies and dangled temptation before the eyes of the lambs. We are thinking of those who perhaps regarded themselves as far more honorable than these moral outcasts, but who nevertheless placed upon the market, without warning to investors, millions of dollars worth of securities of whose speculative character they were fully aware, concerning which, however, the public was quite ignorant. Such men had no sense of the responsibilities inherent in their position, and evidently looked upon it in no other light than as affording them an opportunity to slip other people's money into their own pockets.

What then, in a world of half-lights and shifting views, is the standard of due caution in placing hazardous bargains before the general public. A picture in *Punch* shows two small children emerging from a field to the highroad, each with a pail of berries. The kindly old gentleman, who always happens to be present on such occasions, says to them: "I would not eat that fruit, children. How do you know it is not poisonous?" "Oh", is the reply, "we are not going to eat it, we are going to sell it." The standard of due caution is to sell only what you would be willing to eat. This has been well formulated in the code of the National Leather and Shoe Finders Association, as follows. The vendor "should never advise a customer to buy an article which he would not buy himself if he were in his position." To which are added these words: "Never urge a customer to buy beyond his means. Take advantage of no man's ignorance." [10]

The Law of Caveat Emptor: The Facts

In medieval times the teachings of the church, combined with the discipline of merchants' associations or guilds, and the law of local communities and the state, imposed a strict standard on merchants not merely in making statements about their goods, but also in selling satisfactory goods quite apart from any statements which might accompany their sales. It is of course true that merchants did not universally observe these standards; but they were, at any rate, enforced not only by giving buyers some help in case they were im-

[10] Edgar L. Heermance, *Codes of Ethics* (Burlington, Vermont, Free Press Printing Co., 1924), p. 301.

posed upon, but by penalties and administrative procedure directed toward punishing sellers. As Professor Walton Hamilton has shown, the theory and structure of these early standards underwent a relaxing change under the pressure of ideas developed in the Seventeenth, Eighteenth, and Nineteenth Centuries, in connection with the growth of modern capitalism.[11] The change was parallel to a transformation in the religious and legal treatment of usury and interest, which was produced by the same influences.[12] One can indeed trace the same influences in the development of many other modern ideas, for example, the idea of a natural liberty of contract.

The outcome of this process is the present common-law doctrine. It is stated by Professor W. H. Page as follows: "According to the weight of authority, the mere omission by one party to disclose facts material to the contract which are known to him and not to the adversary party does not in the absence of special circumstances amount to fraud or affect the validity of the contract." [13]

To this rule, however, there are a considerable number of exceptions, which serve greatly to mitigate its rigor. They can be listed under the following headings:—

(1) Active concealment, in some jurisdictions, will be treated as equivalent to fraud. The meaning of active concealment is illustrated by the well-known story of the man who, in selling a horse blind in one eye, kept turning the horse as the prospective purchaser walked around it so that the purchaser did not discover the defect.

(2) "In contracts of sale the vendor is, in the absence of express agreement to the contrary, assumed to warrant by implication the existence of the thing sold, and his title thereto if the property is in his possession." [14] The protection afforded the purchaser by this rule covers a large number of items. For details the reader must consult the text books, especially Professor Page's *Contracts* in the section just cited.

(3) Many courts hold that the seller is under legal obligation to disclose the defects of his goods where the purchaser has been given no adequate opportunity to examine them, or where they are of such

[11] "The Ancient Maxim, Caveat Emptor," 40 *Yale Law Jour.* 1133 (1931).

[12] See Tawney, *Religion and the Rise of Capitalism.*

[13] *Contracts,* Vol. I, Sec. 385; *cf.* Williston, *Contracts,* Sec. 1497.

[14] Page, *op. cit.,* Sec. 392.

a nature that the purchaser could not be expected to discover them for himself. The confusion on this point which exists in American courts is well illustrated by the fact that the sale of cattle infected with Texas fever (see p. 64, above), would be binding in Illinois,[15] but not in Missouri.[16] The decision of the Missouri court turns on the fact that "Texas fever is not easily detectable except by those having had experience with it". The tendency of modern decisions seems to be to extend this rule to cover as many cases as possible.

(4) Certain kinds of contracts have by long-standing tradition been excluded from the operation of *caveat emptor,* notably contracts of insurance.

(5) The agent and the trustee owe a peculiar duty of loyalty to the persons whose interests they are engaged in serving. Thus a trustee who deals with his beneficiary, either in buying or selling, must make a full disclosure of everything the trustee knows which might influence the beneficiary's judgment; and in the absence of such a disclosure, any purchase from or sale to the beneficiary will be set aside by a court.[17]

(6) A court of equity will refuse to enforce a contract if it regards the terms as grossly unfair. In so far as such a contract was brought into existence by the failure of one party to disclose defects, it might be refused enforcement on the ground of its unfairness. This rule would undoubtedly protect the owner of a farm containing valuable minerals who was induced to sell his property at ordinary farm prices because ignorant of the existing minerals.[18] However, according to Professor Page,[19] where a court of equity refuses to order specific performance on the ground of non-disclosure of a material fact there are usually found other facts in addition which render the contract unfair.

There is certainly a growing demand in the community for protection against fraud through silence, and the courts are yielding more and more to this pressure. Where such protection can not be

[15] Morris *v.* Thompson, 85 Ill. 16 (1877).

[16] Grigsby *v.* Stapleton, 94 Mo. 423 (1887).

[17] For an account of a trustee's duty in this and other respects, see Scott, "The Trustee's Duty of Loyalty," 49 *Harv. L. Rev.* 521 (1936).

[18] See Williston, *op. cit.* Sec. 1426, Note 17.

[19] *Op. cit.* Sec. 386.

obtained through the ordinary procedure of the courts, it will be sought through legislation. The sense of the public, that standards at least comparable to those which govern the sale of horses, food, and clothes, should govern, as far as possible, the sale of securities, is expressed both in new state legislation and in the Federal Securities Act and the Securities Exchange Act now in force. The Securities Act of 1933, for example, requires that persons participating in the issue and the original sale of the corporate securities governed by the act, shall make full disclosure of all relevant information in statements open to the public. If misstatements are made, it makes provision for civil actions in which purchasers may recover their losses from some persons in any event, and from others, unless the sellers can show that the misstatements were not due to their negligence. In case of a loss on securities about which a false statement appears in the published information, the person suing to recover for the loss need not prove that he relied on the published statement. Nor is carelessness on the part of the buyer a defense to his action; and only if in fact he knew the true situation is he prevented from recovering.[20]

Whatever may be said with respect to administrative difficulties which have arisen or which may arise under the new legislation, it can not be doubted that it reflects the general conviction that it is desirable to strengthen the sanctions of good faith in business transactions.[21]

The Law of Caveat Emptor: Explanation of the Facts

"The general rule of law is a requirement of good faith in mutual dealings, and . . . the doctrine of *caveat emptor* is an exception to such requirements", declares a federal court in The Clandeboye.[22] What justification, if any, can be offered for the continued existence of this exception, apart from the fact, asserted by Story just one hun-

[20] See a series of articles beginning in 43 *Yale L. Jour.* 171 (1933), particularly Shulman, "Civil Liability and the Securities Act," p. 227.

[21] On this entire subject see Page, *Contracts,* Ch. XIV; Williston, *Contracts,* Secs. 1497–1499, and 1426; Anson, *Contracts,* 5th Amer. Ed., Secs. 189–193; *Restatement of the Law of Contracts,* Vol. II, Sec. 472; *cf.* Secs. 501, 502, 507.

[22] 70 Fed. 635 (1895).

dred years ago that "the old rule is now too firmly established to be open to legal controversy"? [23]

The opinion in The Clandeboye, just referred to, contains the most plausible and most complete answer to this question with which we are acquainted. It reads:

"The doctrine of *caveat emptor* . . . is founded upon special reasons, *viz.* the necessities of commerce and the impossibility of so limiting any other doctrine as to do justice. As Chief Justice Marshall says, 'It would be difficult to circumscribe the contrary doctrine within proper limits.' The necessities of commerce require that enterprise should be encouraged by allowing diligence at least its due reward, and not interfering with any proper and reasonably fair competition for intelligence. Any other course would set the active and the slothful upon an equality.

"Even more weighty is the second reason given in support of the doctrine. The law works with blunt tools. Fallible memories, prejudiced statements, intentional falsehoods, the bias of self-interest, ignorance, and stupidity, are all concomitants of much of the testimony from which she has to make up her judgments. General rules, applicable to the majority of cases, but sometimes having an oppressive bearing upon particular ones, make up the principles upon which, of necessity, she founds her decisions, for the law must be workable. It must be comprehensible to men who live under its rule, and must not be so complex as to overburden the memory with minutiae. Further, were it open, in all cases of contracts, for the dissatisfied party to cry off by saying that the other party had known better than he the value of the subject-matter, or the market price, or some other extrinsic circumstance, there would be no finality in human dealings; and the only limitation to the litigation that would ensue would be that imposed by the diminution of business caused by such want of finality and certainty."

We do not regard it as the part of wisdom for a layman to criticize the procedure of the courts, not because they are sacrosanct, but rather because those persons who stand outside of any complicated system and view it from a distance seldom understand either the excellences or the defects in its workings sufficiently well to enable them to form a useful opinion on the subject. However, when procedure seeks to justify itself by an appeal to ethical principles, the ethicist will not hesitate to raise his voice. Whatever, then, may be said in behalf of the other arguments of the court, one of them is based upon a popular but thoroughly fallacious conception. It reads: "The neces-

[23] *Commentaries on Equity Jurisprudence,* 1st Ed. p. 221; cited in Hamilton (as above), 40 *Yale L. Journ.* 1180.

sities of commerce require that enterprise should be encouraged by allowing diligence its due reward." This is an interesting example of using a principle, valid within certain limits, in total disregard of such limits. It is quite true, as a general proposition, that whether for the purpose of encouraging enterprise or for other reasons, we should allow diligence its due reward. But it is not diligence as such which is entitled to a reward, but diligence exercised for the economic benefit of society. The safe-blower, the forger, and the counterfeiter often show an exceptional degree of diligence. If it is *diligence* as such that must be rewarded, they are as much entitled to compensation as the man who, in selling or buying goods, departs from "the general rule of law [requiring] good faith in mutual dealings".

The failure to discover defects in the goods which one purchases may indeed often be due to carelessness, which is another name for mental laziness; and it may be true that the lazy are not justified in applying to the courts to undo the ill effects of their own shortcomings. On the other hand, such failure may be due to ignorance as to what to look for, which in turn may be due either to inexperience or lack of intelligence. Or, again, the failure to treat the seller as a crook may be due to confidence in his honesty and intelligence. Whatever, then, may be said for the refusal to protect the lazy against the consequences of their laziness the same cannot be said for the inexperienced, the less intelligent, and the trusting. To fail to protect them is unjust. And if it be said that the lazy cannot be distinguished by a court from the other classes just mentioned the conclusion may well be that all ought to be protected.

The above opinion may perhaps seem too sweeping to those who, like the judges, have to meet such problems face to face in the course of the day's work. But however that may be, the refusal of certain courts to protect purchasers against defects which are latent seems to us an inexcusable miscarriage of justice. "The law helps [only] him who helps himself" may—or may not—be a sound practical principle. But a failure on its part to protect those who, through no fault of their own, are not in a position to protect themselves, is an outrage.

CHAPTER VI

KNOWING ONE'S BUSINESS

"You mind your business and I'll mind mine", is a statement or a threat which we have all heard many times. On this view a man's business is a purely personal affair. If he succeeds he is the sole gainer; if he fails he is the sole loser. Such a conception is quite naive. A reputable concern can remain in existence only as it supplies the needs of a considerable number of persons. And the kind of service it gives and the cost of such service is a matter that may concern these customers deeply. Since their interests are involved, directly or indirectly, in all its transactions, they have a claim not merely to be treated honestly, but also intelligently. Accordingly the fact that an intimate acquaintance with every detail of his business is personally advantageous to the owner does not prevent it from being at the same time a social obligation. So clearly has this been recognized that for centuries, in one way or another, the state has considered itself justified in using its power to secure a guarantee of at least minimum fitness in many fields of economic service.

Government Regulation, Past and Present

Thus in 1515, Francis the First, King of France, issued an edict from which the following extract has been freely translated.[1]

"Among other things it has been discovered that there is a great, an excessive, and immoderate number of notaries, of which the greater part are unlearned and are ignorant of the requirements of their office. What is worse, they can neither read nor write, nor record signatures, so that it is only with the greatest difficulty that any of the contracts, letters and orders executed by them can be found to be sound and of value, and without suspicion of vice or fault. Out of this state of affairs have come and will continue to come numerous inconveniences, frauds and abuses, to the loss and

[1] Cauvin, *Documents du Mans,* p. 118. Edit de Francois I[er], du 4 aout 1515, portant order de reduire le nombre des notaires es pays d'Anjou et du Maine, et conte de Beaufort.

prejudice of our good Lady and Mother, and of the public interest, if some provision be not made to correct matters."

There followed an order to reduce the number of notaries to a reasonable quota for each community, and a set of standards for selecting the most competent men for the work.

Francis saw this as a simple problem. He was protecting his society against undesirable tendencies. He did not inquire whether a given servant was a vicious and ill-willed reprobate or merely a well meaning ignoramus. Those who were unfitted to function he cast out.

In the economic life of the present day we act in a similar manner, but only in spots. Our unwillingness to be subjected to the ministrations of ignorance is most effectively displayed in those fields where the resultant harm is to life or health or physical welfare. For many years we have prohibited any individual from practicing medicine or surgery unless, by presenting evidence of extensive preparation in appropriate schools, or by passing examinations under a public board, he is able to give assurance that he can undertake the responsibilities of his profession with the certainty of not harming his patients and with at least a reasonable probability of aiding them.

In most states we do not permit untrained individuals to represent another's interests in the courts, partly because such a practice would disturb procedure and partly because too many people would be badly represented. We do not permit a barber to cut hair or shave a chin, or a "beautician" to give a massage until he has shown a Board of Health that he possesses a knowledge of at least the rudiments of hygiene and allied sciences. Because the work of an amateur electrician can result in a disastrous fire, we usually require that such work be done by qualified experts. In the Summer of 1933 badly designed and maintained plumbing in a Chicago hotel resulted in a nation-wide outbreak of amoebic dysentery; but long before that the connection between adequate plumbing and public health had resulted in regulations which required installation and inspection by experts. No doubt most of the motor conscious people in America, after having seen the engines of their motor cars mangled by an incompetent dolt, would subscribe to the principle that there ought to be legislation guaranteeing that these delicate mechanisms would be repaired and adjusted always by understanding and capable men rather than by some individual whose dubious claim to the title of "mechanic" rests upon the fact that he carries a monkey-wrench in his pocket.

The same desire to protect public interests through insistence on standards of performance will be found in the regulations of the craftsmen's guilds of the Fourteenth and Fifteenth Centuries. An ordinance of 1425 says:

"Because many complaints and objections have been made by various merchants, burghers and inhabitants of this city and the environs to the effect that the laths and tiles which are supplied to cover the houses and edifices are otherwise than good, in that the tiles are badly made and the laths too weak, and not worthy of being sold for their intended use, all of which results in great injury and prejudice to our common reputation, and out of which various damages and inconveniences result, and will continue to result from day to day to the great prejudice of the public welfare, let all people know that, because of these complaints and objections, and for the purpose of remedying these conditions, and for other motives which move us in the consideration of the common welfare and profit, we have ordered and ordained that all laths and tiles which are made in or brought to or sold in this city shall be inspected by the stewards appointed by us to ascertain whether they are good and sound merchandise and worthy of being put to use." [2]

A writer of the Sixteenth Century, criticizing the medical standards of his times, expressed similar sentiments, but in a different way:

"It is certain that drugs, both simple and complex, were not so well known at the time of these writers as they are in our own time. But of what use are books which teach one to know these things if nobody is willing to read them? What good are teachers who would explain them, if nobody will take the trouble to listen? . . . What good does it do to have a wise doctor, capable in his practice, if he sends his prescription to an apothecary who does not know how to read it? I believe that the apothecaries will admit that there are many among them who are sometimes much put to it to read the prescriptions of the doctors. For my own part, I have a recollection that, finding myself one day in a place where I heard an apothecary read the prescription of a physician, I perceived that he said something contrary to what I had learned a few days before at a lecture by M. Sylvius; and having made a wager between us concerning the word on which I had

[2] A. Thierry, *Recueil des monuments inedits de l'histoire du tiers etat.* I Ser., Vol. II, p. 95, Ordonnance de l'echevinage relative au commerce des tuiles et des lattes.

caught him up, we got in touch with the doctor who had written the prescription. He, having asked this apothecary if he was not ashamed at having doubted what I said, added a good deal more to the point that if he had mixed the way he read he would have caused the patient to lose a thousand lives had he had that many. . . . The whole of this applies to the many poor patients, whom they do not fail to charge dearly for the privilege of dying under their hands." [3]

A single principle underlies all these regulations and complaints. As far as possible, the public is to be protected against the ignorance of practitioners in these various fields. In each, and in many others which might be recited, there is the assumption that the possession of certain standards of knowledge and capacity by those engaged in legitimate occupations is a duty, and that he who undertakes to reap the honors and emoluments of a trade or profession must also be able to discharge its obligations in a satisfactory manner.

The intellectual endowments necessary to function efficiently in the fields which have been mentioned are no higher than those needed in the business world today. A system of licensing is neither possible nor desirable as a condition for entering into most commercial pursuits. But the principle which justifies the licensing of physicians and lawyers by the state is of universal application: No one has the right to undertake any work for society for which he does not possess the requisite knowledge and training.

Business Knowledge as an Obligation

We have been talking at length about wilful or deliberate misrepresentation as one of the greatest evils of the business world. But there is an unintentional misrepresentation just as there is an intentional one. And since the primary or direct results are the same in either case, as far as the immediate transaction is concerned, the responsibility is fundamentally the same, provided the ignorance which was the cause of the misrepresentation was avoidable. "He who is really anxious to tell the truth will always be anxious to have the truth to tell." There is thus a duty to know one's own goods, a duty to know what goods the market has to offer, to know what

[3] Henri Estienne, *Apologie pour Herodote,* Ch. XVI, "Des larrecins, des marchands, et autres gens de divers estats."

goods are really the best, at the price, for the various purposes for which customers will use them, and as far as possible to procure such goods.

What, then, are we to think of the bankers who placed on the market certain South American bonds without investigating their value and sold them as first class securities at first class prices? They were so busy making money for themselves that they would not take the time to see whether they were giving value for value. Or they were "easy-going" and were unwilling to take the necessary trouble. The quality of a bond depends upon its security, its yield, and its marketability. It is the duty of the seller to know every relevant fact bearing in any important degree upon these three characteristics. If he neglects this duty he is subjecting his customers to risks which he would never take for himself, and is just as dangerous as and little better than an outright liar.[4]

Such ignorance is not merely a virtual injustice to one's customers, it is a menace to competitors who are conducting their business in an intelligent and honorable way.

A retired bricklayer with some savings decides to open a small furniture store. Knowing nothing more about the business than the fundamental precept that one must buy low and sell high, he finds himself utterly unable to distinguish between mahogany and gumwood. With the best intentions in the world, and with an expansive feeling of self-satisfaction at the service he is performing for the community, he proceeds to sell to his equally ignorant customers, "mahogany" desks and chairs at prices which are the wonder of the neighborhood. It might be claimed in this instance that since the customers get their money's worth their real interests are not harmed in any way, and that as long as they can contrive to remain ignorant and not discover the truth they will remain happy. We need not discuss at this point whether ignorance is really bliss. Let us rather ask, what about the real expert who conducts a business on the next street, who must charge seemingly fantastic prices for his genuine mahogany pieces, and who sells at his new competitor's prices only plainly marked imitations? It is not enough to say that eventually these misrepresentations will be brought to light and that then the

[4] See above, Ch. V, p. 74.

law can be left to take care of the matter. The legitimate merchant has grounds for complaint and is justified in demanding protection against such competition before rather than after the harm has been done. It is small satisfaction to know that the fellow who is cutting your throat will end by cutting his own.

There are, however, other forms of business ignorance just as harmful and just as inexcusable as ignorance of the nature of what one has to sell. Probably the most serious and wide-spread of these is ignorance of costs.

A retail-wholesale company in a small Wisconsin town purchased sugar in Chicago in carload lots and took a discount of two per cent for cash payments. They delivered the sugar by truck from the headquarters in Wisconsin over an area of several counties at a price which was equivalent to the Chicago wholesale price plus the freight to the Wisconsin community. They refused to consider delivery costs and other overhead expenses on the ground that "the trucks would have to make the trips anyway", and were satisfied that they were "making" the amount of the cash discount, that is to say, two per cent. There was no question of predatory intent in this case. They were simply "picking up a little velvet". Their records were not of such a nature that the losses on the sugar sales could be demonstrated, and they were only persuaded by long and disastrous experience that their arithmetic had been very bad indeed. In the meantime, practically all of the dealers in the territory covered by the trucks went out of the sugar business because they had the good sense not to attempt to duplicate this feat of arithmetical legerdemain.

Ought we to take an attitude of casual forgiveness toward the members of this company who blithely spread destruction around them, or ought we to insist that the business man who, through ignorance of adequate methods of determining costs, or through carelessness or indifference, sets prices which are in fact cut-throat prices, is as lacking in appreciation of his social responsibilities as is the man who consciously sets such cut-throat prices with the intention of driving his competitors out of business?

"Ignorant competition is most dangerous to the development and success of our country. . . . The competition which is most insidious and dangerous is that which results from an inadequate knowledge of costs. Laws cannot reach this difficulty. It is a matter of internal organization of each factory, and until the matter is taken up enthusiastically by business men themselves, permanent results cannot be obtained. . . . If this lack of system resulted merely in the elimination of the inefficient it might be regarded as an economic benefit. But in effect it reacts disastrously upon the efficient manufacturer. While the inefficient manufacturer is going down hill to destruction he is cutting prices right and left and demoralizing the market." [5]

The seller thus owes a knowledge of his business alike to his customers, to his competitors, and, we may add, to his creditors. But the buyer owes a parallel duty, not merely to himself but to the business community as such. It is his ignorance that makes it possible for the swindler to mislead him. But every successful act of swindling has a doubly deleterious effect upon the selling community. It confirms the seller in his habits, and makes it more and more likely that he will depend on dishonest methods for results. It tends at the same time to demoralize his competitors. The morally weaker ones will be the first to follow his example, and this may go on until it is all but impossible for honest men to succeed in this field.

Responsibility for Carelessness

Ignorance, whether of the character of one's goods, of business costs, of the state of the market, and the forces at work in it, or what not, may be due to stupidity or it may be due to carelessness in the literal sense of the word, that is to say, indifference. If a man has not been endowed with brains enough to be able to distinguish between fabrics which are all wool and those which are fifty per cent cotton, if he can not see the difference between a Nicaraguan bond and a bond of the Pennsylvania Railroad then he has no more business in the field than a man who is color-blind has to drive a locomotive. His first duty alike to himself and to the world is to get into some other kind of work, and the quicker the better.

It may well be, however, that the greater part of the ignorance that displays itself in the business world is due not so much to stupidity as to carelessness. The legal term is negligence; the every day word is laziness. They all come to the same thing:—"Too much

[5] Edward N. Hurley, *The Awakening of Business* (New York, Doubleday, Page and Co., 1917), p. 15.

trouble". And the explanation is given by the cant phrase: "Why worry?" Why indeed? Why should a man worry when the doctor tells him he has cancer, and he knows this means he will die within a few months, after weeks of agony? The answer is that pain—his own pain,—and imminent death—his own death,—are things he cares about. The sources of laziness and negligence lie in the fact that there are things he does not care about, that he is indifferent to, either his own future financial success or the interests of his customers. More often than not it is both.

Incurable stupidity is not a proper subject of moral blame. We have the right to blame it only when it forces itself into positions which it is incapable of filling. And this usually brings its own punishment—bitter and long-continued. But negligence, or carelessness, or laziness, whichever you wish to call it, is a matter of morals.

When negligence produces serious results, as in an automobile accident or the death of a patient under the care of a physician, it is everywhere recognized as culpable, and in many instances is punishable by law. When the consequences are loss of money or inferior service the principle remains the same. Negligence, as we have said, is due to indifference to others. But such indifference is the source of every criminal act except those which are motivated by malice. The thief steals, the dishonest manufacturer sells dangerous drugs, the racketeer bombs a shop, because he wants the money and because he cares little or nothing about the harm done to others. Similarly the negligent banker sells valueless South American bonds, the negligent real estate broker sells Nevada orchards, because he wants the money, and because he cares so little about the possible harm to others that he refuses to sacrifice ease in order to get together the information that would have prevented the loss. The crooked, the lazy, and the stupid are the pests of the business world; and the lazy are people who do about as much harm as the crooked and the stupid when nature has made them for something better.

CHAPTER VII

THE LIMITS OF PERSUASION

Preying upon Weakness

The Sunday edition of the *New York World* for April 11, 1926, carried an account of the way in which certain New York undertakers were playing upon the feelings of the poor in order to push them into extravagant funerals upon the death of a member of the family. One of its stories was the following. A laborer at small wages for a street railway company was killed accidentally, leaving no provision for his family other than two $500 insurance policies on which he had kept up the payments. An undertaker learned about these policies from the prostrated family and secured their signatures to a blank contract. The bill which he finally presented contained, among other things, such items as a casket for $450; $150 for five automobiles; $30 for palms; and $50 for clothes. The $1,000 of insurance money proving insufficient to cover the entire bill, the undertaker presented an invoice for $74 more.[1]

The ways in which an undertaker can successfully take advantage of a time of intense emotional agitation to play upon grief and pride are suggested with sardonic humor in Mark Twain's account of his conversation with an old acquaintance whom he met on a visit to his boyhood's home. A few years before this man had been in poverty, but was now the possessor of a prosperous and profitable business. The tale is told in *Life on the Mississippi.*[2] The undertaker speaks:—

> " 'A rich man won't have anything but your very best; and you can just pile it on too—pile it on and sock it to him—he won't ever holler. And you take in a poor man, and if you work him right he'll bust himself on a single lay-out. Or especially a woman. F'r instance: Mrs. O'Flaherty comes in—widow—wiping her eyes and kind of moaning. Unhandkerchiefs one eye, bats it around tearfully over the stock; says:

[1] See *The Literary Digest,* May 22, 1926, p. 29.

[2] New York, Harper and Brothers, Ch. XLIII.

" 'And fhat might ye ask for that wan?'

" 'Thirty-nine dollars, madam,' says I.

" 'It's a foine big price, sure, but Pat shall be buried like a gintleman, as he was, if I have to work me fingers off for it. I'll have that wan, sor.'

" 'Yes, madam,' says I, 'and it is a very good one, too; not costly, to be sure, but in this life we must cut our garments to our cloth, as the saying is.' And as she starts out, I heave in, kind of casually, 'This one with the white satin lining is a beauty, but I am afraid—well, sixty-five dollars is a rather—rather—but no matter, I felt obliged to say to Mrs. O'Shaughnessy—'

" 'D'ye mane to soy that Bridget O'Shaughnessy bought the mate to that joo-ul box to ship that dhrunken divil to Purgatory in?'

" 'Yes, madam.'

" 'Then Pat shall go to heaven in the twin to it, if it takes the last rap the O'Flahertys can raise; and moind you, stick on some extras, too, and I'll give ye another dollar.'

"And as I lay in with the livery stables, of course I don't forget to mention that Mrs. O'Shaughnessy hired fifty-four dollars' worth of hacks and flung as much style into Dennis's funeral as if he had been a duke or an assassin. And of course she sails in and goes the O'Shaughnessy about four hacks and an omnibus better."

The popular horror and indignation caused by the publication of the incidents collected by the *World*—even supposing that the charges for materials and services were no higher than those demanded of the well-to-do and the rich for the same things—show that in the opinion of most people there is such a thing as overpersuasion; *i. e.* a use of one's powers of persuasion, which even though they may never overstep the boundaries of truth, is essentially illegitimate. And this means that it is thoroughly dishonorable to urge large expenditures upon those who will have to enslave themselves for months or years to pay the bills.

This does not mean that persuasion may not be a legitimate factor in the selling of goods. It is, indeed, within limits, just as legitimate as the giving of information. Persuasion is nothing more than an attempt to supply such stimuli to the emotions and the will as are likely to induce a person to make a purchase when the mere awareness of the qualities and the uses of the goods will not be sufficient to move him to action. Such an appeal may often be in the buyer's own best interest. We are all inclined to be lazy in mind as well as in body, and for this reason tend to ignore or reject the new; we are unwilling to take the trouble to examine its merits, to get it, or to readjust our modes of living to it. We are creatures of habit, and thus, more or less, slaves to our own past. We are lovers of the old order if for no other reason than that we feel at home with the familiar. In some respects we are far too gullible; but we are likewise often too skeptical. Men thus need to be moved as well as enlightened. Accordingly the attempt to awaken desire through an appeal to the imagination or the emotions may be not merely legitimate but positively laudable; in so far, that is, as it contributes to the enrichment and fuller development of life.

Where Shall We Draw the Line?

Thus persuasion, like any other instrument of power, may be used properly or it may be abused. To state in general terms just where the boundary line ought to be drawn is no doubt difficult. However certain fundamental principles can be laid down which may prove to be not without value as a guide to practice.

The only fair exchange is one that profits both parties. This does not mean that I have any right to determine what other persons' desires shall be, and what they ought to buy or what they ought to refrain from buying. But it does mean that I ought not by my own efforts to push a man into buying today what I believe he will regret having purchased tomorrow, when the emotional glow produced by my words will have evaporated. What this means in practice will become clear, perhaps, if we supplement the above incidents with others which approach nearer and nearer to the line of the permissible but which we think still lie on the wrong side of this line.

A dealer in radio sets, learning that a certain family in poor circumstances has on hand sufficient cash to make a down payment on an expensive instrument, goes to their home, uses all the sales talent at his command, and sells a machine to the family on an instalment contract. The down payment is of sufficient size to insure him against loss in case he is forced to repossess the machine. The family is obviously in serious need of clothing and other necessities, the purchase of which will be, at best, deferred by the purchase of the radio.

In this instance the wrong done, while, of course, not so serious as that of the undertaker, seems to us essentially of the same order. If so it cannot escape condemnation. Should it be asked what the dealer ought to do if a family known to be in want of necessities comes to a shop and demands a radio, we answer that he can not without insulting them refuse to supply them. But he can at least tactfully prevent them from buying an expensive set. And if payment is to be on the instalment plan, he has the right to ask them to make some statement of their financial condition, and he has the duty to set clearly before them the danger that they will be unable to keep the instrument.

The heavy pressure to effect replacement of equipment through fictitious obsolescence which is characteristic of much modern advertising is in our opinion also beyond the boundary line that separates fair from unfair selling. The following example appeared in one of the "smarter" monthlies early in 1936.

"AGE CANNOT WITHER
OH YES IT CAN

"Because . . . even while you read this advertisement . . . something is beginning to wither right in your own kitchen. We mean your electric refrigerator.

"For years it has been delivering refrigeration . . . dependable enough, in truth, but refrigeration without a thrill. And now it is refrigeration for which you will have lost all pride of ownership.

"What has aged it? Why are you suddenly being told that the old 'box' is ready for the second-hand man? Because, with the 1936 De Luxe——, household refrigeration has taken a long stride forward."

A perusal of the advertisement in its entirety reveals that the "long stride forward", apart from fantastic claims for economy which are duplicated by every other manufacturer of refrigerators in the field, consists in no more than a "built in" thermometer.

A second example in this style lacks the feature of misrepresentation which makes the first one not merely vicious but also dishonest, but is in certain respects even more reprehensible. *Business Week* for October 12, 1929, contained the following item.

"A $4,000,000, four year national advertising campaign by the newly organized furniture industry has started. Women are to be made 'furniture conscious'. Low sales are the cause. Billboards will ask: 'Would you drive an auto as old as your parlor sofa?' 'Would you wear a gown as out of date as your dining table?' 'Are your home fashions a handicap in meeting friends?' "

These advertisements are phrased to play upon what is at once one of the most childish, most insatiable, and most devastating impulses of human nature,—the desire to make a better show than one's neighbors. It leads to a never ending competition in every department of human life from clothes to yachts; a competition which in the nature of the case can never produce anything more than a temporary satisfaction. The moment in which you pass a rival may be an exhilarating one. But unless he at least threatens to pass you in turn you soon cease to think anything more about him, and the initial flash of feeling fades into nothingness. When we are recovering from an illness and are allowed to go outdoors for the first time after a long period of confinement in the sick room we compare our present with the past and experience a delicious sense of freedom and well-being. But after a few days we have become used to our condition and are no more capable of feeling delight at our present state of health than in the fact that we are not blind, deaf, or crippled. "The man with the toothache thinks all men with sound teeth are happy." But those with sound teeth know better. So it is in the matter of rivalry. The Browns must get ahead of the Joneses or at least keep up with them; the Joneses, on their part, cannot permit the Browns to remain even on the same level with them. This process creates more anxieties, heart burnings, envy and bitterness of spirit than perhaps anything else in life, and in return yields less satisfaction to the parties in the game. It is, to be sure, a fact of human nature, and it can not be eradicated. But to appeal to it, and to seek to strengthen and extend it on a national scale in the interests of sheer economic waste seems a betrayal of fundamental obligations, not far different from trying to awaken a dormant appetite for whiskey or opium.

These appeals to human weakness, with the consequent encouragement of extravagance and waste, are sometimes excused on the ground that they put money into circulation, and are thus of advantage to the community as a whole. Since this attempted justification embodies an ancient and widely held fallacy, it is worth a moment's attention.

Most people have comparatively small incomes. If they spend money for one thing they will have to contract their expenditures somewhere else. Even if they do not spend all they get as soon as they get it, they do not, under normal economic conditions, put the residue into a stocking or hide it in a mattress. They deposit it in a bank or invest it where it will do work. Accordingly this type of salesmanship has no economic value whatever for society as a whole. Indeed its social—including its economic—effects are thoroughly bad. For it awakens or strengthens desires which can never be satisfied, and which are in no small part responsible for the financial recklessness, the craze for speculation, the dishonesty, in short the determination to get money at any cost, which were among the leading causes of the crash of 1929. Since in a diseased society few or none can prosper, this practice is as unfair to the community as it is to the individual immediately concerned.

A final case will bring us fairly to the border line between the legitimate and illegitimate, and may well be on the safe side of this somewhat elusive entity. It is represented by an extract taken from the discussion of a coöperative advertising campaign of the Wall Paper Manufacturers' Association.

> "The campaign by the Wall Paper Manufacturers' Association has been very successful in a number of different ways. Apparently it has very greatly increased the sale of wall-paper and has done this without decreasing the sale of other wall decorative material. It has made people wall-paper conscious. In the past it has not been uncommon for wall-paper to remain on walls three, five or even ten years, or more. As long as the wall-paper was not torn or ragged or seriously discolored, it was allowed to remain, regardless of how dirty and faded it became. The advertising done by the association has had a most striking effect in shortening the life of wall-paper decoration."

If this campaign really resulted in the change of wall-paper far more frequently than hygienic or aesthetic demands might require, no real interests of the consumers were served. On the other hand, to the extent that such a sales effort might improve the hygienic or aesthetic conditions in homes, it is obviously a step in real education and is serving a useful purpose. The normal effects of the advertising must be used as the basis for judgment upon this effort on the part of the manufacturers to push their wares.

The preceding illustrations have been taken from the field of retail trade and thus of consumers' goods. Estimates of harm done by overpersuasion are here in the very nature of the case somewhat elusive, except in extreme instances. But in the sale of capital goods the situation is quite different. Here gain and loss can be measured in terms of dollars and cents. Here there is no excuse whatever for the more flagrant forms of overselling. Thus a manufacturer finds that his inventory of finished goods has become entirely too high. Thereupon he puts on an additional force of salesmen and sends them out on the road to talk dealers into purchasing the maximum they can be induced to buy—an amount, in many instances, far beyond that which they can possibly sell within a reasonable time. This seems a particularly indecent procedure. The manufacturer overestimates the market and in consequence finds himself with unsalable goods on his hands. By means of the persuasive powers of salesmanship he transfers the risk and most of the losses to his retailers. If the transaction was clearly to the disadvantage of the latter, the mere fact that they could be persuaded or cajoled into accepting the risk is no justification for the practice. Salesmanship is a means of effectively serving customers and not of transferring risks to them.

The Salesman as the Loyal Adviser of His Customers

Despite all the trickery and verbal doping that are common in the selling of goods today, there are salesmen who serve as the loyal advisers of their customers. A few years ago one of the authors of this volume proposed to purchase a pair of lenses for use in a stereoscopic camera and to that end corresponded with the New York representative of a famous German optical company. He wished to purchase a pair of lenses of extreme aperture at a very high price, but the German representative, having discovered the use to which the lenses were to be put, politely but firmly informed him that a set of slower lenses, costing about one third as much, would prove far more satisfactory for his purposes and advised the purchase of the less expensive lenses. After some correspondence in which the advantages and the disadvantages of the large and small apertured lenses were pointed out to him, the author eventually purchased the larger lenses against the advice of the seller. But because he purchased them with a full knowledge of their shortcomings, he has never expected the impossible and has never been disappointed in their possession.

This is by no means an isolated incident. In this same spirit, for example, many high class banks refuse to make loans for plainly inadvisable investments even when the security is excellent and they themselves are fully protected.

To the authors of this book billboard advertising is one of the abominations of the present age. But everyone must make acknowledgment to the spirit which led to the inclusion of the following article in the code of the Poster Advertising Association: "We believe in dissuading a would-be advertiser from starting a campaign when in our judgment his product, his facilities, his available funds, or some other factor makes his success doubtful".[3]

This attitude toward customers is perhaps even more important in the wholesale trade than in dealing with ultimate consumers. For these must depend in most instances upon the retailer; and the average retailer can not be expected to know the qualities and other characteristics of all the hundreds of articles that make up his stock in trade. The wholesale salesman, therefore, can perform a service whose value can hardly be over-estimated if he places at the disposal of his customers the facts which will enable them to make a wise choice among the goods which they carry, and give them the benefit of his best judgment as to the amount of each line which they will be able to dispose of. If in a spirit of optimism a retailer shows inclination to invest in goods too expensive for his clientele the honorable salesman obeys the injunction of the Wholesale Men's Furnishing Code; "Nor shall [customers] knowingly be permitted to select goods not suitable for their stores without a diplomatic word of caution from the salesman".[4]

Such procedure is not merely good ethics, it is good business. For, as has been said thousands of times, the greatest asset of any business establishment is a body of satisfied customers. Perhaps it is not a matter of chance that the house which made every effort to prevent the sale of expensive lenses to one who, in their opinion, would be better served by a cheaper article is a branch of one of the oldest, perhaps the most famous, and presumably one of the most successful optical firms in the world.

[3] Heermance, *op. cit.*, p. 12.
[4] Heermance, *op. cit.*, p. 365.

But a sales policy of this kind is "good business" in a broader and profounder sense than can be measured by success in accumulating financial profits. It helps to make life's everyday activities more enjoyable. For what we want is not merely efficient service; equally with this we crave friendliness of personal relations with those with whom we associate. The normal man would rather have a friend and be a friend than an enemy; he wants to feel good will towards his fellows, and not suspicion and hatred. Every salesman who is genuinely loyal to his customers is doing his part to create this kind of a world.

Summary

In a fair bargain, as we have seen in the preceding chapters, each party must have before him a correct and essentially complete picture, as far as such a picture is attainable, of what he is getting and giving. To this condition we have now added a second: The exchange must be such that on cool reflection and with no change in the situation each party will be glad he agreed to it. This statement must not be misunderstood. Many a man sells a house for less than he had hoped to get. Indeed, whatever the selling price, he would doubtless have liked to see it go higher. Nevertheless he may be very glad indeed that a purchaser came along and offered him such terms as he did. What is wrong is playing upon the shortsightedness and weakness of another. As an English court once declared, to take advantage of a man's weakness is as bad as taking advantage of his ignorance.[5]

To the above conditions a third will be added in Chapter XIII.

[5] Cited in Page, *Contracts,* Vol. I, Sec. 217.

CHAPTER VIII

LOYALTY TO CONTRACTS

What It Means to Make a Contract

Most large scale business transactions and many smaller ones take the form of contracts. Indeed any purchase and sale may be regarded as a contract. "I will give you ten cents if you will give me a Robinson Crusoe cigar." As usually understood, however, a contract involves a promise on the part of one or both parties to do this or that at some later date. It is with contracts in this narrower and more accurate sense that we shall deal in this chapter.

This separation in time between agreement and performance takes place in every department of the business world, but it forms the very essence of many kinds of business relationships, as those obtaining between employer and employee—thus covering the entire field of personal services; between borrower and lender,—the field of credit transactions; between landlord and tenant; and usually between manufacturer and wholesaler and their respective customers. The study of contracts is thus a study of the majority of business transactions.

A contract differs from a promise in that fulfilment is made conditional upon the action of the other party. Each contractor says to the other: "I will do this if you will do that". A promise, in its turn, differs from a mere statement that I expect to do so and so. It is an assertion that I have decided to act in the future in a certain way serviceable to the promisee, and to allow no further consideration of the subject to change my purpose. This assertion may be true or false. We remember the words of Lord Justice Bowen, quoted earlier: "The state of a man's mind is just as much a fact as the state of his digestion". Accordingly, while failure to keep a promise may be due to unwillingness to put through an earlier determination, it may also be due to the fact that when I promised I had no intention to perform.

In this latter case, I was lying; I was affirming something about my state of mind which I knew to be false.

Since a lie is a lie, whatever its subject matter, the same kinds of unveracity may recur in contracts that we have already met in our discussion of intentional misrepresentation. And since one survey of this unsavory subject is quite enough we shall not attempt any enumeration of the forms of evasion which are to be found in the contractual field, whereby weak and flabby minds try to persuade themselves, and crooked minds try to persuade their victims and the courts that they are telling the truth. Most of the confusion of mind which exists on this subject would disappear at once if we squarely faced and truthfully answered to ourselves this question: What expectations did I intend to arouse in the mind of the other party as to what I would do and what I was demanding in return?

When a man enters into a contractual relationship he binds himself to much that is not explicitly stated in the written or spoken contract. In other words, practically every contract carries with it a train of implicit promises. Thus a contract to accept a position as an employee involves a tacit agreement to refuse bribes in exchange for the employer's business secrets. A lease calls for "reasonable care" in the use of the lessor's property, whether anything is said about it or not. A contract requiring under penalty the completion of a piece of construction by a given date is broken when the other party by his actions or failures to act delays the progress of the work. These things are implied promises, because if the employee or lessee or buyer had not allowed the other party to believe that he would act or forbear acting in this way, the contract would never have been made. It follows that when a man contracts, intending to violate any of these unspoken promises, he is one of those liars by silence whose action through inaction we have discussed in an earlier chapter.

Of these implications perhaps the most fundamental is the possession of the ability and power to do what one undertakes to do; this whether you are a physician caring for a patient, a manufacturer accepting an order, or a purchaser giving an order. A manufacturer agrees to deliver a certain amount of goods at a specified date, knowing perfectly well that he can not have them ready by that time. Of course he is a liar. But it must also be noted that he is equally a liar if he agrees unconditionally to a dated delivery when he does not know whether he will be able to get the goods out by the promised date or not.[1] He is "taking a chance", but he does not say so. He represents himself as certain. He would undoubtedly consider himself as being greatly abused if he should discover that the purchaser really didn't know whether he would be able to pay his bill or not, and was also "taking a chance". For similar reasons it is lying to take orders which you are not prepared to carry out satisfactorily because you either lack the skill or equipment, for you are deliberately arousing expectations which you know you cannot meet. The honorable practice in such situations is that represented in the following provisions in certain of the codes. "When we are offered business for which we are not thoroughly equipped and prepared to render efficient and satisfactory service, we will refer such customer to a fellow manufacturer who is equipped to handle it properly." "To each other we pledge that we will never accept a larger order than can be reasonably delivered within the terms of the contract." [2]

The Foundation of Contract

The foundation upon which contracts rest is of course mutual confidence. This confidence is protected by law as far as such protection is possible. But law alone, even if it could ever become 100 per cent effective, can never by itself afford the amount and kind of protection which the contract system requires for its very existence, to say nothing of its successful operation. Recourse to the law is at best so expensive, so time consuming, and so uncertain in its outcome that most persons do not care to employ it except as a last resort. Apart from this consideration a community in which no one could have any confidence in the honor of anyone else would of course have judges whom no one could trust and whose decisions would be determined by the largest bribe. Accordingly the ultimate source of confidence in the fulfilment of contracts is confidence in the voluntary (extralegal) keeping of contracts. This statement holds true, whatever may

[1] See above Ch. III, p. 43.

[2] Code of the Folding Box Manufacturers' National Association and of the Label Manufacturers' National Association, Heermance, *op. cit.*, p. 409; Code of the American Walnut Manufacturers' Association, *ibid.*, p. 309.

be the motive or motives which actually determine the will to keep faith.

The maintenance of community confidence is accordingly in large part a matter of individual effort and thus of individual responsibility. The same thing is obviously true of community morale. As we saw in studying misrepresentation, we all tend to do what others are doing, especially when this happens to be along the line of least resistance. For the preservation of morale among the members of our community we must accordingly look not merely to the courts but first of all to ourselves.

In general the secondary effects of a breach of contract are those of a lie, not merely in that each decreases confidence and increases the number of broken contracts or lies, but in all other respects. These effects serve as grounds for the obligation to keep faith over and above that initial obligation as between man and man which we are taking for granted throughout this book. But in the field of contracts a new feature enters, owing on the one hand to the very nature of a contract as an obligation looking toward the future, and on the other hand to the uncertainty of human affairs, especially business affairs.

When *A* and *B* make a contract of purchase and sale, for example, *A* expects to find his profit in performing his part of the agreement and knows that *B* enters into the contractual relationship with parallel expectations. Why then the formalities of a contract? For several reasons, one of the most important of which is the following. Each knows that the business situation on which the contract was posited may change, and the transaction which looks as if it would be profitable for both may become unprofitable for one or the other. Each party, accordingly, wishes to bind the other to live up to his side of the agreement, however conditions may change, and in order to accomplish this result agrees to bind himself. Refusal to keep a contract, say when prices turn against me, while expecting the other party to keep his contract should prices turn the other way, thus proceeds on the principle, Heads I win, tails you lose. Such a man is the adult prototype of the small boy who, when beaten at marbles, shouts: "No keeps". Any scheme by which I expect the other fellow to shoulder the losses when it is his turn, while I shove them off on him when my turn comes, is certainly gambling with loaded dice. This practice is made the more despicable by the fact that there are always some men who make it a point of honor to keep their agreements at whatever cost. These are the men who, by creating confidence in the given word, really make the institution of contract possible. For, as we have seen, law can never perform this task alone. But one of the basest of human beings is the parasite who lives upon the sacrifices of others, and not merely refuses to contribute his share to the common fund on which he draws but actually depletes it for his own selfish ends.

When May We Seek Release from a Contract?

Notwithstanding what has just been said, however, when conditions arise which could not by any possibility have been foreseen at the time when the contract was made, and which produce an entirely new situation in which the carrying out of the contract will be far more oppressive to the performer than it will be of advantage to the recipient, then the question cannot be evaded, Has the disadvantaged party not the right to ask for relief and has not the other party the duty to grant it?

Before making any attempt to answer this question we should realize exactly what a person asking for relief is doing. "No gentleman", says the code of the National Association of Credit Men, "would ask to be relieved of his obligation upon a note or check, and his contract of purchase and sale should be [regarded] as equally binding." [3] A note, of course, is simply one side of a certain kind of contract. Only a very shameless man would go to a creditor and ask for the cancellation of his debt. To ask for the cancellation of a contract is in most cases to ask the other party to make you a present of money. But even a dead beat never asks anyone to give him money; he asks for a "loan".

Nevertheless there are situations in which it is perfectly proper to beg; and then it will ordinarily be the duty of the other party to give. A clear case is where the burden of performance would be very great, and the advantage to the other party would amount to comparatively little or perhaps nothing. For example you sell some land which you are glad to get rid of, but which you are not compelled to sell at that

[3] Heermance, *op. cit.*, p. 127.

moment in order to meet pressing necessities. Within a few days of the sale the purchaser meets with a serious financial loss which will make the payment of the first instalment of the purchase price or perhaps any payment whatever disastrous to him. Any decent man will permit a delay in payment under such circumstances, and a really humane man will take back the property. Again during a business crisis, at least in extreme instances, permission may properly be asked to return to the wholesaler or manufacturer unsalable but undamaged goods because it is desirable that losses be distributed over the trade as evenly as possible. This lies in the interest of all parties; of the manufacturer who will lose his customers if they fail; the customers themselves; and their creditors and employees.

Beyond these somewhat vague statements it seems impossible to lay down general rules, any more than such rules can be laid down for gifts of charity. "Thy need is greater than mine" would be an ideal standard, alike in relaxing the conditions of contracts, the giving of money to the poor, and indeed in every other situation of life, if it were not for the secondary consequences of such a procedure. But under ordinary circumstances it is positively wrong to give money to those who have less than we, because such a practice, if widely adopted, would produce all the evils that we fear from the dole. Similarly if every contractor relieved the other party from the obligations of his contract whenever they became irksome, this variety of "kindness" would soon come to be expected, and would finally be regarded as an actual obligation. Thereupon contracts would cease to be considered really binding; they would be entered upon lightly, and fulfilled at convenience. In the end contracts would cease to be made because useless.

This leads to a further consideration. In some cases it may be a duty to society—and a binding duty—to procure the fulfilment of a contract by appealing to the law. With too much leniency in the enforcement of contracts there may grow up—as we have just indicated—happy-go-lucky practices in ordering goods. The purchaser loads up beyond necessity with the thought that he can unload whenever he wills without expense to himself. And why study the market and make painful efforts to forecast the future when, whatever happens, you will be taken care of? The manufacturer or wholesaler often dislikes to take a broken contract to the courts. He fears the ill-will of those subjected to this kind of pressure. He shrinks too, at the expense. The Randolph Shoe and Leather Company, in 1920, found that fully 90 per cent of their sales for the season were affected by the cancellation of orders. They thereupon started suits against a small number of the most flagrant offenders. They won their suits in every instance; but one suit for $400 cost them $900, and another for $700 cost $1,600. They were therefore unable to carry this program very far. However, early in 1923, when orders for the fall season again reached the high point, they notified each customer that the company did not want any orders that he did not intend to accept. And in the summer of 1923, although the price of leather had dropped materially below the prices in February of that year, the company had no repudiations of contracts.[4] Failure to enforce at least the most outrageous attempts to cancel contracts is usually due to sheer cowardice, and is prejudicial to one's own permanent interests, to the respect in which one is held by his customers, and to the maintenance of that confidence upon which the possibility of contracts ultimately depends.

The Right to Break a Contract

Circumstances may thus occur in which the contractor is justified in begging for a release from his contract. Are there circumstances under which he is justified in breaking his contract; that is to say, refusing performance contrary to the will of the co-contractor? Our answer is that the moral obligation to fulfil a contract is subject to two limitations.[5]

Before considering these cases we must clear out of the way certain apparent exceptions to the general rule. These are in fact no exceptions at all. The first one is that performance is not required where it is impossible; the second, that it is not required where the adverse party fails to do his part. The first is no exception because where actual impossibility exists, there can be no moral obligation. It can never be my duty, for example, to stop an earthquake. With regard to the second, the failure on my part to perform is not a breach of moral

[4] *Harvard Business Reports,* Vol. I, p. 244. The names used are fictitious.

[5] There is, in fact, still another—somewhat less important—one. But it will be more convenient to discuss this in the following chapter. See p. 115.

obligation when the adverse party fails me, because a contract is a promise in which performance by one party is made conditional upon the performance by the other. There are, indeed, many borderline cases in both classes the examination of which would be at once interesting and enlightening, but limitations of space preclude such a study in this place.

The first of the genuine exceptions to the principle that a contract ought not to be broken without the consent of the co-contractor may be stated as follows: A contract is not binding when the conduct which its execution would require involves wrong-doing on the part of either contractor. The more obvious applications of this truth present no difficulties and can be disposed of in a few words. A contract is not binding when it represents an agreement to wrong third parties, as, for example, to commit murder or theft; and again, when it involves breach of a previous contract or promise, or disobedience to law. What is common to these cases is the agreement to wrong third parties, whether specific individuals or the community as such.

This principle has a second application. *A* sometimes enters into a contract with *B* which is not an agreement to wrong third parties, but where the wrongfulness of the contract consists in the fact that *A* is using it as an instrument for invading *B's* rights. When *A* and *B* unite to racketeer *C's* business, their contract is not binding because they have no right to *C's* money. Similarly when *A* racketeers *B's* business and agrees to refrain from bombing his shop only on payment of $100 a month, the contract is not morally binding on *B*, and he is at liberty to evade it as soon as he can, because *A* has no right to the money. If this statement is not self-evident, consider that we should regard it as monstrous for a court to enforce any such agreement or to assess damages for its breach. But if the contract were a fair one, it would be the court's duty to enforce it.

In popular speech and in law such contracts are said to be without obligation because they are "involuntary", or are the product of "force". But each of these terms is too ambiguous to serve the purposes of ethics—or, for that matter, of law. To be sure, the word "voluntary" as applied to conduct can be given a perfectly definite signification in both psychology and ethics; but the emergent definition would not represent the popular or even the legal usage. In everyday life an "involuntary" act is any act with quite disagreeable consequences. Thus most persons would speak of a visit to the dentist or the sale of a home at one-half its market value in order to escape bankruptcy as involuntary. The word "force" is an equally slippery term. Many persons would unhesitatingly admit that they would not work if they were not "forced" to do so; and some men have declared themselves "forced" to steal in order to supply the needs of their families. The word "forced" in fact, like the word "involuntary", has come to be applied to almost any situation where a man is shut up to a choice between two evils. But even there he can still *choose* between them, and is thus responsible for his choice. And as long as this is the case, he is in a very different situation from one who is seized by a mob or a squad of policemen, bound hand and foot, and carried away whither they will, like a barrel of apples.

Furthermore, the use of "force" may be perfectly legitimate; whether it is, depends primarily upon the purpose for which it is exercised. An employer may threaten an employee with dismissal if he does not arrive at the office more promptly in the morning. The young man may have a strong dislike for early morning rising; he thus finds himself "forced" to get out of bed before he is ready to do so. Similarly a mortgagor may threaten a delinquent mortgagee with foreclosure if he does not pay his interest. He is thus "forced" to pay the money—if he can get it.

In view of these facts we shall do well to eliminate such terms as "involuntary" and "force" from our vocabulary in the discussion of the subject before us, and to confine ourselves to a direct examination of a number of typical concrete cases.

A was a dealer in oysters who was indebted to an express company to the extent of $1,000, a sum which he was able and willing to pay. A member of this express company filed a lying affidavit with the clerk of the circuit court to the effect that *A* owed them $2,996.60, and that he was about to conceal and assign his property in order to avoid meeting his obligations. He thereby obtained a writ of attachment upon $5,000 worth of oysters belonging to *A*, and refused to restore them except on the payment of the sum demanded and a signed release for all damage to the oysters. After considerable verbal conflict, *A*, who did not know that the oysters were already ruined through want of proper care, but who of course did know that they were a perishable commodity, surrendered at discretion, paid the money, and signed the release. Here was an attempt to swindle a man out of $2,000, one move in which involved the destruction of $5,000 worth of property.[6]

A owed *B* $800. Knowing that *B* was on the verge of bankruptcy and needed every cent he could get, *A* informed him that he had taken steps to stop the payment of moneys due him from other parties, and would continue to prevent such payments unless he was given a receipt in full for the amount of his own indebtedness. Face to face with immediate financial ruin, *B* acceded to this outrageous demand. But as soon as possible he sought relief from the courts.[7]

Each of these two instances obviously involved an attempt on the part of unscrupulous men to seize or hold money which did not belong to them. They were foiled in the only way that was open to the victims under the circumstances, namely by signing an agreement which they intended later to repudiate if possible. In our opinion these breaches of contract were justified because a crook has no right to what he obtains by robbing an honest man, whether he does it by pointing a revolver at him or by threatening him with financial injury. The courts, it may be added, took precisely this view. If in consequence of this rule the dishonest should lose confidence in the word of the honest this would be a gain rather than a loss. They would be deprived of their most effective weapon of attack upon the honest.

Let us now turn to another line of cases. A young man executed a mortgage to secure a loan of $100,000 made to his father by a bank and used by the father to improve the joint property of his wife and his son. The young man testified that he signed the mortgage four days after becoming of age at the command of his father, who was a "violent man" of whom he stood in great fear; and that he signed solely "to keep peace in the family". On this ground he prayed the court to relieve him of his obligation. It seems clear that no such plea ought ever to have been entered. Should the bank lose its money because this young man did not care to face a family quarrel with which the bank was in no way concerned? He wanted to have his cake

[6] Spaids *v.* Barrett, 57 Ill. 289.
[7] Vyne *v.* Glenn, 41 Mich. 112.

and eat it. The agreement made by signing the mortgage, distasteful as it was to the signer (and in *this* sense, involuntary) was valid in ethics as it proved to be in law.[8]

Three brothers owned jointly a considerable mining property in Colorado. After years of disputes a written contract was made which was to settle all questions at issue between them. One of the brothers, *A*, signed it reluctantly because of a threat by the other brothers that they would cease supplying the money which had been keeping the mine open, and he had not the capital with which to continue operations alone. Later he applied to a federal court to set the contract aside. Since there was apparently no real violation of any undoubted moral right involved in the settlement, and the conditional refusal to furnish money was entirely within the rights of the brothers, we believe *A* was not justified in seeking to be relieved of his part of the agreement. This, again, was the position taken by the court.[9]

From this brief survey we believe the following conclusion can be drawn. A contract is morally binding independently of whether the alternatives between which the contractor has to choose are distasteful or not. But a contract is not binding where it is employed to deprive one of the parties against his will of that to which he has an unquestionable moral right.

The proposition that a contract is not binding where it is employed to deprive one of the parties of that to which he has an unquestionable moral right supplies the basis for the second exception to the principle that a contract once formed is inviolable. Where it is *A's* imperative duty to release *B* from his contract but he refuses to do so, in extreme cases the right can not be denied *B* to refuse performance. This principle is unquestionably open to serious abuse, since few of us are objective judges of our own needs in relation to those of others, and accordingly we are apt to weigh our own rights and duties in one scale and those of our neighbor in another. But the danger of the abuse of a right can not destroy the right itself. A case where refusal to perform is plainly justified is suggested in the *Restatement of the Law of Contracts*.[10] "*A* contracts with *B* to work

[8] Detroit National Bank *v.* Blodgett, 115 Mich. 160.
[9] Andrews v. Connolly, 145 Fed. 43.
[10] Vol. II, Sec. 465.

for a term in a certain neighborhood. Cholera breaks out in the neighborhood and continues during the term of the contract, giving reasonable ground for apprehending that one working in the neighborhood will catch the disease." Here, according to the eminent authorities responsible for this work, "*A's* [legal] duty is discharged". We should say the same of his moral duty.

CHAPTER IX

WHEN A CONTRACT IS NOT A CONTRACT

The terms of a contract should obviously be as definite, complete, and free from ambiguity as possible. It sometimes happens that crooked men deliberately draw up their contracts in vague and ambiguous language for their own dishonest purposes. Contracts of this sort, however, are less frequently due to dishonesty than to carelessness. In view of the wide-spread nature of the evil—whatever its source—some organizations of business men are taking measures to set up standard forms of contracts for their own industry. The Trade Practice Conferences held under the supervision of the Federal Trade Commission have taken the matter up, and in a number of cases have adopted such rules as the following.

> "The making of contracts which do not expressly cover quantity specifications, time for delivery, inspection, filing of claims and other items necessary to form a complete, unambiguous contract, often results in price discrimination, induces fraud, breach of contract, and constant disputes which create suspicion and ill feeling in the industry, and is condemned as an unsound business practice. It is the judgment of this conference that the industry should adopt, in coöperation with buyers, a standard form of contract which will avoid ambiguity, prevent misunderstanding, and thoroughly protect the rights of both buyers and sellers." [1]

The code of the Woolen and Trimmings Industry makes one provision of a contract absolutely unmistakable:

> "All cuts may be measured not to exceed 37 inches to the yard to allow for possible shrinkage, the intent being to insure the delivering of a 36 inch yard. No claim will be entertained for any length delivered which measures 36 inches to the yard." [2]

A detailed statement of uniform conditions applicable to all contracts in its field has been prepared and accepted by the New Eng-

[1] *Federal Trade Commission Trade Practice Conferences* (1929), p. 216.
[2] *Ibid.*, p. 200.

land Foundryman's Association and will be found in Heermance, *op. cit.* pp. 186–187.

From the preceding discussion we can see what kind of a business contract will be written by two men who are at once intelligent and honorable. It will represent what each party knows with reasonable certainty that he can perform in accordance with the expectations which he has allowed the other party to form; it will represent what each party, having all the more important consequences in view, has firmly determined to carry through; it will represent the will of the two parties in absolutely unambiguous language. Finally, if it is to be a completely legitimate transaction, it will represent an agreement by which each may reasonably expect to profit.

How to Interpret Ambiguous Contracts

With all the care in the world, however, contracts are often written that are so ambiguous that one party can quite honestly interpret them to mean one thing and the other party something quite different. In this situation, to which interpretation has the contractor bound himself? The rule for the interpretation of ambiguous promises and contracts was laid down by William Paley in the classical discussion of the subject which has since been adopted by most, perhaps all American courts. It will be found in his *Moral Philosophy* (1785), Book III, Part I, Chapters 5 and 6, and reads as follows: "Where the terms of the promise admit of more senses than one, the promise is to be performed in that sense in which the promiser apprehended at the time that the promisee received it". The propriety of this rule is all but self-evident. When I make a promise I am arousing certain expectations in the mind of the promisee. But morality is a matter of intent. My obligations to the promisee accordingly depend on the answer to this question: What expectations did I intend to arouse in him? And since—as we have seen—desired results may sometimes be obtained by silence as effectively as by any other means, we must go farther and say: I am responsible not merely for those expectations which I actively strove to create, but also for those which I knowingly allowed the promisee to entertain at the time of the promise. And this is precisely what Paley's definition means.

Contractual Obligations Limited by Intention

From the fact that I am bound to fulfil those expectations of the co-contractor which I intended to arouse, it follows that—as far as this specific transaction is concerned—I have not bound myself to fulfil expectations which I did not intend to arouse. What is true of the offerer holds, of course, for the offeree in accepting the offer.

A few examples will serve to make clear the meaning of these statements. *A,* the owner of a village store, ordered from *B,* by inadvertence, 2,500 needle *cards,* instead of 2,500 needles. Since years might be required for the sale of so large a stock the manufacturer ought to have allowed him to return the difference between his intended and his actual order, providing he would agree to pay all the expenses which his mistake cost the company.[3]

In the preceding incident the mistake had its source in a slip of the pen. In the following it was due to a miscalculation. *A,* in preparing a bid for the construction of a public building, having very little time between the notice of the letting of the contract and the last date for filing bids, in making up the bids from his estimate book in which he had figured the different parts of the work separately, by mistake turned two leaves and omitted an estimate on one part of the work. In consequence his bid as submitted was several thousand dollars lower than he intended. It seems clear that he was not morally bound to do the work for the amount specified since he had not intended to do it at any other price than that which was represented by the sum of his individual estimates.[4]

"The orator conveyed to defendant a lot of land on which was a spring from which the orator by means of an aqueduct supplied his own and other premises with water. This aqueduct was of greater value to the orator than the price he received for the land. By mistake of the orator, who did not intend to part with the right to use the water from the spring, the deed to the defendant contained no reservation to such right. The defendant at the time he purchased had no knowledge of the existence of the spring. *Held* that the orator was entitled

[3] Coates *v.* Buck, 93 Wis. 128.

[4] Board of School Commissioners of City of Indianapolis *v.* Bender, 36 Ind. Appellate Ct. 164.

either to a conveyance from the defendant of a right to use the aqueduct or to recovery of the land on repaying to the defendant the price thereof, and that the defendant might elect which of these modes of relief the orator should have." [5] This quaintly worded decision has a sound ethical foundation.

As will have been noticed, in the preceding cases we have judged there was no binding contract because the verbal contract did not represent the intention. In the following instance our conclusion is that there was a contract because of intention, although the written words did not show it. *A* took out a fire insurance policy on personal property contained in his house, which was located on a country road. Through a mistake of the owner the policy described the house as on the south side of the road, whereas in fact it was on the north side. *A* owned no other house in the county and the fire hazard was no greater on one side of the road than on the other. It is evident that the parties intended respectively to obtain protection for and to extend protection to the contents of *A's* house. The company was plainly liable morally for the loss which the fire caused.[6]

A contract may fail to represent intent because—for whatever reason—the language in which it is clothed does not convey the intention of the parties with accuracy and completeness. It may, however, fail to represent intent for another reason, namely, because one or both of the parties entertain an incorrect or incomplete view of that which forms the subject matter of the contract—the "goods" with which it is concerned. The terms "goods" is here used, of course, in its broadest possible signification, to cover material objects (including land), immaterial objects (as business good will or patents), money, services (including forbearances), and anything else that can be the object of that barter (whether for permanent or temporary possession) which brings into existence the overwhelming majority of business contracts. If there is any truth in the general principles upon which the argument of the preceding sections is based, certain kinds of these incorrect or incomplete views serve to invalidate a contract. Certain kinds, on the other hand, leave the obligation unimpaired. It will now be our task to distinguish between these two classes. As before,

[5] Brown *v.* Lamphear, 35 Vt. 252.

[6] Le Gendre *v.* Scottish Union & National Ins. Co., 88 N.Y. Supplement 1012.

we shall work our way through to our conclusion by an examination of concrete transactions.

A leased an iron mine to *B* on *A's* representation that there was a large quantity of ore in the mine ready to be taken out. The evidence offered was a survey of the mine showing that the ore was within the boundaries of the land to be leased. It transpired, however, that unknown to *A,* the surveyor had made a mistake in tracing the boundaries of the mine and that the deposit in question was located outside of this area.[7] Obviously *B* had no intention of paying money to *A* for iron ore which *A* did not own. He was therefore under no obligation to take over the mine.

In Coppage *v.* the Equitable Guarantee & Trust Company [8] the parties innocently mistook the size of a piece of land thinking it smaller than it actually was. If there was no suspicion of trickery and if the supposed dimensions of the lot were a factor in the determination of the price, the purchaser should have been willing to add to the agreed price a sum proportional to the excess of quantity over that which he had in mind when he entered into the contract. If the new price was more than he was willing to give, the contract should have been rescinded and the land should have been returned to the original owner. On the other hand if a tract of land which is well known to both parties is bought for reasons with which the exact area has nothing to do, for example, as a site for a dam, then a mistake concerning the area can not morally invalidate the sale or create a just claim for a change in price.

The principle exhibited in these cases is clearly of wide application. Apart from the exceptions noted below, a collection of words, representing an agreement to purchase or sell, creates no moral obligation when it calls for the acquiring of or the parting with that which one of the parties did not intend to acquire or surrender.

Exceptions to the Preceding Rule

Consider on the other hand the following transaction. A man buys mining land because he believes it contains enough coal or iron to

[7] Adapted from Chatham Furnace Co. *v.* Moffatt, 147 Mass. 403.
[8] 11 Del. Chancery Reports 373.

render the investment a paying one. He buys a piece of real estate or the good will of a business, or bonds, or stock because he hopes they will give him a good income or because he hopes to be able to sell them ultimately at an advance. A contractor and a city council or a county board sign a contract for driving piles or for constructing a road based on the assumption that there is no rock in the way which will make the operation exceptionally expensive. If, in any of these instances, the expectations with regard to costs or profits are frustrated the loser ought not to ask either the adverse party or the court for relief. As a matter of fact the courts will not grant it.

The reason is clear. The proposition that intention is the measure of obligation, when applied to the objects of barter, holds only for those cases in which the qualities or characteristics of an object are capable of precise determination. Here "capable" means, considering the amount of time, money, *etc.* available for their determination at the time. On the other hand, where the qualities or characteristics in question are a matter of guess-work, both parties are by implication, if not explicitly, agreeing to take a chance; and if one of them loses by the transaction instead of gaining, he can not honorably relieve himself of his agreement. This would be shouting "no keeps" when the game went against him.

If definite knowledge is obtainable and the contractor elects not to trouble himself to get it, the effect is the same; he has chosen to take a chance and must abide by his election. This principle is well illustrated by the following case, a summary of which, with the accompanying comments by the author, I quote from Professor Page's *Contracts:*

"One of the most extreme cases under this subject is Wood *v.* Boynton (64 Wis. 265). In this case *A* sold a stone to *B,* both believing that it was probably a topaz, and both knowing that they did not know exactly what it was. The price was one dollar. It subsequently turned out that the stone was a rough diamond worth about $700. *A* on learning this fact tendered one dollar and interest to *B* and demanded the stone. On *B's* refusal to deliver it, *A* sued him to recover the stone. It was held that *A* could not recover at law, the court declining to express an opinion as to whether *A* could obtain relief in a court of equity. While this is an extreme case, since the actual value was so greatly in excess of the belief of both of the parties, the decision is undoubtedly correct. If the stone had proved to be worthless *B* could not have recovered the dollar paid by him." [9]

[9] Vol. I, Sec. 384.

For the reason stated at the beginning of this paragraph, this decision seems to us ethically sound.

It goes without saying that the boundary line between matters of knowledge and matters of opinion is often difficult to draw. For this reason we may expect to find a large number of border line cases. Since no one is a really impartial judge in a difficult and complicated matter in which his own interests are deeply concerned, the man who wishes to do the honorable and just thing in such cases as these will put the problem up to an intelligent and fair-minded third party, conversant with the situation, and will be guided by his decision.

There is one important exception, however, to the proposition that a contract relating to a matter of opinion is binding. This is when the opinion on which one of the contractors acts is due to wilful misrepresentation or to clearly blameworthy negligence on the part of the other contractor. No one has a right to any gain which is acquired by wronging another. Accordingly, if *A* induces *B* to speculate in land or in stocks by painting what he knows to be purely fanciful pictures of future values, or by making statements which he has taken no pains to verify, *B* on discovering the fact is morally justified in getting out of the contract if he can. And the courts should stand behind him when they can do so without causing more harm in the long run than good.

Apart from the above exception, the rule is that the right to break a contract because the materials which form its subject matter turn out to be different from what we thought they were is limited to those characteristics or qualities of objects which can be subjected to exact determination, or become objects of "knowledge". There is also a second limitation upon such a right which holds for failure of the contract to cover intention, whatever the contract applies to. This is: A mistake must concern a feature of so much importance that if it had been known in advance the contractor would not have entered into the contract, at least in its existing form. Suppose that having bought a farm containing, as both parties supposed, 200 acres, the purchaser discovers that its area amounts to only 195 acres. He is, of course, entitled to the return of a proportionate amount of the purchase money; but unless the exact acreage was of the essence of the transaction, he ought not to use this discrepancy between description and fact as an excuse to turn back the property to the original owner. A contract involves the interests of two parties, and when the contract has once been formed neither may proceed as if the interests of the other party were non-existent.

Indemnification for Negligence in Drawing Up a Contract

Where, as the result of my negligence in formulating or accepting a contract, the words in which it is incorporated misrepresent my intention, and where at the same time its provisions affect my interests adversely, then, according to what we have termed Paley's principle, I am not morally bound to perform. But this does not mean that I am released from all obligations to my co-contractor. In reliance upon my words he may have performed his part of the agreement, or may have involved himself in expenditures which he might otherwise not have made, or refused opportunities of gain, or entered upon a course of action which, but for my promise, he would not have undertaken. For these losses or other injuries my negligence is responsible. But for precisely what and how much ought I to answer? If as a result of careless driving I smash into another car and do $100 worth of damage, this is the amount which I should pay. If I happen to hit the bumpers and do no harm, I am under no obligation to pay anything. In neither case, assuredly, am I bound to buy the owner a new car. Precisely the same thing is true in the field of contracts. An honorable man will pay for all losses which are due to his negligence in formulating or accepting a contract; he should not be expected to do more.

Indemnification for loss sustained through another's negligence will take various forms as circumstances dictate. In some instances it will involve cancellation of the contract; in others, compensatory payment. If, as a result of a "change of position" of the adverse party or for other reasons, cancellation or compensation would not cover the losses, performance becomes morally obligatory. Where goods have been prepared and delivered which can not be returned, or services have been rendered before the discovery of the mistake, the rule in morals is that which has been long accepted and applied by the courts: "If the parties can not be placed *in statu quo* the one who has received the property or services of value must pay a reasonable compensation therefor, irrespective of what his understanding of the terms was".[10] In practice "reasonable" will ordinarily mean average.

What ought to be done when both parties are negligent? Where the negligence is, as far as can be judged, equal, the loss should be equally divided; otherwise, in proportion to the amount of fault, in so far as this proportion can be estimated. This provision is vague, but frequently it represents the best that can be done. Sometimes, however, a more definite solution is possible. (1) Where the offerer may properly be supposed to have special knowledge, the negligence of the offeree may properly be treated as, for practical purposes, zero. Thus the directors of a bank erroneously, but in good faith, made a statement as to the condition of their bank which they would never have made had they examined the bank's books with any care. In reliance on their statements innocent purchasers bought its newly issued stock. In morals, as in law, they were at liberty to return the stock to the bank and get their money back. (2) Where one of the parties is guilty of fraud the other should not be treated as negligent for believing him. For, even if negligence as to one's own interests be considered culpable, it is certainly not so culpable as lying for the purpose of swindling another person. And a crook should never be permitted to urge, either in law or morals, that if his victim had made a careful examination he might have discovered he was dealing with a crook and have taken the appropriate precautions; for this is saying: "You have done me the honor to trust me; therefore I have the right to betray that trust".[11]

The principle that in negligence the damages are to be paid by the party through whose negligence the loss takes place ought to be tempered in morals—whatever may be true in law—by another principle. This is that burdens should be carried by those who can bear them most easily. If a Model T Ford belonging to a poor man smashes the car of a millionaire, and the former does not carry insurance (of course he is negligent for not doing so, and if he can not afford to he has no business to be driving a car—but let him who is without carelessness among us cast the first stone) it would be a very churlish or a very brutal millionaire that would deprive the former of the results of,

[10] Page, *Contracts,* Vol. I, Sec. 274.
[11] Cottrell *v.* Krum, as cited above, Ch. V, p. 68.

perhaps, years of saving in order to obtain compensation. Under exceptional circumstances this principle may apply also to the negligent formulation of a contract. No general rule can be laid down for the application of this principle, any more than in the somewhat similar case of giving money to charity. But no statement of the problem of contractual liability would be complete which ignored it.

Summary

Our conclusions as to the relation between moral responsibility and intention in the performance of contracts may be summarized broadly as follows: (1) In forming a contract I am assuming an obligation to perform or to refrain from performing such actions as are contemplated in my intention. My intention, it will be remembered, includes all expectations which I am knowingly arousing or allowing to exist in the mind of the other party. (2) I am assuming no obligation in the way of actions and forbearances which were not contemplated in my intention; but I am morally liable for all losses of whatever kind which are due to my negligence in making the promise.

A collection of words which has externally the form of a contract but which does not represent my intention, as the term intention has just been defined, is not in the proper sense of the term a contract. A contract involves a "meeting of minds", as the lawyers phrase it. This means that both parties understand the obligations involved in the same sense. Where this condition does not exist a refusal to perform is not a breach of contract.

The Law of Contracts

The law of contracts has so many ramifications and is otherwise so complicated that we shall here attempt no more than to offer a few statements concerning such of the fundamentals as are directly related to the topics of the present and the immediately preceding chapter.

Promises, as Such, Are Not Enforceable in Law. Promises, as such, are not enforceable in English and American law. Thus in a leading Illinois case a written agreement to keep an offer to sell land open and firm for a stipulated time, led the person to whom the offer was made to investigate the land and to go to some expense in making inquiries. He might indeed have made the most elaborate arrangements on the faith of the promise, adjusting his own and other persons' affairs on the faith of the undertaking contained in the offer; and it would have made no difference. Since the man who made the offer and the promise to keep it open did not receive compensation in exchange for his promise, the promise is said to be without consideration and unenforceable.[12]

There is no inherent necessity for the court's refusal to act in a case of this kind. For the courts of Continental Europe enforce the fulfilment of promises as a matter of course. The principal reason—or rather cause—for the failure of our courts to follow their example is doubtless historical in nature. It simply has never been done. A better ground, however, may be found in the following consideration, presented by Sir William Anson, one of the leading authorities on the law of contract. He writes:

> "We need some means of ascertaining whether the maker and receiver of a promise contemplated the creation of a legal obligation. . . . The rule or doctrine of consideration is the most general existing test for this purpose, one that has grown and maintained itself through several centuries of judicial development. It may be questioned whether the general convenience is not better served by adopting this test in its logical completeness than by allowing distinctions and subtilties to refine the rule away." [13]

It is true that in matters serious enough to be brought before a court a merely casual or unconsidered promise ought not to bind a man to undertakings which he will deeply regret after the momentary impulse or the passing attack of blindness has disappeared. Against such a mischance the formality of "consideration" may sometimes prove to be a real protection. It is also true that the consideration may be quite nominal in character and amount, and thus the demand for it need involve no real hardship for those who have any acquaintanceship whatever with law. Nevertheless in the end we shall have to admit that the failure of our law to enforce promises as such places it at this point in a position of manifest inferiority to Continental law as an instrument of justice.

The Interpretation of Contracts. The fundamental principle em-

[12] Corbett *v.* Cronkhite, 239 Ill. 9 (1909).

[13] *Principles of the Law of Contract,* 5th Amer. Ed. (1930), Sec. 121.

ployed by the Common Law in the interpretation of contracts has been stated by Professor Page as follows:

"The nature, effect, and meaning of [an] offer depend upon the meaning which an ordinarily reasonable man would attach to the words and to the outward acts of the parties. . . . The intention is thus a standardized intention; and while the courts say that it is the intention of the ordinarily reasonable man, it usually is the intention which the court itself would attach to such words and acts." [14]

The reasons for this procedure are clear and at bottom sound. The leading one is the fact that "the law works with blunt tools".[15] In consequence the real intentions of the parties concerned are most likely to be realized in the majority of instances if the parties are held rigidly to their words and acts, rather than to the actual but unexpressed intentions, where the two diverge.

However, if this rule were carried through to the bitter end, much serious injustice would result. Hence the policy expressed in the following statement:

"Though the [legal] obligation of a contractor depends upon his expressed, not his actual intention, it is desirable that as little violence should be done to his actual intention as is consistent with two things: 1. Fairness to the co-contractor, who may have been justified in assuming an intention different from that which actually existed. 2. A reasonable certainty of proof of the terms of the contract." [16]

In accordance with this policy many courts will on occasion make exceptions to the general rule and go back to the original intention, employing not infrequently Paley's formula (p. 110, above) as an instrument of interpretation.

Where the failure of the verbal agreement to represent the essential intention of one party is due to misrepresentation of the other party, the courts will find for the misled contractor—where the misrepresentation is intentional, in all cases; where it is unintentional, in the majority of cases. Coercion by threats of serious harm, whether bodily or financial ("duress"), will also ordinarily release a contractor from the obligations of his contract, as in Spaids *v.* Barrett and Vyne

[14] *The Law of Contracts,* Vol. I, Sec. 83.

[15] See above, Ch. V, p. 78

[16] Williston, *The Law of Contracts,* Vol. II, Sec. 608.

v. Glenn.[17] Other exceptions to the rule that contracts will be enforced, and enforced according to their letter, do not concern the problems of this book, except the fact that the courts will make allowance for "changed conditions", where the effects of enforcement would be very harmful to one party and of no comparable value to the other. The case quoted on page 107, above, from the *Restatement of the Law of Contracts,* will serve as an illustration of the attitude of the law towards situations of this kind.

[17] For these two cases see pp. 105, 106 above.

CHAPTER X

THE ETHICS OF CORPORATE MANAGEMENT

The Problems

The corporation is as characteristic a feature of the modern commercial world as are contract and competition. Evils it has undoubtedly brought in its train—what creation of man has not?—but the advantages it offers are so great that it is assured of as long a life as the present economic system. Its role today is so commanding that no study of business ethics would be adequate that failed to examine the special moral problems which it raises.

There are thousands of corporations in the United States which, apart from the legal provision of limited liability, are corporations only in name. They are actually private business establishments, owned and operated nominally by three or more persons; actually, sometimes, by one or two. But the provision of limited liability in the law of corporations has made possible the bringing together of large sums of money to serve as capital for great business enterprises which for the most part would have been beyond the power of any individual or any small group of individuals to undertake. Such enterprises the stockholders can not themselves operate directly. The determination of general lines of policy is placed by them in the hands of a board of directors, and this board in turn names the higher executive officers. Thus there takes place, from the necessity of the case, that divorce between ownership and management which is one of the outstanding features of contemporary business life.

How complete this divorce is in the giant corporations few people realize. In 1929 the largest single stockholder of the Pennsylvania Railroad owned only .34% of the outstanding stock, while the twenty largest held together but 2.7%. In the same year only .6% of the outstanding stock was held by the principal stockholder in the largest utility corporation in the world, the American Telephone and Telegraph Company. The largest holder in the United States Steel Corporation held only .74% of the stock, and the twenty largest holders owned but 5.1%.[1]

Corporations whose owners manage the enterprise for themselves raise one set of ethical problems. Where ownership and management fall into different hands other problems present themselves. It is these latter that we are to study in this chapter. The principles which we hope to develop, however, are in most instances applicable to the corporate system as a whole.

The "management" of a corporation consists of the higher officers and the directors. The former are salaried, full-time employees, engaged, for the most part, in work of an administrative character. The directors, on the other hand, are representatives of the owners—the stockholders. Their function may be described as legislative and supervisory. They are expected to devote only a small part of their time to their directorial duties; and at least in the United States, they serve practically without compensation.

The problems with which we shall concern ourselves may be formulated as follows: (1) What are the responsibilities of the managers to the public; specifically to the customers and competitors of the corporation? (2) What are the responsibilities of the stockholders to the public? (3) What are the responsibilities of the managers to the stockholders?

The Responsibilities of the Managers to the Public

We begin our discussion with the first question, and lay at its foundation a proposition so flat and obvious that we should be ashamed to state it if we did not know that it is constantly ignored, often only half realized, and sometimes absolutely denied. We shall lead up to it by a story which we assure the reader neither we nor anyone we know would have had brains enough to invent.

It was tax paying time in Madison, and at this period in its history most citizens paid in person, instead of by mail. Consequently there was a queue of considerable length in front of the treasurer's

[1] Adolf Berle, Jr., and Gardiner C. Means, *The Modern Corporation and Private Property* (New York, The Macmillan Company, 1935), Table XII, pp. 107–109.

cage. One of the number was a harrassed looking woman who, while waiting for her turn, harangued her fellow citizens upon the iniquities of municipal waste and extravagance. It happened that the city had just acquired some land for a new park. This provided her with the climax of her Philippic. As she stepped forward to the fateful counter and took a last longing, lingering look at the cash in her hand she turned to her audience with the words: "And then there are those parks. Why do *we* have to pay for them? If the city wants parks why doesn't the city pay for them?"

Evidently this excellent woman thought of Madison as a kind of entity that acquired property and paid out money "of itself". Similarly many people talk, at any rate, of corporations as if they were living creatures that operated automatically, apart from all human beings. Of course this is the rankest sort of mythology. No corporation as such acts. "Its" actions are the actions of one or more men; and the responsibility for such action, just as everywhere else, rests upon the men who make the decisions.

This fact knocks the foundations from under a very widely held view as to the responsibilities of corporation managers. This is that there exists a double standard of morality, one for the rulers of corporations in their capacity as rulers, the other for the rest of the business world. A very intelligent man who was for many years president of one of the greatest railroads in the United States, once said to a friend: "I have done many things as president that I would not do as a man." The statement was doubtless strictly true. A man of honor as soon as he had turned his back on his office in the afternoon, he changed his skin at nine o'clock every morning, and then, as presiding genius of the corporation, did with a perfectly good conscience what he would never have allowed himself to do as a private individual. Now this assumption of a double personality is preposterous. Every human being is responsible for the foreseen consequences of his acts, and for all of them. He can not dodge responsibility by saying that between nine a. m. and five p. m. (with an intermission for lunch) he is the president of a railroad, while the rest of the day he is a man.

But this notion of a double standard of morality may perhaps have a deeper foundation than a myth which ought not to deceive an intelligent child. Our railroad president might have said, in his effort to whitewash his record, that his first duty was to protect the interests of his stockholders; and that this justified anything he might do with this end in view. Unquestionably he was appointed and paid to look out for a certain group of stockholders. He was therefore bound not to use his high position to help himself to money which belonged to them, as did Stewart, president of the Standard Oil Company of Indiana.[2] He might not loot the treasury, as has unfortunately been done more than once, by forming organizations to sell supplies to his company at extortionate prices. In short he had in effect pledged himself, or, if you prefer, contracted to place the interests of his company above his personal advantage. But there is a definite limit to what he may do for the benefit of his stockholders. For no one has a right to contract to wrong third parties; and no man, in his capacity as a stockholder or in any other capacity, has the right to ask anyone else to trample for his benefit on the rights of others. If this statement is not self-evident imagine what you would think and how you would feel if you should discover that your house-maid's "boy friend" had asked her to steal your silver-ware for him.

These facts are so simple and so obvious that we can only suppose that failure to see them is due at bottom to wishful thinking, the desire to have your cake and eat it, to wrong others and yet keep your self-respect. When thorough-going crooks lead their companies into iniquitous practices they are merely acting in their official capacity as they would act outside of it. But when an essentially honorable man like our railroad president does the same thing we are justified in inferring either that he has a yellow streak in him and is afraid he might endanger his job if he threw away a chance to hit below the belt, or else that he has become so infatuated with the game that, like some football players, his desire to win stifles the inhibitions of his better self. Such a man, however, must keep his self-respect at all costs, and so he uses his "obligations to his stockholders" as an alibi.

[2] See below, p. 132.

The Responsibilities of Stockholders to the Public

We have been speaking of the responsibilities of the managers. What of the responsibilities of the owners? For the most part the responsibilities of the ordinary stockholders of large corporations are few, because in the main they do not and can not know what is going on; and if they did, could not do anything about it. But they have a real even though limited responsibility just the same. They ought never to condone and always to disapprove of all brutality, oppression, crookedness, and wrong-doing of every kind which their managers have initiated and of which they may learn; to denounce such actions to their fellow stockholders where opportunity offers, and to make the opportunity, when doing so has any chance of producing results; to protest to the management under similar circumstances, either jointly or severally; and to join with others who are seeking to replace unworthy leaders with honest men. If the management consists of men who really wish to act justly and honorably but are afraid of their stockholders, such action can not fail to strengthen their hands and is sure to be welcomed.

The Responsibilities of the Managers to the Stockholders

The Managers Occupy a Position of Trust. The large corporation is the most significant and important feature of contemporary business life. There may well be limits beyond which mere size becomes a liability rather than an asset.[3] But the fact remains that in very many fields the best results require extensive aggregations of capital. Apart from exceptional cases, the necessary cash and credits can not be supplied by one or even a few persons who are prepared to devote their time as well as their money to the actual conduct of the business. Hence arises the divorce between ownership

[3] Consult Eliot Jones, *The Trust Problem in the United States* (New York, The Macmillan Company, 1921), Ch. XIX; Myron W. Watkins, *Industrial Combinations and Public Policy* (Boston, Houghton Mifflin Company, 1927), Bk. I, especially Chs. IV and VI.

and management which in turn gives rise to the directorate. This restriction of power to a few individuals is the source of grave dangers and inevitable evils as well as unquestionable advantages. Whether we like it or not, however, the way back to owner management is, in great areas of the economic world, practically closed. The only possibilities we need consider today are control by a small group, or by government, or by both combined. The second possibility means straight socialism; the third, if extended beyond certain rather narrow limits, means virtual socialism.

Here then are the basic facts. The large corporations not merely exist; they are and will remain an essential feature of the capitalistic system. Whatever else happens, the determination of policy and the supervision of salaried administrators must remain in the hands of the owners. But the owners, as a body, are absolutely incapable of exercising this function. Hence it must be taken over by a small group of persons serving as their representatives. These men constitute the board of directors.

The directors thus occupy the position of trustees. People have placed money in their hands in trust to be spent by them for the common advantage according to their best judgment. When a man accepts membership on the governing board of a corporation he has thereby assumed the responsibilities which were implied in the surrender of the money to him and his associates. If it had been certain or probable that he and his colleagues would not have been true to these obligations the money would never have been forthcoming. He was not bound to take upon himself the responsibilities of the office, any more than he was bound to serve on the city council. But having once accepted the position, he has by implication—just as has the councilman—pledged himself to the performance of the attendant duties. This means that he has at least implicitly promised to do his part to see that the money entrusted to his care is honestly and wisely expended, and that the profits are divided equitably among the investors. If men can not be found who will accept these responsibilities, and, upon acceptance, be loyal to them, the corporate system, and with it capitalism, will necessarily collapse.

Apparently certain lawyers look at this matter from a different angle. They claim that when a man invests in stock he is or ought to be aware of the possibility that the directors may loaf on the job or help themselves to his share of the profits. He elects to take this risk. Therefore if the dice fall against him he has no right to complain. To this contention the reply is a very simple one. When a man deposits money in a bank he knows that the president may run off with the funds or squander them in speculation. This fact, however, does not make defalcations right. There are two kinds of misfortunes which can be brought upon us by the conduct of others, those which are unintentional and those which are intentional. The first—except those due to culpable negligence—are injuries; the second, where they involve a breach of faith, are wrongs.

A second line of attack upon our position might consist in pointing out the fact that a large amount of the country's corporate stock is in the hands of speculators who buy today and sell tomorrow, and have no more stake in any one organization than has the passing tourist in the hotel in which he spends a night. Such an objection could never come from any but those who spend their lives watching the ticker. Stocks are held by investors and speculators, and of course by many persons who play both roles. It is the existence of the great body of more or less permanent investors that creates in the corporate world the relation of trustee and those who trust. The advantages which thereby accrue to speculators may be looked upon as a by-product.

Plain Graft. Certain of the moral evils that afflict the present day corporate world are clear cases of dishonesty. As such they require no extended discussion in this place. Where the high officers are members of the board and dominate its policies the simplest way of picking the stockholders' pockets consists in voting themselves and their accomplices enormous salaries and bonuses. Perhaps the most notorious instance in recent years is that of the Bethlehem Steel Company. Unknown to its stockholders, this organization presented its president, Eugene G. Grace, with $3,200,000 in bonuses during the years 1925 to 1928 inclusive; this at a time when the company was declaring no dividends on the common stock. In 1929 this same gentleman received a bonus of $1,623,753, and other officers in proportion, making a grand total of $3,425,306.[4] The bonus system has a legitimate place in the business world. But especially when it is kept a secret it offers grounds for suspicion.

A less sensational method by which the directors can help themselves to the earnings of the stockholders consists in certain manipulations whereby the earnings are routed to one class of stock in which the directors are interested to the disadvantage of other classes in which their holdings are insignificant or nonexistent. The *modus operandi* is described in detail by Messrs. Berle and Means in *The Modern Corporation and Private Property,* Book II, Chapters I to IV; and at sufficient length by Professor W. Z. Ripley in *Main Street and Wall Street,* Chapter II. Again the legal and the illegal may look much alike to an external observer. For when additional capital is sorely needed and is difficult to attract, the corporation, that is to say the associated owners, may be profited in the long run by a readjustment in the distribution of earnings to the different classes of stock. But in morals, as we have said again and again, intention is everything. And where this device is adopted —as it sometimes is—for the purpose of enriching a favored class at the expense of those who have no friends at court, the transaction is clearly fraudulent.

Disloyal Selling. A more difficult problem arises when a man who is a member of more than one board of directors is compelled to decide between the claims of conflicting loyalties. One corporation, for example, is a railroad; the other manufactures rails. As a representative of the first he is bound to see that materials are obtained at the lowest possible rates; as a representative of the second he must aim to get the maximum price obtainable. What shall he do? When he is voting or otherwise acting as a director of the railroad he has clearly bound himself to represent the interests of the railroad. The alternative is to refrain from voting and otherwise attempting to determine the decision. The latter is the position which most honorable men will take. They will excuse themselves from voting on the ground of their adverse interests, and will carefully refrain from influencing the votes of their colleagues through

[4] John T. Flynn, *Graft in Business* (New York, The Vanguard Press, 1931), p. 195 ff.

pressure, log rolling, or any other method calculated to deflect the judgment of the directorate away from the merits of the case.

Why not meet the situation by resigning from one of the boards? This solution is, broadly speaking, neither possible nor desirable today. The activities and relationships of a large modern corporation ramify in a hundred directions. It needs the ablest and most experienced men obtainable to guide its destinies. Such men are relatively few in number. It therefore lies in the public interest that the services which they are capable of performing should not be confined to a single organization. This fact is recognized in many, perhaps most corporate charters. It not infrequently offers a cloak for all sorts of disloyalty, trickery, and downright and outrageous graft. But a board of directors that lived up to the spirit expressed in the following provision of the charter of the Ward Food Products Corporation would be beyond criticism, as far as this particular issue is concerned.

> "A director of this Corporation shall not, in the absence of fraud, be disqualified by his office from dealing or contracting with the Corporation, either as a vendor, purchaser, or otherwise, nor in the absence of fraud shall any transaction or contract of this Corporation be void or voidable or affected by reason of the fact that any director, or any firm of which any director is a member, or any corporation of which any director is a member, or any corporation of which any director is an officer, director, or stockholder, is in any way interested in such transaction or contract; provided that at the meeting of the Board of Directors or of a committee thereof having authority in the premises to authorize or confirm said contract or transaction, the interest of such director, firm, or corporation is disclosed or made known, and there shall be present a quorum of the Board of Directors or of the directors constituting such committee, and such contract or transaction shall be approved by a majority of such quorum, which majority shall consist of directors not so interested or connected".[5]

Routing Purchases by Way of the Manager's Pocket. The use of one's position as a director in one organization to enrich oneself through supplying it with goods or services at exorbitant prices is

[5] William Z. Ripley, *Main Street and Wall Street* (Boston, Little, Brown, and Company, 1929), p. 57.

unfortunately a not uncommon occurrence. It seems to have been one of the factors which, in 1925, forced into a receivership the once great and prosperous Chicago, Milwaukee, St. Paul and Pacific Railroad. The entire affair was investigated by the Interstate Commerce Commission. Among the causes of the crash the Commission lists the excessive rates charged for the electric power used in certain portions of the new section of the road running through the mountains. The companies involved were controlled and to a large extent owned by Thomas Fortune Ryan, with William Rockefeller as a very substantial stockholder. Both of these men were directors —the latter, apparently, the most influential director—of the railroad.

The devices employed were several in number. But the basic one was the requirement to pay for a certain minimum of power, whether it was actually used or not. Such a requirement is reasonable enough in itself; but in this instance the minimum was placed at such a point that, in the words of the Commission, "The St. Paul paid during the years 1921–4 inclusive at least $1,500,000 for power which it was unable to use." [6] Another of the devices employed was the formation of the Intermountain Company for the purpose of purchasing power from an already existing company with a considerable surplus on its hands, and selling this power to the railroad at a handsome profit. Said the Commission with reference to this deal: "There does not appear to have been any good reason for interjecting the Intermountain into this situation. The only purpose it has served has been as a vehicle for profits to Ryan and his associates." [7]

We here see members of the management of a corporation, in the process of obtaining supplies for their organization, first snapping them up for themselves and then selling them to the company at a substantial advance. The best known example in recent years of this malodorous practice was afforded by the records of the Tea-

[6] *Reports of the Interstate Commerce Commission,* Vol. CXXXI (1928), p. 644.
[7] *Ibid.,* p. 649.

pot Dome Investigation. We recite the story in some detail and without comment.[8]

Colonel A. E. Humphreys struck oil at Mexia, Texas, in 1921, when the price for oil was at a twenty year top. Colonel Robert W. Stewart, Chairman of the Board of the Standard Oil Company of Indiana, together with H. N. Blackmer, president of the Midwest Refining Company, a subsidiary of the Standard Oil of Indiana, and James E. O'Neil, president of the Prairie Oil & Gas Company, another affiliate of the Standard Oil of Indiana, wished to obtain supplies of oil from Humphreys for their corporations.

After lengthy negotiations Blackmer came to an agreement with Humphreys to purchase 33,333,333⅓ barrels at $1.50 per barrel for a total of $50,000,000.

The preliminary meetings for the arranging of the contracts were attended by Blackmer, O'Neil, Harry F. Sinclair, Colonel Humphreys, and counsel, and the original drafts of the contracts designated the Prairie Oil & Gas Company, and the Sinclair Crude Oil Purchasing Company, of which Harry Sinclair, H. N. Blackmer and Colonel Robert Stewart were in control, as the vendees.

Blackmer, Stewart, Sinclair, O'Neil, Humphreys and others met at the Vanderbilt Hotel in New York City on November 17, 1921, for the purpose of signing the contract. At this meeting Blackmer stated that the Continental Trading Company, Ltd., would be the vendee. To this proposal Humphreys objected until Blackmer and Sinclair promised that the Sinclair Crude Oil Purchasing Company and the Prairie Oil & Gas Company would guarantee the contract. Thereupon the contract was signed.

On that same day Sinclair, Stewart, Blackmer and O'Neil made a contract by which the Continental Trading Company, Ltd., which had just purchased 33,333,333⅓ barrels of oil at $1.50 per barrel, resold the same quantity to the Sinclair Crude Oil Purchasing Company and the Prairie Oil & Gas Company for $1.75 per barrel.

[8] *Leases upon Naval Oil Reserves: Hearings before the Committee on Public Lands and Surveys.* U.S. Senate, 68th Congress, 1st Session. 3 vols., 1924. Government Printing Office.

Leases upon Naval Oil Reserves: Activities of the Continental Trading Company of Canada: Hearings before the Committee on Public Lands and Surveys. U.S. Senate, 70th Congress, 1st Session, 1928. Government Printing Office.

The Continental Trading Company, Ltd., was incorporated in Toronto on November 16, 1921, the day before these memorable contracts were signed, by one H. S. Osler. Osler and four clerks were its only officers, each holding one share of stock.

The only activity in which the Continental Trading Company, Ltd., indulged was to receive, on the 10th of each month, $1.75 per barrel from the Sinclair Company and the Prairie Company, and to remit to Humphreys at the rate of $1.50 per barrel. The difference of 25 cents per barrel was invested in 3½% U.S. Liberty Bonds. These bonds were invariably delivered to Osler divided into four equal packages. It was subsequently shown that these packages were delivered to Stewart, Blackmer, O'Neil and Sinclair.

The subsequent tragic history of these individuals and others who became mixed up in the accompanying transactions need not concern us here. What is of interest is the reaction of their stockholders when they learned of this roundabout way of milking their corporations.

The contracts were, as a matter of fact, approved by the directors of both the Sinclair Company and the Prairie Company. Mr. H. L. Phillips, the president of the Sinclair Company, commented upon the situation as follows, "We have every confidence in Mr. Stewart and Mr. Sinclair, and that what they did was for the best interests of the company".

Stewart, in his own defense, said: "Maybe we could have gotten that oil for 25 cents a barrel less, but my stockholders certainly did not complain if the contracts have been fairly profitable to them".

The prospective profits of these four individuals, profits to be taken directly from the rightful earnings of their own companies, was to have been eight and one third millions of dollars. As a matter of fact, only $3,080,000 of the fateful Liberty Bonds had been delivered by June of 1923, when the Senate disclosures brought ruin upon the scheme.

So little feeling was aroused among the stockholders of the Standard Oil Company of Indiana, even after the details of these transactions were known, that even the tremendous power of the Rockefeller family was taxed to its limit to depose Colonel Stewart from his position in the corporation. It is true that Stewart's dexterity in the dispensing of strategic dividends and in utilizing all of the resources of the great corporation in his fight for proxies had much to do with the apparent loyalty of his stockholders. Even allowing for this, however, the callousness with which most stockholders regarded their superior's lapse from duty, even when the lapse worked against their own interests, is one of the most disquieting signs of the times.

Disloyal Buying. What is true of selling to one's company obviously applies to buying its property. The Burland Lithographic Company having become insolvent, Burland bid for and purchased all the assets of the company in four lots, paying $21,564 for lot 1. This lot he shortly afterwards sold for $60,000. Minority holders felt that this was unjust and sued for recovery of $38,436. The court held that Burland need not reimburse the minority holders, but said in the course of its decision: "It may be that a person of more refined self-respect and a more generous regard for the company of which he was president would have been disposed to give the company the benefit of his purchase. But their Lordships have not to decide questions of that character. The sole question is whether he was under any legal obligation to do so".[9] This statement differentiates clearly between the legal and the moral judgment in such cases. The moral judgment must be that a man under whose leadership an organization becomes a failure is bound to do all he can to extricate from the wreckage those unfortunate persons whose money he has agreed to care for.

The Right of Managers to Deal in the Stock of their own Corporations. A problem somewhat less simple than any of the preceding has to do with the right of an officer or director of a corporation to sell or buy the stock of the corporation which he serves during his incumbency in office. The question is sometimes asked in the form, "May an officer or director buy or sell the stock of *his own* corporation?" The connotation of the words "his own" is perhaps unfortunate, but it seems to fit the case; for on more than one occasion in the recent Senate investigations of corporate activities, officials who had enjoyed the rights of dictatorship over a corporation for long periods of time without owning more than a very small frac-

[9] Burland *v.* Earle, A. C. 83 (1902).

tion of the stock were compelled by the driving attorneys to admit that they had never before appreciated the fact that "they didn't actually own the damn company".

It has been reported elsewhere in this volume that Judge Gary introduced the practice of holding directors' meetings of the United States Steel Corporation after 3:00 o'clock in the afternoon, the hour at which the stock exchange closed. "I have always thought," he is reported as saying, "that this use of inside information by directors was akin to robbery of their own stockholders".[10]

We believe that Judge Gary was right. From the very nature of his position an officer or director is constantly coming into possession of information concerning circumstances which will affect the value of the stock; and he comes into possession of it before the stockholders have had an opportunity to learn of its existence. Thus a series of new and very profitable contracts may quite suddenly offer themselves after a period of depression has driven down the price of the stock. The only way in which he can get additional shares is to buy them from present stockholders. This means he must deprive of prospective gains those whose interests he has agreed to represent; and he does this by using as if it were his private property information which essentially belongs to them. If for any reason such information must be held for a time then he has no right to use it himself till the occasion for secrecy has passed. To transmit information to the stockholders of any large corporation is in effect to make it public. This affords us a simple formula for our conclusion: An officer or director has no right in connection with dealings in the stock of his corporation to take advantage of information which is not at the disposal of the public.

What is true of a prospective rise in value holds equally for an anticipated drop. Under such circumstances, of course, no one acquainted with the situation would buy except at a readjusted price. The question whether a man may rightly seek out ignoramuses for the purpose of gaining through their loss has already been discussed at length in Chapter V, and need not be further considered. But in

[10] Flynn, *op. cit.*, p. 15. How low prevailing standards are in this matter is shown by the fact that some directors still take advantage of the circumstance that the San Francisco Exchange closes two hours later than that of New York.

the case now before us there enters another factor. The only way in which the official can dispose of his stock with advantage to himself is to find someone else who will agree to become a stockholder. This means, in effect, that he must find someone who does not yet know of the disastrous information. The officer thereupon invites this person into the corporation to assume his losses. All that is needed to make a perfect picture is for him to write the victim a letter of welcome into the fold, together with pious expressions describing the zeal with which the management will care for the interests of the newcomer.

Our conclusion does not mean that a manager ought not to buy or sell his company's stock under any conceivable circumstances. It means he may not deal in it on the strength of information not available to the public. He may find himself in great need of more capital in his private business, and for perfectly legitimate reasons prefer to sell a part of his holdings rather than to borrow on them. He may discover better opportunities for investment elsewhere and wish to avail himself of them. A sale under such circumstances need not involve taking undue advantage of any other stockholder. In fact no purchase or sale by an insider can be considered illegitimate when he has no reason by virtue of the information which his position gives him to expect a change in market price.

Direct or Resign. An evil in the management of American corporations more common than positive breach of trust is neglect to perform the duties for which one has made himself responsible. An effective board must be small; a corporation can not be governed by a mob. All of the ten or twelve members of a directorate should recognize that it is the combined knowledge, experience, and judgment that are necessary for the successful guidance of the organization. No one is justified in accepting such a position unless he expects to do his share of the work. The board needs not merely his knowledge, experience and snap judgments; it needs his diligent attention. For some of the worst swindles in the history of American corporations, as the looting of the Milwaukee Road, were due as much to the negligence of certain directors as to the crookedness of the others. Had the former group attended properly to their business that great and flourishing organization could never have been reduced to a receivership.

This is not too onerous a demand, particularly for a man who is willing to content himself with participation in the management of one or two corporations instead of allowing his name to be trumpeted abroad as a member of the directorates of twenty or thirty. "The real function [of a board of directors consists not in managing all the details of the business but in] selecting the right officials, outlining policies, and passing well informed judgments from time to time as to the efficiency and honesty of the management." [11] A member of one of the greatest accounting firms in the United States informs us that under ordinary business conditions this should not require more than the equivalent of a week's time *per annum,* even in the case of the larger corporations.[12]

We believe that some, at least, of these negligent directors would feel their responsibilities more keenly if we adopted the European custom of paying directors an adequate salary for their services. It should be—as in Europe—on the percentage basis. Even where they are the possessors of great wealth, so that the compensation received, however considerable in itself, might seem relatively insignificant to them, we believe this statement will still hold true. In the first place, apparently, few men of wealth despise even small sums of money. In the second place, directors, like other men, are very complicated creatures. The obligations of an unpaid service might not move them to action. Furthermore, as experience has demonstrated again and again, a stake in the organization as stockholders does not necessarily provide adequate motive force. On the other hand there are those who would consider it dishonorable to accept remuneration for a piece of work and not perform it. The fact that they are not moved by the five or ten or twenty dollar bills which they now get for attending a meeting proves nothing; this is widely regarded as something of a joke. We believe this policy would

[11] W. H. Lough, *Business Finance* (New York, Ronald Press, 1917), p. 41.

[12] How careless directors can be in meeting their obligations is indicated by the fact that in recent Senate investigations more than one of these great men was forced to inquire of his secretary whether he was actually the director of a given corporation or not.

not merely conduce to diligence. It would remove one excuse—even if it be a very poor excuse—for getting profits out of the position by illegitimate means. It would certainly make the community take a more serious view of directorial negligence when it was shown to be a leading factor in any serious financial disaster.

The Basis on which Directors should be Selected. The majority of directors are undoubtedly chosen for their business ability and for their capacity for directing the affairs of the company. Many others, however, are selected because they possess a name which will impress the public. Still others are given a place on the board solely because they "can bring business along with them".

Selection on the first basis is the only proper one. Selection on the second basis, where likely to be accompanied by ignorance of the business, want of good judgment, or neglect of duty, is simply dishonest trickery and rank misrepresentation, and is as reprehensible from the moral point of view as is any other form of dishonest advertising. Selection on the third basis represents a method of playing upon the personal element in business which is very difficult to fit into any theory of fair competition. Corporations should select their officers, both executives and directors, solely on the basis of efficiency and then pay for all the services they require.[13]

[13] For a brief and clear statement of the legal obligations of management to stockholders see Berle and Means, *The Modern Corporation and Private Property*, Bk. II, Chs. V and VI.

FAIR TREATMENT OF COMPETITORS

CHAPTER XI

FOUR PROBLEMS

The present and the following chapter have as their subject matter fair dealings between competitors, in distinction from fair dealings between buyer and seller. As we pointed out in Chapter I, no hard and fast line can be drawn between the two, for they are often merely different sides of the same transaction. We have classified such incidents as the misappropriation of the name Waltham Watch, or such practices as full line forcing under the head of unfair selling simply because the first blow falls on the customer. It may easily happen, however, that the worst blow is directed to the competitor.

Fair competition has already been defined.[1] It consists in the attempt to succeed by supplying better goods or services than your competitors; or more briefly, trying to succeed on your merits. The problems discussed in the present chapter may be formulated most conveniently in the following terms: How far does fair competition exclude this or that mode of treating a competitor? We begin with truthful disparagement of a competitor's goods, services, credit, or character.

Truthful Disparagement

The Fundamental Principle. We have already said so much about lying that we need not stop to discuss false disparagement. There are, however, a good many students in our business ethics courses, and there appear to be many people elsewhere, who believe that all disparagement in the business world is unfair. Most of those who maintain this position, however, confine this prohibition to competitors. This view is worth examining.

If taken literally and in its most sweeping form it would require the elimination of credit information by banks and by credit institu-

[1] Ch. I, p. 12.

tions; it would condemn the campaign once waged by *Collier's Weekly* and the *Ladies' Home Journal,* and the almost continuous attacks directed by the American Medical Association against one of the biggest of American frauds, the fake patent medicine. It seems almost unnecessary to discuss such a proposition. Can the average person be expected in these days to discover, by his own investigation, the credit rating of those with whom he must do business, or to know at first hand all about the qualities of the thousands of articles now upon the market? On what basis can it be maintained that he is not to be protected? The seller gets his right to a place in the economic world by serving society; if so, he certainly loses this right when he prostitutes his position by robbing its members or ruining their health. And if it be urged that the government ought to protect you, and the government alone, it might as well be claimed that I have no right to warn my neighbor directly that a thief is trying to get into his garage or his cellar, but must instead go home and telephone the police.

Probably those who profess to believe that all disparagement, from whatever source, is unfair, have never tried to think the matter through. But there are a good many who persist in the view that disparagement, however true its statements, is aways wrong when it is the work of a competitor. For example the *Z* company, which had published and was advertising a new encyclopedia, printed the following statement: "We hereby guarantee: that everything in the *Z* encyclopedia was especially written for it. . . . That this Encyclopedia was undertaken as a purely original work, and that it is not founded upon, copied from, or based upon any other encyclopedia, domestic or foreign". Thereupon the *Y* Company, publishers of a rival encyclopedia, printed and distributed widely a pamphlet of over one hundred pages, containing in parallel columns extracts from the *Z* encyclopedia and from an encyclopedia published fifty years earlier. The practical identity of the material in the two columns demonstrated that at least some parts of the later were copied from the earlier. A considerable proportion of the members of our classes who think this exposure would have been justifiable on the part of a grocer or a bond salesman think it very wrong when put out by a rival publisher.

We ourselves have never been able to see the justification of any such position. No book, no medicine, no article of commerce of whatever kind, has any right to exist except as it can do reasonably well what it pretends to be able to do. The person who is most likely to know whether this is the case is precisely the man's competitor in the same field. Furthermore, if one of these does not do it, it will usually remain undone for lack of adequate motive.

This brings us to the objection always urged: The intention of the competitor is wrong because he is presumably aiming at the ruin, or at least the injury of his competitor, not for the sake of the public but for the sake of building up his own business. And if motives have anything to do with morality this is wrong.

This apparent difficulty can be met, however, by considering a parallel case. There are doubtless a good many business men who pay their debts for egoistic reasons only. They wish to maintain their credit rating, so that they may be able to borrow when they need money, and they want to keep clear of the law. If they could squirm out of their debts without subjecting themselves to these penalties they would jump at the chance. Now when such men pay their debts they are not entitled to any particular credit, in the moral sense of the term; and yet we may quite properly say they have done right. Their creditor has a rightful claim upon them, and they have met this claim. It is true that they have not acted from the highest motives, the motives that would operate in a thoroughly honorable man; nevertheless they have performed, with whatever motive, an act they were bound to perform. Morality is, strictly speaking, internal, as was pointed out in Chapter II, but it exhibits itself normally in outer acts. A man therefore who pays his debts merely to maintain his credit rating and to keep out of the clutches of the law is internally not on a very high plane; but externally he is performing precisely the same kind of an act that a man of honor would perform without compulsion. His paying his debts, looked at from the moral point of view, is inwardly of no particular moral worth; we might perhaps call it morally indifferent; but externally it is right.

The same thing applies to the action of the *Y* Encyclopedia Company in showing up the *Z* Company, in so far as the material used was not open to misinterpretation. It is externally the right thing to do, whatever the motive, in that it violates no rights of the Z Company. Indeed we may go farther. It is not merely my right but also my duty to society and to myself to defend myself against the trickery of competitors. An exposure carried out in this spirit would acquire a positive moral flavor. In addition it would represent what the highest type of publisher would do out of regard for the public interest.

The Limitations of the Preceding Principle. Is it, then, our conclusion that it is the duty of any man, competitor or not, who knows that the goods, or the solvency, or the character of another business are not what they ought to be, to trumpet forth these facts to the world? By no means. The limits within which true disparagement of a business concern is justified can best be exhibited by considering a much discussed problem in the ethics of the medical profession.

As is well known, the Code of Medical Ethics unreservedly condemns all criticism in the presence of laymen by one physician of the work of another physician, whether such criticism be well founded or not. The reasons offered for this prohibition are the following. Medical diagnosis and treatment, are, to a large extent, a matter of judgment, and two equally good doctors will often take different views of the same situation. Furthermore the layman is apt to believe the critic rather than the object of his criticism, and to do so quite uncritically. Statements made to a layman, therefore, condemning the methods used by a fellow-physician, even when made in perfect good faith, are as likely as not to be misleading; and should the practice of making them become general, would undermine the confidence of the public in the entire medical profession. Such practice, accordingly, is, on the whole, a source of more error and injustice than truth, and as such is forbidden.

This rule is based upon an important distinction which we have already used several times, namely that between matters of fact and matters of opinion. It is a matter of fact that on a given date a certain stock sold on the New York Stock Exchange at sixty. It is a matter of opinion that it will rise in value during the next six months. The former belief can be verified at any time; the latter represents guess work. Every man has a right to a good reputation if he deserves it. Therefore no other person has a right to attack it unless he can verify and has verified his statements by objective evidence. Disparagement, therefore, should be confined, as an all but universal rule, to matters of fact.

To be sure the distinction between matters of fact and matters of opinion, like most other distinctions in life, is not a hard and fast one, and difficult problems are certain to arise as one approaches the boundary line. But it will prove to be a valid and a useful one, none the less.

There is, however, another factor which we think ought to enter into consideration. Disparagement of a competitor should not merely confine itself to matters of fact—*i. e.* those which the specialist could verify; it ought to be further restricted to such matters of fact as the general public, if it wished, would also be capable of verifying. Thus the "Exhibit" of the *Y* Encyclopedia Company shows the facts in such fashion that anyone sufficiently interested could determine the truth of its statements for himself. The only objection to their actual procedure is that they failed to state—as they were bound to do—how much of the material was thus borrowed, and whether the borrowed articles were quoted in their entirety or whether they were supplemented by new material. This was a very serious omission indeed. But the underlying principle upon which they acted was a thoroughly sound one. Anyone is entirely justified in protecting the public against fraud on the part of a competitor or any other person if he confines himself to verified facts, which can also be verified by the prospective purchasers themselves.

This conclusion has found its perfect embodiment in the Code of the Electric Power Club, as follows:

> "Comparisons favorable to one's own product are justifiable if they are confined to strictly truthful statements. But neither generally nor specifically disparaging statements concerning a manufacturer or his product should be made beyond those involved in a clear-cut comparison of similar facts. It is proper to make comparison of one's product with that of a competitor when such comparison is based on information secured through bulletins available to the public, articles appearing in the public press, information derived from the reports of competent, independent testing organizations, or upon data which can be readily verified by the prospective purchaser, such, for example, as weights and dimensions." [2]

[2] Heermance, *op. cit.*, p. 150.

Sometimes the public is protected against wishful thinking or deliberate misrepresentation on the part of rivals by the fact that if their statements are not true their falsity will presently be demonstrated by the course of events. Here, then, we may say that something approaching objective evidence is available to customers, and that where the disparager himself has definite evidence at his disposal he is justified in proceeding. This is what happened when a corporation manufacturing a complex mechanical contrivance was going out of business because of lack of capital, and was making every effort to dispose rapidly of all stock on hand. The salesmen of competitors met this with a campaign of disparagement, describing vividly to all prospective purchasers the undesirability of being in the position of owning an "orphan" machine, and stating truthfully the financial status of the concern and its forthcoming dissolution. In consequence the company lost its market. But, if the conclusions of Chapter V are valid, it was not unjustly treated; those who would otherwise have been purchasers were protected against future inconvenience and loss; and nothing was done which would shake the confidence of the public in those permanently engaged in this line of business.

If you are at once certain of the dishonesty or incompetence of your competitor and unable to present evidence of the fact which would be accessible and intelligible to the public; and if at the same time you regard his methods of doing business as a menace either to yourself and your associates or to the community, the proper course of action, if you are a member of a business men's association, is represented by the following provision of the International Association of Milk Dealers. "It is to be considered the duty and not an unfair practice or objectionable in any sense of the word, for a member to make a confidential report of unethical conduct, unsatisfactory conditions, or illegal practices, to the Secretary of this Association in writing, and to supply the Secretary with all the evidence that the report may be substantiated".[3] If your association has no machinery to take care of such cases you should see that it is introduced.[4]

[3] Heermance, *op. cit.*, p. 136.

[4] For the law of disparagement see Jeremiah Smith, "Disparagement of Property", 13 *Columbia L. Rev.* 13, 121 (1913).

Inducing Breach of Contract

We pass now from statements made in disparagement of competitors to the field of contracts. Observance of contracts has already been dealt with at sufficient length. One practice in this field, however, remains for considerations, that of inducing breach of a contract made by a third party with a competitor. While the principles involved are none other than those presented in the discussion of partnership in lying,[5] the extent of the practice and the failure on the part of many persons to recognize its true nature seem to warrant a brief survey of the subject.

Inducing breach of contract may best be described, if it needs description, by an illustration. One of the most famous of English law suits is that of Lumley *v.* Gye. Miss Wagner, a singer who was a favorite with the London opera going public, signed a contract to sing for a season exclusively with a company managed by Mr. Lumley. Thereupon a rival manager, Mr. Gye, induced her by the offer of a larger salary to break her contract and to join his company. Miss Wagner, it must be premised, had no justification whatever for her part in the affair, and her only motive was to get more money.

The principle upon which rests the solution of the problem raised by this incident has already been stated in the chapter just cited. A person is responsible for every consequence of his act which is included in his intention, that is to say, which is foreseen. One consequence of Mr. Gye's action was the loss on the part of Mr. Lumley of a valuable advantage to which he had acquired the right, *i. e.* the services of Miss Wagner. Mr. Gye is thus responsible for the loss. The mere fact that he acted through Miss Wagner is irrelevant; just as much so as where a burglar steals the silver ware by bribing the servant to get it for him. The gist of the matter can be put in a dozen words: Mr. Gye attempted to appropriate for himself services which belonged to someone else.

We have said that the fundamental principles of ethics can be most easily seen in a murder case. Accordingly if a person who is facing a decision involving moral issues really wants to see things as they are

[5] See above, Ch. IV, p. 56.

instead of merely throwing dust into his eyes, let him translate the situation into terms of murder. Applying this method to the solution of the problem concerning the responsibility of Mr. Gye yields the following result. Police Lieutenant Becker, according to the findings of a New York jury, hired four gunmen to kill the gambler Rosenthal, who was supposed to have had something "on" him. The part played by the gunmen was never seriously questioned. They were accordingly sent to the electric chair. When the jury found that Becker had bribed them to commit the murder, was he permitted to go free on the ground that he himself had killed no one? On the contrary: he went to the electric chair along with his tools. Admitting the facts, did anyone ever regard the execution as unjust? No one that we have ever heard of.

Of course we do not mean that depriving a man of services to which he has a right is as bad as murder. What we mean is that when one person bribes or otherwise induces another person to wrong a third party he is just as responsible for the consequences, whatever they may be, as the direct actor. Indeed he is worse. For he is not merely responsible for the ultimate consequences; he is also responsible for putting temptation before another person, and thus doing his part to debauch that person's character. "Lead us not into temptation", points to one of the most important and fundamental articles in the code of an honorable man.

It would be unprofitable to attempt to enumerate the different forms which this kind of theft may take, for they are as numerous as the various kinds of contract. One of the commonest varieties is inducing purchasers of machines or other goods, bought on the instalment plan, to stop further payments, return the machine to its maker or wholesaler, and put in its place a rival machine. The seller, on his part, agrees to compensate the purchaser for the instalments already paid, and to protect him against a suit for breach of contract. The seller, it need hardly be said, would feel that he had been very unfairly treated should the purchaser break this contract and install a third machine sold by another rival.

Another variation on this theme is represented by the manufacturer who induced the owners or lessors of buildings used as stations by his competitors to break their contracts by ousting the lessees.[6] Another is causing a person under contract to deliver goods or perform services to break his contract by threats of physical or economic harm. Illustrations from court cases are: Sunwalt Ice Company *v.* Knickerbocker Ice Company,[7] and Doremus *v.* Hennessy.[8] Still another form is bribing another man's employees to purchase or to recommend the purchase of your products, to sell you their employer's secrets, to injure his goods or machinery, *etc.* For, as we have seen,[9] he who enters a given employment thereby implicitly promises loyalty to his employer.

Is it our conclusion that no one ought to make an offer unless he knows that the party approached is not under contract with someone else to perform the same service? It means that he ought not to make an offer where he has *reason to believe* such contract exists. The Linde Air Products Company instruct their salesmen never to approach with a view to making an immediate sale a possible customer who is known to be under exclusive contract with another firm to purchase from the latter the article in question. He who follows this rule will ordinarily have done his full duty in this matter.

Lumley *v.* Gye was decided in favor of the plaintiff by a divided court in 1853. While there was some pretense on the part of the majority that the decision was simply an extension of the ancient common law principle which forbade the enticement of another's servant, it represented, as a matter of fact, the introduction of an entirely new principle of law; the principle being that of "according to promises the same or similar protection as is accorded to other forms of property".[10] In 1893 the principle was applied to another form of contract besides that of personal services in Temperton *v.* Russell, namely, an agreement to supply building materials. Since that time it has been extended to all other forms of contract, regardless of their nature. It is therefore a firmly established principle of English law.

In our own country the doctrine of Lumley *v.* Gye has met a dif-

6 *Federal Trade Commission Decisions,* VIII (1927), 450.

7 114 Md. 403.

8 176 Ill. 608.

9 P. 98, above.

10 F. B. Sayre, "Inducing Breach of Contract", 36 *Harv. L. Rev.* 675 (1923).

ferent fate in different states. The majority of them, however, follow the English rule. In this number is now included (since 1918) the State of New York.

Outside Selling

The Present Situation. "Outside selling" means selling outside the traditional sequence from manufacturer to wholesaler, to retailer, to consumer. It has become an especially acute problem because of certain changes in merchandising methods that have been going on the past thirty or forty years. During this period the functions of the wholesaler have been assumed more and more completely by the manufacturer at one end of the series and by the retailer at the other. This process has gone so far that many people are expecting the wholesaler to be crushed to death between these upper and nether millstones; and most of them apparently suppose this will result in great economies to the consumer.

Whatever may be the fate in store for the wholesaler, consumers' hopes for extensive economies are unquestionably doomed to disappointment. For the functions hitherto performed by the wholesaler can not be destroyed as long as our present marketing system endures. These services cost money as they always have cost, and the chief question at issue is not: How shall the expenses of a given service be eliminated, but who shall get the profits, the specialist who has been supplying the services in the past, or the manufacturer and the retailer? Of course if the manufacturer or the retailer is the gainer the public may get some of the profits in the form of lower prices; just as when a department store puts in groceries and meat the public may get the benefit of a part of the earnings. But the common notion that the consumer has any really large savings to look forward to as the result of the possible elimination of the wholesaler appears to be an error—though a widespread one.

The average grocer carries from two thousand to three thousand items on his shelves; there are in the United States over ten thousand manufacturers of food stuffs from whom to buy. Thus there is involved a choice of producers on the part of the grocers; and there is equally involved a choice of grocers on the part of the producers. For credit standing, the special nature of the retail market, and much else must be determined by the latter before profitable trade relations with the retailer can be established. The wholesaler performs these functions, finding the right kind of producers for the retailer, the right kind of customers for the manufacturer; "right", that is, from the point of view of the particular needs and situations and policies of each.

The retailer must have near him some depot from which he can get goods on a few hours notice; this is especially true today with the growth within the last decade of "hand to mouth" buying. Someone must supply storage facilities, and they must be situated near the retailer. Furthermore large shipments of goods from the factories to the wholesalers involve a very considerable number of economies, as compared with scattered small shipments from factory to retailer. These economies have been made possible by the wholesaler's warehouse.[11]

Today many manufacturers are, in effect, adding a wholesale department to their business; and many retailers are doing the same thing. Among the latter are to be counted, as everyone knows, the chain stores, the larger department stores, and the mail order houses. In addition many retailers are forming coöperative buying associations. These changes are by no means eliminating the wholesaler. In Manhattan, for example, according to a table supplied by Dr. Beckman,[12] the number of wholesale dealers more than doubled between the years 1900 and 1922. He suggests that "If the [wholesalers] would be willing to effect necessary changes in organization, merchandise control systems, and methods of doing business, rather than to adhere to plans and policies which have long outlived their usefulness—there is no reason why they should cease to be one of the most economical links in the chain of distribution of manufactured products".

Whether these innovations are on the whole a good thing for the consumer remains to be seen. Like most other changes in life they have their good and their bad side. But from the point of view they are, of course, wholly bad. For while they can not elimi-

[11] See Theodore N. Beckman, *Wholesaling* (New York, The Ronald Press, 1926), Ch. II.

[12] *Ibid.* Ch. V, p. 70.

nate him they narrow his field and tend to restrict it to the smaller retailers and, perhaps less completely, to the smaller factories.

Is There a "Sacred Way" from Manufacturer to Consumer? This, then, is the situation. Is there anything unfair about it? Many wholesalers have complained that it is unfair for the manufacturer to sell directly to the retailer and for the retailer to buy directly from the factory. They regard themselves as the victims not merely of an injury but also of a *wrong*. Is this true?

In answering we may look at this problem from either of two points of view—that of the wholesaler or that of the community. The former presumably never hesitates to take on another line if he thinks he can "make a go of it", regardless of its effects upon his competitors. A wholesale drug house will add chemicals to its repertory, the wholesale grocer, hams, bacon, and sausages; the dry goods house, shoes,—*if it will pay*. What is more to the point, hundreds of wholesalers have gone into the retail business themselves. Why then should not a chain store system or a department store take on another line, namely the functions hitherto subserved by the wholesaler, as far as supplying themselves with goods is concerned? What is there "sacred" about the province of the wholesaler? He sees with perfect equanimity a clothing store take on the shoe business, and perhaps buys his shoes at this new outlet. Is it possible that he has one standard where he is consumer and another where he is producer? To this the wholesaler will perhaps reply: How about the interests of the consuming public? To us the following seems to be the proper answer. Over a large area the wholesaler is indispensable, and he will therefore continue to occupy this field as long as the present system of distribution lasts. On the other hand, the question whether he is indispensable in certain other fields is now being determined in the most convincing way possible, namely by experience. In the meantime he has no more right to cry: "Unfair competition" than the shoe dealer when the clothing store begins to sell shoes, or the restaurant keeper when the drug store serves lunches.

In certain fields, to be sure, the wholesale and the retail business ought to be kept absolutely and completely independent of each other. This holds, particularly, for the marketing of stocks and bonds. The underwriter is essentially a wholesaler. It is his duty to see that the securities which he markets are sound, and in general are such that they can be disposed of without misrepresentation. But he is under no obligation to confine his offerings to the small number of the very strongest and most profitable investments. For if all did this the overwhelming majority of business enterprises would starve to death. The distributor, on the other hand, is constantly being called upon to serve as the confidential adviser of his customers. It thus becomes his duty to pick out and recommend what he regards as the best available material which the market affords; the "best", of course, of the kind which the given customer wishes to own. He must therefore be in a position to survey the entire investment field with a cold and calculating eye. But this would be almost impossible if he were actively engaged at the same time in pushing a particular group of securities.

We see, then, that the considerations which would prevent an honorable man from engaging in the wholesaling and retailing of securities have nothing to do with the supposed existence of a "sacred way"; but depend, instead, upon the fact that the legitimate interests of the wholesaler are likely to warp his judgment when he becomes a retailer, and thus to render it impossible for him to do justice to the obligations which he takes upon himself in the latter capacity.

It is sometimes urged that the wholesaler who sells at retail is unfair to the regular retailer in that he skims off the cream, leaving to his competitor nothing but the blue milk. Thus if he is in the lumber business he will sell the lumber required for building a house, but not the few boards needed for repairing the veranda. But if the retailer is reduced to selling nothing but "kindling wood" he will presently be forced into bankruptcy; and then the community will find itself without a supplier for its most frequently recurring even if not its most important needs.

To this contention it may be replied that while outside selling on the part of wholesalers will doubtless result in the elimination of some retailers in certain fields and thus cause much hardship to them and occasional inconvenience to purchasers, nevertheless, as far as consumers are concerned the matter will sooner or later regulate itself automatically in the larger cities. Furthermore, owing to the existence of the modern car and its cousin the modern truck, practically all places are now for business purposes parts of some large city. Unfortunately all progress, whatever its nature, injures some persons. But on the whole a business practice is justified which in any degree lowers the enormous costs of getting goods from the original producer to the ultimate consumer.

In the struggle to maintain their territory intact many wholesalers are demanding a special discount from manufacturers, apart from the amount of goods purchased. For example, if a wholesaler orders from a manufacturer the same amount of goods as does a chain store, where the latter receives a ten per cent trade discount, the former is to receive, say, fifteen per cent. Manufacturers not offering this special discount are thereupon black-listed by the wholesalers' trade associations and then boycotted.

Now whatever may be said of the boycott any fair-minded person will admit that for a body of men to get together to force their will upon another person by threatening him with ruin is a very serious affair. There must, at least in our opinion, be some real injustice that needs righting before this procedure may properly be resorted to. Certainly all business men take this view of strikes, which are a form of the boycott. Why is it unjust for the manufacturers to refuse special discounts to wholesalers? The answer is quite simple: It is not. Wholesalers are no more entitled to special protection than anyone else, for example, the small retail shoe dealer. If in his own interests the manufacturer chooses to offer a certain class of customers a differential rate, this is one thing; but to demand this as a *right* is a very different matter. Our conclusion is that a manufacturer who chooses to treat wholesalers, chain stores, department stores, and retailers' co-operative buying organizations exactly alike, and to give discounts based on size of order only is not merely within his rights, but is ordinarily and perhaps always performing an important social service; that a boycott to prevent this can not be justified; and that, in principle, such boycotters are doing the same kind of a wrong as that of the working-men who, with precisely the same provocation, smash the newly invented machinery which is "stealing" their jobs from them. What applies to the wholesaler when the manufacturer threatens his economic existence applies equally when the wholesaler becomes the devil in the picture and sells at retail.

All this may perhaps seem a hard saying. Nor will one who has never been subjected to such a temptation wrap about himself the cloak of a Pharisaic self-righteousness and thank God that he is not as other men. But however much allowance we may be disposed to make in judging the wholesaler or retailer who, seeing his business threatened with ruin through the introduction of more economical methods, resorts to the boycott; however much allowance we may make for the working-man who meets a similar crisis in his life by sabotage; the fact remains that if they are fighting against the coming in of a more efficient economic order they are doing wrong. The courts are therefore bound to interpose their veto, as they invariably do; and those persons, at least, whose interests are not directly involved must recognize that the repression exercised by the state is essentially just.

The fundamental principle of fair competition is: Let the best man win. The tendency of our selfish nature is to say: Let me win, whether I am the best man or not. When it dares to be consistent, this spirit will lead a man to commit murder if this is the most effective way of getting rid of a rival. Such a man of course represents the worst type because he will go to any length in order to win. But just as certainly as such a man stands at the bottom of the moral scale, just so certainly does he stand at the top who, however insistent the temptation, wills from start to finish to play the game according to the rules, and whatever happens acts on a level with the standard: Let the best man, the best goods, and the best methods of doing business, win.

A Question of Geography

Is it unfair for a producer to take advantage of his geographical location by offering lower prices than his less favorably situated competitors? Since fair competition consists in attempting to succeed by giving better services, which of course include rates, than one's competitors, the question may seem too simple for discussion outside of the kindergarten. Perhaps it is. But the current practice and opinion in a number of industries point to the acceptance of a position by certain very prominent business organizations which makes an examination of this subject worth while.

This practice took its classical form in the notorious Pittsburgh Plus system in the steel industry under the domination of the United States Steel Corporation. The essence of this scheme was quite simple. Let us say that *A's* price for steel at his mill in the steel producing district around Chicago was *m*; and that *B's* price for the same commodity at his mill in Pittsburgh was also *m*. By arrangement within the industry, however, the price quoted to the purchaser *C* had to be for steel as delivered at the purchaser's door. Let us suppose his place of business was Chicago. Under normal conditions *A* would receive the order because freight rates from his factory were lower than those from Pittsburgh. But for *A* to take advantage of this fact would be "unfair" to his competitor *B*. Therefore in order that they might compete on a plane of equality *A* must quote a price which was *m*, plus the cost of transportation from Pittsburgh to Chicago, call it *n*. The Pittsburgh company was now in the running, for its delivered price was also *m* plus *n*. Thus both could offer *C* precisely the same terms; and the resulting situation was one that would have justified fully the recent boast of the American Iron and Steel Institute that "every purchaser has at his disposal at the same price every source of production in the United States".[13]

In the period shortly after the World War the Federal Trade Commission devoted a good deal of attention to this method of pricing. At the conclusion of its study, in 1924, it ordered the United States Steel Corporation, whose case was the one under consideration, to "cease and desist from using the Pittsburgh Plus system of quoting prices." Contrary to the expectations of the Commission, this order did not destroy the system. It resulted rather in its modification, whereby Pittsburgh was replaced by a considerable number of "basing points", as they were called. This is the situation today. Certain evils have doubtless been eliminated by the change, but the principle is still insisted upon in the steel and some other industries. It is this principle in which we are here interested.

We repeat, accordingly, our original question: Is it unfair for a producing organization to avail itself of the advantages of its geo-

[13] Quoted from the *Report of the Federal Trade Commission to the President with Respect to the Basing Point System in the Iron and Steel Industry,* November 1934, p. 3.

graphical location in order to undersell its less favored competitors? If the answer is Yes, certain conclusions follow which the steel industry has not hesitated to accept. Suppose a steel plant happens to be located on a river. In that case some of its customers could often profit by the inexpensive water transportation thus made available. But a reduction of prices resulting from this condition is "unfair competition". The man who has a plant on a river will take business away from those who have their plants on the rails, and will do this apart from their relative efficiency as producers. This, it is declared, is the very essence of unfair competition. To prevent such activity the practice in the industry requires not only that the quoted price shall include freight charges from the basing point to the destination, it requires also, in the case of products moving by rivers, that quoted price should include *railroad* freight charges between the same two points.

Thus if a manufacturer on the Ohio River orders steel from Pittsburgh it probably comes down by barge, unless he insists otherwise. He nevertheless pays the full railroad freight. The Pittsburgh producer, however, pays the river freight and pockets the savings. Accordingly while the customer is not given the advantage of his location, the steel man who happens to be favorably located can reap an additional profit out of it. Any attempt on the part of the latter to pass some of this saving along to the customer is regarded as an unfair trade practice.

The fundamental fallacy in the reasoning of the members of the Institute has its source in their implicit conception of competition. They think of it solely in terms of rivalry between men engaged in the same occupation. But competition can also be defined in a broader sense as a system for supplying the economic needs of society. Under the former conception the public interest gets only secondary attention in the definition of the term. Under the latter the public interest is made the controlling consideration.

As has been shown in another chapter, our principle of fair competition requires that the work of society continually gravitate into the hands of those best fitted to perform it; that in the broadest social sense, the most efficient should win. Just what do we mean by "efficiency"? Surely we cannot be tied down to a narrow concept which regards it merely as the ability to run a machine economically. The term "efficiency" must be correlated with the whole of our social interests, and, in the last analysis, it means getting the most out of life with the smallest expenditure of human time and energy. In business it must be measured by the combined net result of a production system, a distribution system, and a consumption system. In a far flung empire or nation, transportation becomes one of our most important physical problems; and where goods are produced at one point and consumed at another, efficiency in production can not be gauged without a consideration of the problems of transportation.

Under these conditions, such advantages as nearness to a source of materials, nearness to markets, nearness to cheap means of transportation are physical advantages which produce actual benefits just as truly as do the latest mechanical or chemical marvels which come from the shops or laboratories. To set up a condition which limits such advantages is comparable to the suggestion that we destroy our spinning machinery and go back to hand weaving, or that we build our highways with hand shovelled instead of machine laid concrete. These advantages are the natural resources of the communities in which they are found; frequently the only considerable natural resource which the communities possess. To insist that the advantages be "shared", as the steel industry might put it, is to insist that they be neutralized or destroyed. The "sharing", where it is accomplished, is always a loss to the immediate community and it is never an advantage to any other. Only the steel industry, or more properly, only certain portions of the steel industry, benefit by the process. For to admit that the situation requires the acceptance of the Institute's definition is to put an obstacle in the way of the mill which produces primarily for a nearby market. Such a mill can frequently cover its local markets at lower prices than can distant plants, not because it is more efficiently organized, but merely because it can avoid much of the handling and transportation costs. A natural barrier is built around it by the rapidity with which freight rates on bulky products can eat up a slight advantage. Nevertheless, within its natural territory, it is the more efficient producer, if efficiency be measured according to the ability to "*produce and deliver* steel in the market".

Of course, if a large number of local markets are to be handed over to local independent producers who have no advantage other than that of their location, a good deal of business will not be available to the larger but more distant centers of industry such as Pittsburg and Youngstown. It was partly to place such centers on a par with the local producers that the basing point system was developed. Originally it was used to guarantee a market for the Pittsburg area. Nowadays it guarantees a market for a larger number of basing points. But the practice which permits the plant with a natural disadvantage of location with respect to the markets to force others to share its disadvantage still prevails.

We have confined our attention in this discussion largely to the steel industry. But it must not be forgotten that the problem arises, and is bound to arise, in every field of production where transportation charges form an important factor in the cost to the purchaser, and where, because of the standardized nature of the commodity, competition turns chiefly on the factor of price. The difficulties that arise in such a situation ought not to be ignored and may call for a certain amount of sacrifice on the part of the consuming public. How the necessary adjustment (if it *is* necessary) shall be made is a different problem for each industry. But it can not be decided solely by a group of magnates within the industry who, while using such purely ethical terms as *fair* and *unfair* where their private interests are concerned, are either blind or indifferent to the social implications of these same terms. If we are to talk about fairness at all, we are tied up inescapably to the principle that fair competition means that the competitor who can give the best service is the one who ought to win. And an important factor in determining what service is best is often geographical situation.

If this conclusion be denied consider the consequences. One factory has at its disposal a cheap and abundant supply of water power. Another is located in a small town where the cost of living is low and where wages are in consequence below the average. Another is next door to its chief source of supplies. Is it unfair for these producers to undersell their less favored competitors? This question answers itself.

CHAPTER XII

PREDATORY PRACTICES

Interference with a Competitor's Production or Distribution Processes

False disparagement and inducing breach of contract, bad as they are, are not so raw in their intent or—ordinarily—so disastrous in their consequences as the direct attempt to cripple or destroy a competitor's business. This is what is called predatory competition. It may take a number of forms. We shall deal with two: Interference with a competitor's production or distribution processes; selling below your own cost of production until, in the effort to meet your prices, your competitor has exhausted his resources, and is thus driven from the field.

The Ways of the Wild Beast. Certain methods of interfering with the production and the distribution processes of a rival are so obviously wrong that they require no comment. In an early English law suit (Garrett *v.* Taylor) it appeared that the defendant kept workmen away from his rival's quarry by threats of violence. In what was essentially the same sort of a thing the defendant blocked the road leading to his competitor's colliery (Iveson *v.* Moore).[1] Among the more modern methods of accomplishing the same end are breaking up his employment staff by fomenting strikes; enticing away his key employees, or a large group of his employees, not because you need them yourself but because he needs them; bribing his employees either to betray his business secrets or to sabotage his products; bribing railway employees to give you information about his shipments, or to destroy, limit, or otherwise hamper his transportation facilities. Some of these acts involve inducing the breach of an implicit contract, and in this capacity were referred to in the preceding chapter.

Perhaps a somewhat newer device is putting your competitor to unnecessary expense. A unique method of accomplishing this end is

[1] Cited by Bruce Wyman, *Competition and the Law*, 15 Harv. L. Rev. 440 (1902).

described in the *Decisions* of the Federal Trade Commission, Vol. V, p. 451. The Chamber of Commerce of Missoula, Montana, the majority of whose members were retail merchants, carried on a campaign to hamper the business of inconvenient mail order houses by announcing that thereafter a local motion picture theater would accept in lieu of tickets of admission for children under fifteen years of age the catalogs of any mail order house, and that certain cash prizes would be offered to those presenting the oldest, the most used, and the latest catalogs. As a result they obtained possession of several hundred such works of reference, which they thereupon promptly burned.

All these methods of competition are exactly on a par with doping a rival's horse as a means of winning a race. We do not expect very much of the men who find their chief interest in life in horse racing; but the majority of them are at least above this level. These practices do not represent trying to win by giving the best services you can, but the poorest that you can get away with. No one who has caught the spirit of our standard will suppose that its claims upon us are met by making your competitor's services worse than your own, instead of making yours as good as you can possibly make them.

Hiring a Competitor's Employees. The only one of these activities that can cause a moment's honest perplexity to a decent man is the attitude to be assumed toward a competitor's employees. Taking his key men away from him when you do not need them yourself is clearly just one way among others of wantonly crippling his business. But when we pass this point there are difficulties. Thirty-two of the 133 codes in Heermance's collection make pronouncements on this subject. It may be of interest to see what attempts the employers concerned have made to solve this problem.

High ground appears to be taken in the code of the National Confectioners' Association: "It shall be considered an unfair trade practice to offer a competitor's employees higher wages for the purpose of enticing them away from their employer." [2] But this looks at the interests involved solely from the point of view of the employer. It is as if two farmers should agree not to steal each other's cattle; and it suggests all too plainly what is frankly stated in the otherwise ex-

[2] Heermance, *op. cit.,* p. 119.

cellent code of the National Restaurant Association: "Hiring employees away from a competitor or inducing them by other means to leave a service is thoroughly unethical. Bidding for the services of those already in employment demoralizes the local labor conditions, and tends to raise the cost of labor to all restaurant men." [3] Somewhat more humane is the statement of the Iowa Concrete Products Association: "We shall not offer employment to our competitor's employees unless, without solicitation on our part, they ask for employment." [4] By the side of this may be placed the provision in the code of the Refrigerating Machinery Association: "The services of an employee engaged with a competitor should not be solicited by any of us without first notifying said competitor and securing consent to such solicitation".[5]

Here for the first time we approach something reasonable. A man is not a commodity or even a mere animal. On the other hand the employer has his rights also; the employee may be under contract for a specified time; furthermore, an employer is entitled to protection against a raid by a competitor. However even the last two provisions, cited above, are not entirely satisfactory; they still leave the employee too completely in the hands of the employer. Much better in this respect is the rule adopted by the American Institute of Accountants: "No member or associate shall directly or indirectly offer employment to an employee of a fellow member or associate without first informing said fellow member or associate of his intent. This rule shall not be construed so as to inhibit negotiations with anyone who of his own initiative or in response to public advertisement shall apply to a member or associate for employment".[6] More comprehensive are the following provisions of the National Association of Building Owners and Managers: "No member shall, directly or indirectly, by letter, interview, telephone, or otherwise, personally solicit the employees of another member. Nothing herein contained shall prevent a member from soliciting other members' employees by newspaper and other impersonal and general forms of advertising, nor shall anything herein contained prevent the solicitation or employment of

[3] Heermance, *op. cit.*, p. 466.
[4] *Ibid.*, p. 76.
[5] *Ibid.*, p. 459.
[6] *Ibid.*, p. 6.

another member's employee where said employee shall take the initiative in applying for a position; but in every such event any member knowingly taking on another member's employee must notify said other member, and then not take on said employee until said employee has complied with any agreement, if any, which he may have made with said other member, in reference to giving said member advance notice of a desire to leave his company".[7] Finally, the most imperative of this class of obligations is expressed in the following words: "No manufacturer of steel office furniture shall induce any of the officers, agents, salesmen, or employees of any competitor to violate their contracts of employment; nor shall any such manufacturer entice away the officers, agents, salesmen, or employees of any competitor in such numbers or under such circumstances as to constitute an appropriation of the good will of such competitor or of any property right or value created at his expense".[8]

If we bring together the best features of the above codes we shall get a regulation which will read somewhat as follows: No employer shall directly or indirectly offer employment to the employee of a competitor without first informing the competitor of his intention. Under no circumstances shall he induce an employee to violate his contract with his employer. Nor shall he under any circumstances entice away the employees of any competitor in such numbers or under such circumstances as to constitute an appropriation of the good will of the competitor or of any property right or value created at his expense. Nothing herein contained shall prevent an employer from soliciting a competitor's employees by newspaper and other impersonal and general advertising, nor shall anything herein contained prevent the employment of a competitor's employee when the employee shall take the initiative in applying for a position. But in every such event anyone knowingly taking a competitor's employee must notify the competitor, and then not take on the employee until

7 Heermance, *op. cit.*, p. 457.

8 *Federal Trade Commission Trade Practice Conferences* (1929); Steel Office Furniture, p. 211. The phrase "appropriation of good will" refers to the practice of enticing away a competitor's employees who have a following of their own which they can deliver to the new employer. "The appropriation of a property right" refers to the information acquired by the employee during the course of his employment. This complicated and difficult subject is discussed below in Chapter XVI.

the latter has complied with any agreement which he may have made with his employer in reference to giving him advance notice of a desire to leave his employ.

Blocking the Roads to the Market. There are certain less violent methods of ruining a competitor than those enumerated in the opening paragraphs of this chapter which often pass unrebuked even by intelligent and honorable men, although they are performed with exactly the same intent, are the product of exactly the same spirit, and have exactly the same results. The intention is to win, if not by merit then in some other way, and no matter at whose expense; the spirit is the spirit of ruthless egoism; the results are normally the undeserved ruining or crippling of a legitimate business organization.

The most reprehensible of these devices is the practice of making arrangements with other parties that will shut off one's competitor from access to the market. This may be accomplished with equal effectiveness in either one of two ways. The first is cutting him off from his customers. This constitutes full line forcing, where some patent or specialty is used as a club to keep possible customers out of the reach of his offers. This subject has been considered at sufficient length in Chapter II. The other method is the converse of this. It consists in inducing people to refuse to sell to him the things which he needs for the conduct of his business.

The American Can Company, soon after its formation, acquired almost complete control over automatic can making machinery through a series of "deals" of which the following is typical.

"By the terms of the contract with the E. W. Bliss Company the American Can Company agreed to pay $100,000 a year to the Bliss Company for a period of six years. The Bliss Company agreed that during and throughout the aforesaid term and period hereof it will not devise, construct, and manufacture or deliver any automatic can-making tools or machinery except for and to the first party, except for export elsewhere than to Canada. During the six years that this contract was in force only $117,954.76 worth of machinery was delivered to the American Can Company, so that it appears that the American Can Company paid close to half a million dollars in order to prevent the Bliss Company from supplying independents with automatic machinery. Similarly, the six-year contract with the Ferracute Machine Company, running from 1901 to 1907, provided that the American Can Company should pay to that organization $10,000 a year, although the Can Company's purchases did not exceed $5,000 during this entire period." [9]

The results obtained by offering a reward may be secured just as effectively by threatening with loss. Some years ago in a certain Minnesota city, the owner of a department store, who was also the president of the principal local bank, succeeded in preventing the proprietor of a rival store from getting a loan not merely from his own bank, but also from every other bank in the city. The credit of the rival was excellent, and the securities he offered perfectly satisfactory. But the other banks were given to understand that they could not make the loan in question without "offending" the local financial magnate, and they did not have the courage to risk the chance of becoming the object of his wrath.

Intimately allied in spirit with the preceding is the threat to withdraw patronage if supplies are sold to a competitor. A common form is that of threatening to withdraw advertising if the advertisement of a rival is accepted. The lowest depths of depravity are reached when a competitor's customers are actually threatened with the ruin of their business if they continue to trade with him.[10]

As a final item in our catalog of shame we chronicle the device of bidding up the prices of your competitor's necessary supplies, at a loss, if need be, to yourself, till you have thereby driven him into bankruptcy. This may take several different forms, such, for example, as an agreement for exclusive purchase provided the competitor is charged a higher price. But the underlying principle is sufficiently illustrated by the following case from the *Decisions* of the Federal Trade Commission.[11]

The Brown Rendering Company was engaged in the business of rendering and refining animal fats in Trenton, New Jersey. Their materials, consisting largely of bones, suet and other animal fats were purchased for them by traveling buyers directly from the retail butchers. For a time they confined their operations to Trenton and

[9] William H. S. Stevens, *Unfair Competition,* p. 144. *Cf. Federal Trade Commission Trade Practice Conferences* (1929), p. 86, Rule 14 (buying motion pictures to prevent a competitor from displaying them).

[10] See, for example, The Standard Oil Company *v.* Doyle, 118 Ky. 662 (1904).

[11] Vol. III, p. 284 (1921).

its vicinity; but later, having built up a considerable trade in this territory, they decided to expand. Accordingly they entered the Philadelphia market for the purpose of purchasing raw materials. Thereupon the Philadelphia renderers got together, formed a purchasing organization, which they located in Trenton, and informed the Brown Company that if they did not cease buying in the Philadelphia territory they would invade the Trenton field. As the Brown Company continued operations as before, the Philadelphians sent agents into the Trenton district, who, at a loss to themselves, bid up prices to such a point that their rival was unable to secure materials at a cost which would permit profitable operations. In consequence they were forced out of business.

Predatory Undercost Selling

The competition of which the Brown Rendering Company was the victim consisted in the purchase by competitors of materials at a rate high above the current market price, that is to say, at a loss to themselves. A more widely employed device for ruining a competitor consists in selling your goods at a price below his and your cost of production until his resources are exhausted, and you, the assailant, are left in possession of the field. This is called predatory undercost selling.

The Meaning of the Term. The large rôle played by overhead in modern business makes it at first sight appear difficult to define this term with precision. Thus in times of economic stress producers often make sales at any price they can get above the additional cost involved in the particular transaction. Or they may do the same thing in order to meet competitive prices. Here, however, the aim is not predatory. Predatory undercost selling means the adoption of a price policy which, if continued, would bankrupt the aggressor himself, with the direct intent of ruining a rival or at least driving him from the field.

As practiced by the great national organizations popularly known as the trusts this procedure takes the form of what is technically called local price cutting. This consists in selling below one's cost of production in one locality where competition is keen and at correspondingly higher rates where competition is either non-existent or comparatively innocuous. Thus in the case of the old Oil trust,

"The prices charged in various localities appear to have been governed rather definitely by the percentage of competition to be met in each section. . . . [For example on] October 15, 1904, the Standard Oil Company's profits and losses on water-white illuminating oil ranged from as high as 6.48 cents per gallon profit in Albuquerque, New Mexico, with 7 per cent of competition, and 6.1 cents per gallon profit in Spokane, with no competition, to as low as 3.16 cents per gallon loss in Los Angeles with 33.4 per cent of competition and 1.35 cents per gallon loss in New Orleans with 51.2 per cent of competition." [12]

Local price cutting is the exclusive prerogative of those great organizations which have wide flung markets. But the practice of predatory undercost selling presumably did not await the coming of the "trusts". It has doubtless been with us ever since the beginnings of our present economic order. Certainly most small towns in the United States have witnessed the spectacle of an old established store putting on a vicious price slashing campaign in order quickly to dispose of a newly established competing shop. In this case it will have to recoup its losses not elsewhere but elsewhen—after the rival has been forced into bankruptcy or has abandoned the field. But whatever and wherever a business establishment may sell, and whatever may be the means by which it plans to get from the red into the black, the essence of the act is always the same. It is the selling of your goods at such a price as would, if continued, reduce you to bankruptcy, with the intent of ruining a competitor, or at least driving him out of your particular field, before you get to the bottom of your own pocket.

Why It Is Wrong. The wrong in such predatory selling lies in the fact that the outcome of the competitive struggle is no longer based upon the comparative efficiencies of the producers, but upon their respective financial powers. Fair competition, as we have seen, justifies itself and the incidental damage which it brings to the less able producers because it develops efficiency in all phases of economic life. If competition is to be fair, it must be so adjusted that the most efficient producers shall hold the market. But where predatory practices prevail mere efficiency is no defense against commercial annihilation. Superior force in the form of financial resources which enable one to stand unnecessary losses for a great length of time decides the

[12] Stevens, *op. cit.*, p. 11. For various devices whereby predatory undercost selling is concealed or its effects upon the aggressor minimized see the same work, Chapters I to III.

struggle, and the ability to produce well and cheaply has, at bottom, nothing to do with the matter. It follows then that this practice can not fall within the limits of our definition of fair competition.

To this contention it may be replied that whatever may be the injury inflicted upon the defeated competitor, society, at least, reaps the benefit of the conflict. Does it not profit by the lower prices? Where the battle rages, and as long as it rages, Yes. But no farther and no longer. For such losses must be made up somewhere and somewhen. And since the intent is usually to create or maintain a monopoly, the losses of the victor are likely to be more than offset by his gains. Certainly he will not undertake a war of this sort unless his calculations lead him to believe that this will be the outcome.

Under exceptional conditions, to be sure, the financial losses involved need not be recovered by markedly higher prices than those which ruled before the campaign began. The price cutter may return to his old scale after victory, recouping himself simply by the resultant larger volume of sales. This is certainly not the usual outcome, but it is a possible one.

Even in such exceptional cases, however, predatory undercost selling remains a thoroughly illegitimate business practice. The reason is that it normally deprives the community of useful servants who would otherwise survive and prosper, and it is thus unfair both to competitors and consumers. For it is the peculiar vice of this form of competition that, like a Mississippi flood, it sweeps away indiscriminately everything that stands in its path.

The Survival of the Fittest. To this assertion we may expect the reply that it shows us to be ignorant of the simplest elements of modern science. Is not every intelligent person supposed to know that the source of progress is the "struggle for existence", through the "survival of the fittest"? Our answer is that "the survival of the fittest" has been used as a catch phrase for the last fifty years by a lot of people who are apparently unaware that it is primarily a technical term in biology bearing a highly specialized meaning. To the biologist the tape-worm represents a far more perfect type of fitness, *i. e.* adjustment to the biological conditions of its existence, than the greatest business man or any other kind of human being that ever lived. Consequently anything that a biologist may say about "fitness" has noth-

a man do what he wills with his own? The answer is, no society that has ever existed has ever recognized any such absolute right. If it had, it would have promptly ceased to exist. No society has ever admitted that a man has an absolute right to anything, not even to life, else it would have been compelled to renounce the right of military conscription to prevent annihilation by its enemies. Similarly it has never permitted its citizens unlimited licence in the use of their property. In a modern city, for example, you may not put up on your own property a wooden building within the "fire limits". You may not go and come to and from your own home as you please when a member of the family has scarlet fever. According to an old English court decision you may not stand on your own property, and, with your own gun and your own powder, shoot into the air, when the consequences will be to frighten away ducks from the decoy pond of a neighbor who makes his living by supplying a city market with wild ducks.[15]

If there is anything in the world that is your own it is your name. But you may not use your name, for example, in labeling the products of your factory, in such a way as to lead the public to believe they have their source in someone else's plant. This is well established in law, and if there is a word of truth in Chapter III of this book, it holds equally in ethics. For it is manifestly unfair that the mere accident of a man's bearing such and such a name should enable him to mislead the public and help himself to the good will of one who, through years of service, has built up a reputation worth perhaps hundreds of thousands of dollars.[16]

As against any alleged unlimited right to do what you will with your own we may set the fact that in the eyes of both law and ethics a going business is a piece of property. This is obvious. If I have some unregistered stock in my safe or safety deposit box, and the safe is blown and the securities abstracted, I rightly consider that I have been robbed. But stock is nothing but a certificate of part ownership in a business corporation. A business may be sold, and if it has been successful, the chief part of the value will lie in the good

[15] Keeble *v.* Hickeringill (1707), in Ames & Smith, *Torts,* Vol. I, Pt. II, p. 736; the same, in Nims, *The Law of Unfair Business Competition,* 3rd Ed., p. 436 ff. See also below, Notes, Ch. XII, p. 297.

[16] For the experience of Walter Baker and Company, chocolate manufacturers, with this kind of parasites see Nims, *op. cit.,* Sec. 70, p. 170.

will or the name. Any attempt to destroy or cripple a business is thus theft, far more serious in its consequences, ordinarily, than if you wrecked the machinery in the factory or stole all the material goods that happened to be piled up in the warehouse. There is just one thing, therefore, that justifies you in using your own in such a way as to injure the business of another, and this is superiority of service which attracts prospective customers from him to yourself.[17]

Furthermore you may inflict an injury by what you refuse to do just as much as by what you do, by the refusal to sell, as in full line forcing, or by the refusal to buy, as from those who are selling to your competitor. The William of Orange incident [18] should serve as a sufficient illustration of this fact, but the matter is so important that we venture to offer a second. The Jains are a sect in India who believe in carrying to the extreme limit the prohibition, common to the Hindu religions, against taking animal life. So when a Jain peasant finds his bullock is growing too old for work he merely leaves it in the stable (where it would spend all its leisure time anyway, since India has no pasture lands) till nature has done its work; and then, after giving the poor beast a decent burial, with the clearest conscience in the world he buys a successor.

Perhaps William of Orange and the Jain peasants seem a long way off. So we return to our own time and our own land.

"In Davis *v.* New England Railway Publishing Company, defendant corporation published a directory of local express companies, and intentionally omitted plaintiff therefrom, although requested to include his name, being induced to do so by the false statements and threats of certain individuals, competitors of plaintiff, who were joined as defendants. Plaintiff was held to be entitled to injunction."

Said the Court in rendering its decision:

"The ground on which the plaintiff seeks relief is not that he has a right to compel the defendants or either of them to do anything for his benefit, but that he has a right to have them refrain from intentionally doing anything, without legal justification, to his injury. The defendant corporation professes to give the public a full list of all the reputable ex-

[17] On the recognition in common law of the fact that a business is a piece of property see Bruce Wyman "Competition and the Law", 15 *Harv. L. Rev.* 440 (1902). The case which settled this doctrine once and for all in American law was Allgeyer *v.* La., 165 U.S. 578 (1896).

[18] Ch. V, p. 65, above.

press companies doing business in Boston. While it does not say in express words that the list is complete, that is the meaning which the publication is intended to convey and does convey. Its list is false and misleading, to the plaintiff's injury. * * * The direct effect of the false statement is to point those who want the services of an express company to other companies and to divert them from the plaintiff's. * * * The gist of the plaintiff's action is the wrong done him by intentionally turning away from him those who would otherwise do business with him." [19]

Must we—or indeed dare we—say it again? In morality, intent is everything; and oftentimes an aim can be most effectively accomplished precisely by refusing to act.

[19] Nims, *op. cit.*, p. 493.

FAIR PRICE

CHAPTER XIII

FAIR PRICE AND FAIR WAGE

Is There a Fair Price?

We have more than once had occasion to say that the common law of England and the United States represents, on the whole, the greatest and most authoritative collection of moral judgments in the possession of the English speaking people. It is a settled principle of this law that there is such a thing as a fair price. Indeed one of the standard functions of the courts is to determine a fair price for the services of the public utilities and the railroads. In the competitive field, to be sure, the regulation of prices is left to the automatic workings of supply and demand. But where competition is either undesirable or impracticable, the courts claim and exercise the right to declare certain rates fair and others unfair; and they have been doing this now for several hundred years.

Whatever the rest of us may think, therefore, our judges proceed on the assumption that the term "fair price" means something and that it can be applied to business transactions. This assumption, moreover, has very important implications. Though the courts have the last word, as far as any individual case is concerned, there is an authority more powerful than they, and this is public opinion. It can do nothing—apart from revolution—to help or hinder the cause of any particular plaintiff or defendant; but if it comes to regard a line of decisions as grossly unfair it has a ready remedy at hand. The law making power can modify, annul, supplement, or change any principle of judge-made law at will.

Since no such fate has befallen the decision declaring certain prices to be fair and others unfair, we may conclude that whether we are expressly aware of it or not, we are all committed to the existence of this distinction. This remains true whether we have any clear ideas, or any ideas whatever, as to how to determine what a fair price is.[1]

Popular language testifies to the same fact. We speak of an "outrageous" price, of "extortion", and of "profiteering". These terms carry with them a flavor of *blame;* we mean to indicate a *wrong,* and not merely an *injury.* Most persons, when told that the X safety razor which used to sell at five dollars cost some ten cents to manufacture, would call this profiteering. And it is certain that the Company, if called to account, would never have attempted to answer by declaring: "We intend to get the highest price we can possibly squeeze out of the community". Instead it would have presented a long list of expenses, and an equally long list of risks, connected with placing the goods on the market. These, it would hold, justified the price demanded. The actual "justification" might be valid or not; but the point is the company would feel that it had to justify itself somehow.

There may be much difference of opinion as to what constitutes profiteering; but in any clear cut instance condemnation is emphatic. This is what happens when a speculator or group of speculators succeeds in cornering the market for some essential commodity and bleeds the public to the last drop. Try the experiment of reading to your friends an account of one of these transactions, say the attempt to corner gold on "Black Friday", by that unholy trinity, Drew, Gould and Fiske. Or, if it is too much trouble to look up the material, try Genesis, Chapter XXV, verses 29–34. You will find most persons ready to agree that a price may be unfair even though no element of misrepresentation or overpersuasion enters into the transaction. Those who do not, we venture to predict, will reject the idea only because they do not see how it can be applied to the field of competition.

Price Reduced to Wage

Compensation for material goods is called price; for services, broadly speaking, wage. We shall find it desirable to conduct our study of fair price by reducing the problem to one of wage. Here the term wage is used to include compensation for any kind of service rendered, whatever form such service may take. It includes "wages of

[1] For the right asserted by the state to regulate rates outside of the field of public utilities and transportation systems see Notes, Ch. XIII: 1, p. 297.

management", which, at least in the smaller business establishments, ordinarily go to the "entrepreneur", or owner of the business. The owner must be paid not merely for his actual labor but also for the risk he assumes, in that he receives his share of the returns only after all other expenses have been paid. Taken in this broad sense, wage obviously plays the dominant role in the determination of price, at least in the competitive field.[2]

In view of this fact the price of a material thing may be regarded, for our present purpose, as the sum total of the wages of those who have brought it into the state in which and to the place at which it is purchased; that is to say, of all those who have produced it and placed it on the market. The conclusions we derive from the study of wage can thus be applied directly to price.

"Everyone Has an Absolute Right to the Fruits of His Labor"

Many persons who have not given much thought to the subject are disposed to take a view of fair price which amounts in fact to the denial of its existence. They hold with John Locke—though they may never have heard his name—that every man has an absolute or unlimited right to the fruits of his own labor. He is therefore justified in parting title with them on such conditions and only on such conditions as he himself may choose to set. "May a man not do what he wills with his own?" [3]

We say this proposition is in effect a denial of the existence of any

[2] We are not here denying the view, held by a very distinguished school of economists, that in the last resort wages are determined by demand. We mean merely that by adding wages together you get a total which represents the greater part of the price. Thus in manufacturing, salary and wage earners received 87.8 per cent of the returns in 1925, leaving approximately 12 per cent for "interest on funded debt, dividends on stocks, rents and royalties received from leased property, and profits withdrawn from their own enterprises by individual entrepreneurs". This last item, of course, belongs in part under wage, as we have defined the term. See Willford I. King, *The National Income and Its Purchasing Power* (New York, National Bureau of Economic Research, Inc., 1930), Chs. IV, V, VI, especially p. 124. The proportion of gross earnings devoted to salaries and wages varies markedly in different fields of industry and is greatest in manufacturing. However manufacturing is in certain respects the most typical of our industries, and is distinctly the largest, measured by the value of its products.

[3] On this question see above, Chapter XII, p. 172.

such thing as a fair price. For on this basis Jacob was perfectly justified in refusing Esau the famous mess of pottage except on his agreement to surrender his title to his birthright as the first born. On this basis a surgeon in a territory where medical skill was scarce would be justified in refusing to perform an emergency operation that would save a man's life except for so much of his property as he would consent to surrender rather than die. If the surgeon thereby reduced the patient to beggary he could not be criticized. He had a right to make such terms as he chose for the fruits of his labor. In other words, a monopoly price, whatever its amount, is perfectly fair. And,—this is the only possible inference—when the government enters the field with its heavy hand and puts an end to my profits as monopolist it is depriving me of an inalienable right, the right to get from another in exchange for the fruits of my labor whatever, without misrepresentation, I can induce him to give.

The Objection from Economics

The first thing to remark about this theory is that at best it could be applied only in a very primitive society. When a pre-Columbian Indian, having provided himself with stone axes and fire sticks made with his own hands, fared forth into the forest to build a canoe, the resulting canoe might perhaps be called the fruits of *his* labor. For it represented the results of his own industry and his own skill, in addition, of course, to his luck in finding a tree suitable to his purpose. But in our present highly complicated economic system all labor is social, in the sense that it involves the coöperation of a great number of persons. And it is impossible to determine what is the proportionate amount which each worker has contributed to the completed whole. Consider, for example, how many persons' work enters into the making of a loaf of bread at a bake shop. The chief organic ingredients, wheat and yeast, have come from farms, by railroads and trucks, through mills and factories, to the shop. The salt was mined, packed, and sent on its way from Michigan. The water was supplied by the labor of those connected with the city water works. The building, without which the bread could neither be made nor sold, the furnace, the coal in the furnace, the containers,—these are essential features in putting the bread on the market, and they involve the labor, directly or indirectly, of thousands of persons. An integral part of the process is the bank, which takes care of cash received and lends money when extra funds for running expenses are needed. The fire department helps by keeping down the cost of insurance; the police department, by keeping down the cost of protection; and both of these are inconceivable today without a highly developed municipal government. The state and national governments do their part,–among other ways by compelling the payment of debts and by keeping counterfeit coins out of circulation. Each of the preceding operations, in its turn, is a meeting place for a great aggregation of productive and marketing activities. The farmer, for example, must have his farm machinery, and this implies iron mines and steel mills. All this is but the barest suggestion of the almost inconceivably great multitude of economic processes that are connected, directly or indirectly, with the simplest business enterprise. And every one of these has its part in determining the price of the finished product.

When we turn to mechanical inventions, whether the machinery used in the creation or transportation of goods, or those which directly produce consumers' goods, as electric lights, telephones, and radios, the attempt to trace the effects of any one man's labors becomes still more hopeless. For in addition to all the complications involved in manufacturing and marketing, as above enumerated, there is the problem of the inventor. Who invented wireless telegraphy? Not Marconi. All he did was, by a comparatively few steps, to convert a series of great scientific discoveries by Hertz, Lodge, and Righi, into a paying investment. The foundation upon which these discoveries were built was the experimental production of an electric wave by Professor Hertz in the physics laboratory of the University of Bonn. But he devised and built his apparatus because he was led to look for the wave by the mathematical calculations of Clerk-Maxwell. He in turn got his data from the experiments of Faraday and Lord Kelvin; who in their turn started where a number of early experimenters, including our own Franklin, left off. Thus the trail goes on back for some three hundred years, at least, to the first systematic student of magnetic phenomena, Gilbert, the physician of

Queen Elizabeth, and one of the creators of modern science. In short wherever electricity and steam are at work, there will be found machinery whose present form can be traced to the labors of generation after generation of men, great and small, most of them unknown to us today.

One thing more. The fruits of the labor not merely of the owners of factories, transportation companies, systems for the transmission of information, and allied industries, but the fruits of the labor of all of us, depend fundamentally upon the general social, economic, and political system into which we happen to have been born, and which even the greatest of our contemporaries have done almost nothing to create. We live, for example, in a country of enormous area, secured through our constitution to freedom of trade, whose growth and prosperity have been largely determined by the outcome of two wars fought and won by the blood and agony not of our generation but of those who came before us. All this and much more has been said in words more impressive than any at our command in *The Outlook,* as follows.[4]

> "The American youth enters active life a member of a society which has made for him out of a wilderness a rich country, has secured precious rights for him at a large cost of treasure, toil, and blood, has accumulated for him stores of gainful knowledge and power, has trained steam and electricity to serve him, has given him an education, costing far more than his parents paid for it. Where his predecessors cleared the forest and defended their settlement from the savage, the open doors of an industry, an art, and a commerce he had no part in creating, invite him to share freely in rich opportunities. One who stands thus on the shoulders of others and plucks from the top of the tree its ripest fruit and calls it his own, needs to remind himself how it came to his hand."

The Objection from Ethics

But even if the share of any one individual in producing a loaf of bread could be measured, the theory that every man has an absolute right to the fruits of his labor and may therefore set upon them any price he pleases, would have to meet an objection from ethics just as serious as that urged by economics. The nature of this objection will become clear if we return to our Indian and remember that the

[4] LXXXI (1905), 12.

qualities of his canoe—good and bad alike—were determined by three factors: (1) his industry; (2) his skill; and (3) his luck in finding or failing to find the proper material for his purpose. We shall examine each of these three factors in turn with a view to appraising its claims to serve as the basis of a fair wage.

The Right to the Fruits of One's Industry. With regard to the first item, almost everyone will agree that the worker who performs a service for others is entitled to a reward for his industry. Indeed this statement will probably seem self-evident to most readers. But since some few persons deny it,—notably Bernard Shaw in his *Intelligent Woman's Guide to Socialism and Capitalism*—it may be worth a brief examination.

By way of introduction, it must be noted that the term "industry" is here used to mean every quality of will which enters into labor. It includes not merely hours of work, but also, what is usually far more exhausting, intensity of work; that is to say, concentration upon the business in hand. It involves, in addition, carefulness, perseverance, patience, willingness to "take it out of one's self", and reliability and integrity in all their forms. In persons who have large and serious responsibilities, as in administration, it involves, in addition, sustained attention over long periods of time, and concern not merely for the problems of the moment, but for those of the future also. If "industry" seems too narrow a term for this large group of qualities, it may be replaced with "devotion to the task", or "effort".

In the first place, then, speaking generally, men must be paid for their industry in order to induce them to do the best work of which they are capable. If society could count upon getting "from each according to his ability", spontaneously and without pressure, the problem before us would be a very different one. As it is, however, most men will not work, or at any rate will not work with the requisite "devotion to the task" without the prospect of some external reward. It is true that a minority who have jobs that are intrinsically interesting will work without reference to the pay check as they will without reference to the clock. It is also true that there is a small percentage of men who would do their share of the world's work and do it well, from a sense of duty or from public spirit. But as the experience of contemporary Russia has proved, and as unbiased observation in our own country will show, such persons form too small a proportion of the population to enable society to depend upon them for the supply of its economic needs. In the interests of production, therefore, the economic system must be such that income bears an intimate relation to amount of industry.

We may look at this subject from a different angle and reach the same conclusion. When one of two partners in a business enterprise throws all the hard work and most of the rest of the burden upon the shoulders of the other partner and thereupon demands half the profits, we have no difficulty in seeing the injustice of such a proposal. But this is exactly what would be happening in a society where the loafer and the near-loafer received the same income as the industrious. No one has a moral right to be a sponge. Therefore a man may not complain when he is not permitted to play that game.

If, then, the above reasoning is sound, workers performing useful services for others must be and ought to be paid for their industry. At what rate remains still to be determined.

The Right to the Fruits of Economic Chance. Omitting for the moment the consideration of the second factor in our Indian's success, we pass to the third—the chance play of economic forces. By "chance" is meant that which is beyond our power to control. If the canoe builder was lucky enough to be born in western Oregon the first tree he came to would serve his purpose admirably. If on the other hand fate placed him in central Nebraska he might look long and carefully and not find anything that was more than halfway satisfactory. Once more, if he had happened to be an inhabitant of Wisconsin he would have had no difficulty in finding a passably suitable tree, but might or might not have come upon one completely adapted to his need. So it is in the business world in which we live. As will be set forth in detail later, and as everyone ought to know without being told, chance, in the sense defined above, is a leading factor in determining actual income. As has already been said, it plays at least as large a role in this field as it does in determining the score in an evening's game of contract. But no thoughtful person will assert for a moment that a man has any moral claim to a "reward" which comes to him as the result of chance.

It may indeed be argued that since a man must suffer the consequences of bad luck he ought to be allowed to hold on to the fruits of good luck. This is true enough as far as it goes. But it is very undesirable that anyone should be the victim of bad luck; and society ought to reduce the number of such casualties to the minimum possible. There has been much progress in this direction during the past hundred years, notably through the introduction of various forms of insurance. In so far as success attends such efforts, society may properly restrict and ultimately wipe out the "rewards" of good luck also. But whether or not it succeeds in the endeavor to narrow the range of luck, good and bad, the fact remains that the distribution of the good things of life by what is, in effect, a throw of the dice is an unmitigated evil, and the less there is of it in the world the better.

The Right to the Fruits of Intellectual Ability. We now come to the second factor determining the character of our canoe, intellectual ability or mental power. Its maker's facility in the use of his fire stick and his flint hatchet represents one form of intellectual ability, since all so-called muscular skill is an effect of the nervous system, operating under the control of the brain. Now the amount of intelligence which a man brings to his daily work at any given period of his career is in part the product of past industry. For our mental powers can be greatly improved by cultivation where there is the will to do so. A "trained intellect" is by definition a product of training, while all training is in the last resort self-training. But what is patently true of athletic skill, as running or jumping, holds equally for our intellectual powers; there is a barrier set by inexorable nature which renders progress beyond a certain point impossible. This point is located at different places for different persons, but it is always there—somewhere.

The position of this barrier is determined for each one of us by our native endowment. This, in the main, is a matter of inheritance. It is thus something which is given, like sex, not something worked for. In other words native endowment is due to chance, as we have defined the word chance. But as we have just seen, the possession of advantages which are due to chance affords no just ground for claiming rewards.

This conclusion must not be misunderstood. Society is bound to create and maintain a system which will offer adequate compensation to industry. And practically the only available method of measuring industry, crude as we have shown it to be, is through the results which it produces in the form of goods or services. Now these results are determined as much by intelligence as by industry. The fruits of industry and of intellectual power, however, are not easy to separate. They usually form an indivisible whole. Accordingly even a society that is earnestly seeking to get as near to absolute justice as possible will find itself compelled to incorporate into its economic system payment according to results; and this means, according to the amount of intelligence as well as industry involved in the performance of the work. This admission does not contradict our former statement. Industry alone has a direct claim for reward. The claims of intellect rest solely upon necessity. Society is justified in including the fruits of chance in the pay check only because there is no practicable way of excluding them without doing a great deal more harm than good.[5]

How Much Ought a Man to Be Paid for His Industry?

Our conclusion raises at once another question. How much does justice demand that a man be paid for his industry? For example, should those who work to the limit of their powers receive a thousand dollars or ten thousand or a hundred thousand per year?

As the long history of the controversy on this subject shows, we shall never be able to answer this question except as we recognize squarely the principle which is now accepted, in one form or another, by practically every living ethicist, and upon which the state bases its right to control monopoly prices. This is the proposition that no individual has any right to any thing, the possession of which is harmful to the common welfare. In the pursuit of his own good a man may not harm another man.[6] Much less may he claim a right to the enjoyment of any good where this conflicts with the requirements of the good of society as a whole.

The significance of this statement in its application to the problem before us will appear if we ask what these requirements of social wel-

[5] For the objection that after all qualities of industry are also a matter of chance see Notes, Ch. XIII: 2, p. 298.

[6] See above, p. 172.

fare would be if it were not for the necessity of paying men for their industry. Let us, accordingly, picture in imagination a society where each member works according to the full measure of his ability, without having to be driven to it by the expectation of external reward. Under such conditions the best system of distributing economic goods would be that which most completely met the needs of the members of the society in question. By "needs" is here meant "ability to put wealth to good use"—the ability to employ it effectively and wisely. This principle has been put into the form of a famous slogan: "To each according to his needs".

How this slogan might work out in practice in a restricted society like a family, is shown by the following bit of biography. In the early part of the Nineteenth Century two brothers, "Zeke" and Daniel, were helping their father to eke out a scanty living on a rocky New Hampshire farm. Zeke was a youth of ordinary good intelligence, but Daniel, as everyone recognized, was a genius. The father would have wished to educate both of his sons; but this, he knew, was absolutely impossible. After long thought on the subject he finally approached the older brother, pointed out the financial impossibility of sending both of his sons to college, and asked him if he would think he was being unfairly treated if the family resources were pooled, and the younger brother given the chance which both coveted of a college education. Zeke not merely accepted this view of the situation, but all through the long period of his brother's preparation and undergraduate study did his part loyally to make it possible to carry out the plan. This is how Daniel Webster was able to go to Dartmouth College.

The attempt, however, to apply this principle to a social group of any size would raise some very difficult problems. For in the world outside of the family, it would prove well nigh impossible to adjust men's incomes to their needs because no one could really tell who had more needs than another, and how much greater they were. Even an ideal society, therefore, unless it were composed of omniscient beings, would be compelled, as a general rule, to treat different persons' needs as for all practical purposes equal. And this means that our ideal society would have to be satisfied with equality of income for all its members as the nearest approach to a satisfactory system of distribution which the ignorance of man would permit.[7]

This conclusion prepares the way for the answer to the question: How much ought a man to be paid for his services to society? As we have seen, we must and ought to reward industry as such. Apart from this consideration the moral ideal requires equality of distribution. How, then, shall we combine these two demands? The answer is, in principle, quite simple. A differential is allowed for industry primarily, at least, in order to produce certain desirable results. Therefore allow so much and only so much of a differential as is needed to get these results. In other words, allow so much compensation for industry as experience shows to be necessary in order to get the desired amount of production. The following, then, will be the resultant formula for social justice. That system of distribution is just which departs from equality so far and only so far as is necessary to supply the spur required to raise production to the maximum desirable. The inequalities which belong to such a system will of course be just also. And those returns will be just which come to the individual as a result of the workings of the system.[8]

The nature and amount of the excess return may and probably will vary from one occupation to another. The aim is to get the work done. And if rewards must be higher in one occupation than another in order to attract the requisite number of persons and to induce them, when there, to do their best, such returns for their services will be justified. Furthermore the nature and amount of these returns may vary from generation to generation according to changes in conditions, such as the relative intrinsic attractiveness of different fields of labor, the amount of physical or mental effort involved, *etc.;* so that no one specific system is ever likely to remain eternally just as far as its concrete workings are concerned. The most we can say is that that system is just at any given time which most successfully maintains such a ratio between the demands of production and those of distri-

[7] For a practicable step in the direction of payment according to needs see Notes, Ch. XIII: 3, p. 299.

[8] For the significance of the term "maximum desirable" see Notes, Ch. XIII: 4, p. 299.

bution as will best serve the economic interests of all concerned, while at the same time sacrificing to economic ends none of the higher elements of human life.

Fair Compensation in the Competitive System

The definition of a just system of distributing wealth offered in the last paragraph may sound rather remote from anything which can be applied to our own economic system. As a matter of fact this system represents a serious attempt to meet the conditions stated in the definition. Taking human beings as we find them, it is necessary to offer special inducements in order to get the world's work done. These inducements are what we have been calling the rewards of industry. But unfortunately, as we have noted, industry can not be measured directly, so that it would be possible by consulting a meter to discover that *A's* industry was 25 per cent greater than *B's*. However, there has grown up through the ages a system of barter in which, *everything else being equal,* reward is automatically proportioned to industry. This system is none other than our competitive system. In so far, then, as competition is the best industrial system at present available, that is a fair wage today (or the nearest practicable approximation to a fair wage) which is obtained by fair competition in an open market. "Fair competition" is that form of competition in which success is won on the basis of effective service. An "open" market means one which is not artificially closed by law, agreement, ignorance, *etc.,* and which is reasonably accessible to a large number of persons prepared and willing to serve and be served. If this is a correct definition of a fair wage, it is equally applicable to a fair price for a commodity, in so far as its price represents the labor which has been expended upon it.

The Defects of Competition as a System of Distribution

If the competitive system were a perfect instrument for the creation of economic justice the definition of fair price and fair wage as that obtained under fair and open competition would be final. But unfortunately this system, like every other institution of society outside of Utopia, has serious imperfections, some of which go down to the very foundations.

In saying this we are not thinking of violence, brutality, dishonesty, trickery, and favoritism; nor of stupidity, short-sightedness and the rest of the long list of intellectual defects which are at least as numerous and harmful as the moral deficiencies; for all these are common to every form of economic society, and will continue to be so as long as average human nature remains at its present mediocre level. We are thinking rather of those imperfections which are inherent in the nature of the competitive system itself, and which create inequalities of income which can not be justified on the ground that they serve as a spur to industry.

The nature of these defects has already been foreshadowed in our examination of the ethical assumptions involved in Locke's formula. The fundamental flaw in the working of our present economic system is the enormous role played by chance. Its two major forms have been already pointed out. They are, as will be remembered, the following.

The first is the wide range which the system leaves open to the uncontrolled, and, for the most part, uncontrollable play of economic forces. The chief factors involved in this wheel of fortune have been enumerated by Adolph Wagner,[9] as follows: (a) Variations in the receipts from harvests, affecting both the farmers and the consumers through the rise and fall in the price of foods, clothing, materials, *etc.*, and in addition producers of other classes of goods, through variations in the amount which others have at their disposal to spend for their goods. These forces not merely affect the total income of the community, but their effects are apt to be distributed throughout the community very unevenly. (b) The introduction of new methods of production. This affects the value of all existing machinery in that particular field, and the products of such machinery. Its most important single consequence in our day is technological unemployment. (c) Changes in the means of communication and transportation, whereby the value of certain lands and of transportable articles is profoundly affected, sometimes for better, sometimes for worse. (d) Changes of opinion with regard to the usefulness of goods. Changes

[9] *Grundlegung der politischen Oekonomie* (3rd Edition, 1892–1894), Vol. I, pp. 386–398.

in fashion, taste, *etc.* (e) Changes in the conditions of production and sale of goods and also of credit which depend upon the general conditions of trade and the confidence we may have placed in them; depressions. (f) Changes in the laws relating to the conduct of business. Corn laws in England, the tariff, corporation law, financial legislation. (g) Changes in the local distribution and general economic relations of population; feverish demand for certain lines of labor, while other lines are a glut in the market. (h) Changes in the general social and economic condition of entire classes of society through the rise and fall of wages, of rates of interest, *etc.* This changes the nature of all economic demand, and this, in turn, affects capital in all its branches. The preceding is by no means a complete presentation of the role of chance in the interplay of economic forces, but it suffices to suggest its extent and importance. These forces give rise to both unearned gains and undeserved losses.

What makes the matter still worse is the fact that as a result of the importance of capital in business, the effects of chance, both good and bad, are cumulative. For, as has been pointed out by Professor F. H. Knight, "The effects of luck in the first hand or round, instead of tending to be evened up, in accordance with the law of large numbers, in the further progress of the game [of business], confer on the player who makes an initial success a differential advantage in succeeding hands or rounds, and so on indefinitely".[10]

The second great defect in our economic system is even more deep seated and more serious than the first. Whereas our formula for justice demands that pay should vary from equality solely in proportion to industry, our economic system permits the workers to reap the advantages of their intellectual ability as well.

The rewards of service in the present economic system are thus parcelled out between chance—that which lies outside the power of the individual directly concerned,—and industry, which is within his power. But a wage in which chance plays so large a role is far from representing a satisfactory outcome to the worker for all the labor, effort, and physical and emotional strain which he must put into his daily task. Again, looking at the matter from the point of view of so-

10 *The Quarterly Journal of Economics,* XXXVII (1923), 609. The same in *The Ethics of Competition* (New York, Harper and Brothers, 1935), p. 64.

ciety, payment to its members for the luck that has happened to come their way obviously represents a pure waste of community resources, except in so far as it is absolutely unavoidable.[11]

The gradual narrowing of the range of chance as a source of income, coupled with a corresponding enlargement of the range of industry, represents one of the most important lines of economic and moral progress which is open to human society. The element of chance could be, to a very large extent, eliminated if the characters of all men, or the great majority, could be developed to a point where without outer constraint from either hunger or government they would work to the maximum of their ability. For then we could introduce a social order somewhat like that of which many Socialists dream; only it would be an order resting not on force, as in Russia, but on free consent. Here, since each worked according to his ability, each would receive, not indeed in exact proportion to his needs (for that would require an omniscient mind), but (the next best thing) equally with others. In such an order everyone would be better off, for we should be relieved from the many serious evils which flow from inequality of income, evils which affect not merely the poor, who are after all the great majority, but also in many ways the well-to-do and still more, the rich. But for such an economic millennium we must wait until there is a very great advance in character. Laws and institutions, however cleverly conceived, supply no real substitute. And only in a society in which character reaches a very high level can there be any near approach to an equitable distribution of wealth.[12]

[11] A further discussion of the role of chance in economic society will be found in Notes, Ch. XIII: 5, p. 299.

[12] On some of the evils resulting from inequality in the distribution of wealth, see Notes, Ch. XIII: 6, p. 300.

CHAPTER XIV

THE STATE AS THE DETERMINER OF FAIR PRICE

The purchasers of services may be divided into two classes. On the one hand there are private individuals and groups of individuals, such as partnerships and corporations; on the other hand there is the state with its subdivisions.

The state aims to be, or pretends to be, or at any rate ought to be, a fair-minded employer, anxious to treat with justice all its employees. On what principles, then, ought it to determine the wages of these servants? Again the state, as the greatest of monopolists, determines the rate of pay for certain services which are performed, not by its employees in the strict sense of the term, but by those who have invested their capital in business undertakings "affected with a public interest"—notably the public utilities and the railroads. It claims to aim at fair treatment of these organizations also, and thus at a fair wage for them. What, then, is a fair return for the services of a public utility?

These problems supply the subject matter of the study immediately before us. We select them for examination partly because of their own intrinsic importance; still more because we believe their solution will throw much light upon a wide-spread theory of fair price which flatly contradicts the definitions of the preceding chapter. According to this theory a fair price (or wage) is one which is the result of an exchange of "equivalents"; that is to say, of things of equal value. This view we shall subject to a careful examination.

What Is a Fair Price for the Services of a Public Service Corporation?

Our first objective will be the determination of the fair return for the services of a regulated monopoly. We begin by studying the actual procedure of the state. After this, we shall be in a position to deal more concretely with the question, What ought it to do?

What Is the Actual Procedure of the State? When a group of individuals dedicate their property to a public use, as in creating and maintaining a public utility or a railroad, the charges for their services, according to English and American common law, must be fair. Furthermore, as we have just indicated, it is the function of the state, and not of the owners of the capital, to determine what rates are fair. In the United States it is now settled doctrine that the final arbiters in this matter are the courts. We shall accordingly examine their findings. It must be noted that the principles which they follow in their work of regulation are identical for the railroads and the public utilities.

The problem to be discussed resolves itself into two. In the first place the appropriate commission, subject to review by the courts, must determine the amount of the investment upon which the rate is to be based. Secondly, they must decide what percentage of return shall be allowed upon such investment.

We begin our study of their procedure with their treatment of the latter problem. Here we find complete unanimity of opinion. The courts regard that return on the invested capital as fair which yields a profit equal to that of the average yield in the competitive field in that particular locality when the amount of the capital in question and the amount of risk involved are taken into account.[1]

As an illustration of the use of this principle the following may be cited.

"In Spring Valley Waterworks *v.* San Francisco, where an ordinance passed by a board of supervisors would reduce the annual net earnings below 4.40 per cent on the value of the property necessarily employed in the service, or 3.30 per cent on its stock after deducting proper charges, its enforcement was enjoined as fixing a rate so low as to be a taking of private property for public use without just compensation. Judge Morrow said: 'The next question to be considered is, what will be a fair and reasonable income for the complainant to receive as a just compensation for the public use of his property? A number of bankers have testified as to the usual and customary net income from investments of $10,000,000 and upwards of capital in corporations of a quasi-public nature, where judiciously managed. The affidavits of four bankers of long experience and well-known

[1] Bluefield Water Works Co. *v.* Public Service Commission, 262 U.S. 692 (1922). *Cf.* Beale and Wyman, *Railway Rate Regulation*, 2nd Ed. (1915) by Bruce Wyman, Sec. 220. This is still a standard work on the subject, as far as our purposes are concerned.

character and standing fix the rate at not less than 7 per cent per annum. . . . The affidavits of five bankers of like standing and character and similar experience fix the rate at not less than 6 per cent per annum for large investments. . . . The affidavit of one banker of large wealth and experience fixes the rate of net income from such investments at between 4 and 5 per cent per annum. The weight of evidence is clearly in favor of a rate of not less than 6 per cent per annum.' "[2]

The value of the capital on which return is to be allowed may be appraised in any one of several ways. It may be determined (1) by the original cost, when cleared of all expenditures chargeable to investments unwisely inaugurated or badly executed; (2) by the value of the property at the time of appraisal. This is defined as the cost of reproduction less depreciation. (3) A third method takes both of the preceding standards into account in the attempt to combine them to an unassignable extent. This is the procedure now employed by the United States Supreme Court.[3]

Having determined the percentage of profit to which the server is entitled, and the amount of invested capital upon which this percentage is to be calculated, a third problem remains: How are the rates for individual services to be adjusted?

According to the decision of the United States Supreme Court in Northern Pacific RR *v.* North Dakota,[4] the price which may be charged for any particular kind of service, as carrying tea or coal, must equal the cost to the railroad of this class of service plus something above a nominal profit. But how much above the cost line each class of traffic may go is left to the discretion of the producers or carriers, provided the total net profits are not thereby increased beyond what has been determined to be a fair total. The reason for permitting this liberty is to be found in the enormous role played by overhead costs in all public utilities. This is particularly true of the railroads, where these costs are estimated to represent eighty per cent of the total expense of any given service. Every class of service will of course be charged a rate which will cover the special cost which it involves; but the amount which it contributes to overhead will

[2] *Op. cit.,* Sec. 314.

[3] See Los Angeles Gas and Electric Corporation *v.* Railroad Commission of California, 289 U.S. 287 (1933).

[4] 236 U.S. 585 (1915).

necessarily vary according to the relation of the value of the article to its size and weight. Otherwise the expense involved in transporting heavy and bulky commodities of relatively low selling price would be prohibitive. Coal, for example, can not be charged the same rate per pound as tea. Accordingly the latter will be allowed to contribute a much larger sum to profits than the former. In other words, "Traffic which will continue to come even at comparatively high rates . . . will be taxed high, [while] traffic for which the demand is sensitive to price and which can be got only at low rates will contribute little".[5]

Are the Resulting Rates Fair to the Corporation? This is what the courts, as representatives of the state, actually do. What are we to think of the fairness of the resulting rate? We shall take up in order the several features involved in the transaction.

The attempt to find a satisfactory method for determining the value of the capital which is to serve as the basis from which rates are figured, involves problems of far greater complexity than anyone can realize who has not made a detailed study of the subject.[6] As it does not concern our present purpose we pass it with a single remark.

The most important practical difference between the first and second methods for determining the fair value of the capital involved is as follows. Where there is a long period of advancing property values, the investors gain by the second method; where the reverse movement prevails they lose; while by the first method profits are unaffected by these changes. Thus suppose the original cost of a given railroad property amounted to $100,000,000. Suppose further that the courts authorize rates that will yield 6 per cent on the investment. The use of the first method would permit rates capable of yielding a net income of $6,000,000. Suppose, on the other hand, that the second

[5] F. W. Taussig, "Contributions to the Theory of Railway Rates", in *Railway Problems,* edited by W. Z. Ripley (Boston and New York, Ginn and Co., revised edition, 1913), p. 120.

[6] The reader who is interested in this subject is referred to an article by Gerard Henderson, "Railway Valuation and the Courts", 33 *Harv. L. Rev.* 902, 1031 (1919–1920), and to the very able dissenting opinion of Justice Brandeis in Southwestern Bell Telephone Co. *v.* Public Service Commission of Wisconsin, 262 U.S. 289 (1923). A more recent discussion will be found in the *Journal of Land and Public Utility Economics* for August 1927, in an article by Professor Martin G. Glaeser, entitled "The Valuation Doctrine at the Crossroads".

method of determining rates is adopted by the courts, and that in the course of ten years a general rise in the level of prices brings the value of the property up to $120,000,000. Rates then can be adjusted to yield $7,200,000. On the other hand, should there be a general drop in prices, reducing the value of the road to $80,000,000, rates would have to be lowered so as to yield a maximum of $4,800,000. Accordingly, in a community in which wealth is steadily increasing it will be to the advantage of the public to adopt the first method of valuation. But should a period of long drawn out decline set in it would be a piece of rank injustice for the state to jump from the first method to the second, or, for that matter, to the third. This, however, is precisely what is likely to happen.

We now turn to the simpler problems of determining the rate of return. There are two reasons, both good, why the courts are justified in regarding a fair return on the capital of a public service corporation as identical with the average rate obtained on similar investments in the competitive field. In the first place a lower figure would end in disaster. For it would fail to attract capital in sufficient amounts to enable the corporation in question to give effective service. On the other hand, since the rate, by definition, is high enough to secure the desired services, it may be said, as it has been said: "The government is a trustee [for the public] and is recreant to its trust if it permits a private purveyor of a public service to impose a higher rate".[7]

In the second place investors in the field of public service are getting on the average and in the long run neither more nor less than they would have obtained had they invested their money in the competitive field. Therefore if the competitive price is the fair price they are getting a fair price. If on the other hand the workings of the competitive system do not produce, on the average, a fair price the courts may well say: If the community is dissatisfied with the results of the competitive system let them change the system; but this is properly the function of the legislature, not the courts.

How ought the price of any particular service, or rather class of service, to be determined? Again, essentially as the courts have de-

[7] J. E. Orton, *The Independent*, LXXII (1912), 671. The precise significance of this statement, as we interpret and accept it, will appear from page 204, below.

cided it should be done. Remembering that the total net return is supposed to have been fixed, the question is how to adjust the tariffs on particular classes of goods so as to obtain this total. The best system is certainly that which will encourage traffic to flow most freely, whether the traffic consists in coal or tea. For this traffic simply means the bringing of the necessities, comforts, and luxuries of life from their points of origin to the consumer. A low rate on heavy and relatively inexpensive goods, and a correspondingly high rate on light and expensive goods is the only one that will accomplish this end.

Are the Resulting Rates Fair to the Customer? Up to the present we have been looking at the problem of rates solely from the point of view of the carrier or the producer. We have asked what is a fair price for him to receive for his services. To this method of approach it will be objected by many that we have ignored entirely the rights of the shipper or customer. We ought to have asked, not what is a fair return to the provider of the service, but what is the value of the service to the receiver. Some authorities assert that the latter is the only just principle governing railroad and utility rates. Others—including many judges—assert that it is at least a coördinate principle with the other.

As far as the judges are concerned, when we turn from what they *say* to what they *do* we find that as a matter of fact all their decisions are based on the wage to be given to the supplier. Specifically a railroad will not be compelled to carry any commodity for any distance to any market which the shipper may select for a price which will enable him to make a satisfactory profit, or indeed any profit at all. Thus the Interstate Commerce Commission has refused to order the roads to carry the grain of Western farmers to the Eastern markets at a price which would enable the farmers to earn a fair return from their crops, on the ground that to do so would require rates so low as to represent a loss of money to the carrier.

Again, the courts will not require rates to be based on the utility of the goods carried. If they did grain and coal would have to be charged higher rates than silk and tea.

The conclusion is that notwithstanding all the dicta of the judges about charging what the service is worth, the actual decisions are based on what they regard as a fair return to the server, *and to that alone.*[8]

This procedure is ethically justified, because the theory that a fair price is determined by the value of the goods to the purchaser is fundamentally false. Ultimate values, even in material goods, can not be measured in terms of dollars and cents. What, for example, is the value of food to me, the consumer? The answer is that without it I could not live. To be sure if I have a somewhat limited and fixed income I can tell—roughly—which goods I prefer to others at current prices. But if I could not get food, shelter, fuel, and clothing, at the present prices I would pay higher prices and go without the comforts and luxuries in which I now indulge. And if I could get food only on the condition which Jacob presented to Esau, I should certainly accept the proposal.

Furthermore the money value of any commodity is relative. It depends for me upon how much money I possess altogether. If I have an income of $100,000 a year, an orange at just the right time, when I am hungry and thirsty, might well be worth five dollars to me; that is to say, I would cheerfully give that amount in exchange for it.

It is thus impossible to build up a system of fair prices on the basis of the value of the goods or services to the receiver. This is why the men who believe they believe that value to the receiver is a standard of justice, and who are called upon to apply their standard to actual and living situations, have been compelled, without wishing it and apparently often without knowing it, to abandon this point of view.

Are we then left with no standard for a just rate? By no means. Rights and duties are correlative. This means that *A's* rights against *B* are *B's* duties toward *A*. If *A*, a house owner, makes a contract with *B*, a painter, in accordance with which *B* agrees to paint *A's* house, then *A* has a right to this service; and his right is simply the other side of *B's* duty to do the painting. After the work is done, *B* will have a right to the amount of money provided for in the agreement; and *B's* right to the money is the other side of *A's* duty to pay it. All rights are rights against some person or persons or group of persons. And

[8] See H. W. Edgerton, "Value of Service as a Factor in Rate Making", 32 *Harv. L. Rev.* 516 (1919). *Cf.* Beale and Wyman, *Railroad Rate Regulation,* 2nd Ed., Ch. VII.

to each right there corresponds a duty on the part of the other either to do something, or to refrain from doing something. For example my right to a sum of money corresponds, as we have seen, to the duty of someone to pay me that money. My right to life corresponds to the duty of everyone to forbear from murdering me.

If, accordingly, a given railroad company has a right to receive a certain return for its services it is *ipso facto* the duty of those thus benefited to pay to the server the amount which he ought to receive for them. Where else should it come from? And if they can not afford to pay the sum in question they must do what the rest of us do—apart from special circumstances calling for gifts of charity—namely, go without.

Summary. The most important conclusions to be drawn from the preceding discussion are as follows: (1) Society, as was pointed out in Chapter XIII, recognizes the fact that there is such a thing as a fair (and therefore unfair) rate or price. This rate, organized society (*i. e.* the state) stands ready to enforce. But such enforcement would be outrageous tyranny if it were not a rate which it was just or right for one party to pay, and for the other to receive, entirely apart from any compulsion. (2) Fair rate or price can not be determined by asking what is the value of the service to the receiver because no real answer to such a question is possible. It is determined rather by inquiring what constitutes a fair wage for the server; and this problem turns out to be capable of solution. A rate which is fair for the server to receive must be, in the very nature of the case, one which it is fair for the customer to pay. (3) The courts declare that a fair rate for the services of a railroad or a public utility is that which, as a whole, yields a return equal to the average return obtained by a business operating under the same conditions of risk, size of investment, *etc.*, in the competitive field. In other words, society recognizes that, broadly speaking, fair price is definable as that which is obtained by fair competition in an open market.

What Is a Fair Wage for a Public Servant?

What is a fair salary for a judge? Here we again see the absurdity of the theory that a fair wage is determined by the value of the service to the receiver. For a court composed of upright, able, and learned judges is valuable beyond all possibility of computation in terms of dollars and cents. Accordingly we can only resort to the principles and methods of the preceding section, and ask, what are the lowest terms at which men of the requisite character, intelligence and training can be obtained? But we must take one more factor into consideration. Upon the shoulders of the judges rest most serious responsibilities. Their profession calls for all but unremitting toil of the most exacting kind. They must accordingly be paid enough to relieve them of financial anxieties, which would certainly impair their usefulness by drafting time and attention away from their judicial duties. In other words the state must pay its officials, whatever their position, not merely enough salary to attract the kind of men needed for the position, but also enough to enable them to do their work with maximum efficiency.[9]

These conditions are not Utopian. They have been met in the case of the United States Supreme Court and in some of the state courts.

May we carry this principle all the way down the line? Ought the state, for example, to apply it to its janitors or the city to its unskilled laborers? All branches of state and municipal government ought to aim to be the ideal employer. But the ideal of distribution is equality, modified by the necessity of rewarding industry. Therefore in the case of the lowest paid occupations the aim should be to raise the level as far as possible, rather than to push it down to the lowest attainable point. To be sure, the attempt to carry this program into practice will meet great complications. The wages paid by the state come from tax payers, many of whom are just able to keep their heads above the financial waters. Furthermore if the wages of the unskilled were allowed to rise above a certain point, it would tend to produce a dislocation in the wages of the skilled. The state, the county, and the city are not the only employers in the community, and they can

[9] It is often said that allowance must be made in paying the higher officials for the time, expense, and labor involved in preparing them for the exercise of their profession. This item is included, however, in the amount required to attract them away from private practice or other business into the service of the state. For the entire level of professiona' incomes is affected by the necessity of a long and expensive period of preparation as a prerequisite of entrance into the profession.

not proceed without reference to what the others can afford to pay. Still the ideal should never be lost sight of: To those who are able to command salaries above the average of the incomes in the community, pay as little as possible consistently with obtaining the requisite amount of ability, training, character, and efficiency; to those whose salaries will in any event be below the average, raise them as near to the average as circumstances permit. The duty of the representatives of the community to get the most that can be got for the money, whether in setting railroad rates or salaries, is thus not an absolute one. It applies rigorously only to those in the upper levels of the income receivers. When it comes to the lower levels the ideal of social justice calls for precisely the opposite procedure.

Application to the Work of an Arbitration Board

The community is constantly being called upon to determine, through its arbitration boards, what constitutes a fair wage for great bodies of workers such as coal miners or locomotive engineers. As is well known, this method of settling industrial disputes has of late been losing favor because the boards, sometimes by their own confession, have been unable to find any standard of fairness toward which to move. Their findings have therefore tended to represent merely a more or less arbitrary compromise between conflicting demands. With all due recognition of the enormous difficulties of this class of problems, this outcome does not seem to be a necessary one. For the principles which hold for the judge and the day laborer hold equally for the coal miner or the locomotive engineer, though the actual working out of the problem in the latter cases happens to involve complications of which the former are quite innocent. The wages of locomotive engineers, like those of judges, ought to be sufficient to fill each grade of the service with the requisite number of men possessed of the necessary ability and character. They should furthermore afford a man with a family of average size sufficient means, reckoned by the year, to keep him permanently in the physical condition necessary for a proper performance of his duties, and of course to maintain the same standards of living for his family. These items should be a first charge on all transportation. But there is another factor. If the annual income, thus reckoned, should turn out to be less than the average annual family income of the nation as a whole, the men would have a *prima facie* claim to an advance up to this point. It goes without saying that the duty of society to honor these claims may be limited by other conflicting considerations. It must take into account the effects of any proposed advance upon the real wages of the remaining members of the community who must pay the charges. The effects upon the industry as a whole must of course be counted, and much else which it is unnecessary to mention in this place. All that we here attempt is to formulate a first approximation to a standard. And this, notwithstanding the questions it leaves unanswered, should not be a futile method of spending one's time. For without a standard, whether formulated or implicit, the economists and other experts, the "representatives of the public", and all the other members of the arbitration boards are like the Irish horseman who was "going at a divil of a pace" but didn't know where he was going.

CHAPTER XV

THE ETHICS OF BARGAINING

In the field of public employment the state, in virtue of its sovereign power, sets wages, and thus prices. In the competitive market, however, the private individual must make or find his prices. This operation may involve the process called bargaining.

The Place of Bargaining in the Competitive System

Bargaining consists in an attempt on the part of a would be buyer to induce a potential seller to exchange his goods or services for the smallest attainable return—usually in the form of money. Similarly it consists in an attempt on the part of a would be seller to induce a potential purchaser to buy, and to buy at the highest attainable price. When conducted by a person of intelligence and experience it will include a survey of the market, and this is its most legitimate and healthy form. But whatever the form, the attempt to sell to or buy from another party on the most favorable terms to self is the essence of bargaining.

Since this is the foundation on which the competitive system rests it is, broadly speaking, as legitimate as the system itself. One of the prime advantages of competition consists in the fact that where it takes place on a sufficiently broad scale—that is, in the "open market" —it drives the price of commodities down to the lowest point at which they can be produced continuously. Where the pressure is severe it calls for rigid economies and the elimination of all wastes, and forces profits down to the minimum. This last statement means it forces profits to a point below which the majority of suppliers either would be compelled to close up or would prefer to withdraw, either temporarily or permanently, rather than to continue business in this field. When we say "competition" forces prices down we mean of course individual buyers and sellers, who are exerting and resisting pressure in the process of coming to an agreement. When this process is conducted fairly we believe that it results, on the whole and for the most part, in the nearest approximation to fair price which the present structure of society permits us to attain.

While, then, we recognize bargaining as in principle an entirely legitimate method of determining price we nevertheless cannot overlook the fact that it assumes at times certain forms which call for careful examination. To this task we shall devote our attention in this chapter.

"Brutal Buying"

A fair bargain, whatever else it may be, must be one by which both parties profit, in the sense that each is better off for the transaction than he would have been had it not taken place. Anything else represents what Mr. Arthur J. Eddy calls "brutal buying".[1] Thus a millionaire boasted that in building the tiled roof for his new house the contractor lost $3,000. This is getting something for nothing. Success in the pursuit of such a policy may be the bargainer's heaven. But if this is what he is looking for, he is about on a level with the robber and the thief. They make getting something for nothing the business of their lives. Of course there is a difference between actual theft and an oppressive bargain; for the two have very different secondary effects. But as far as the underlying spirit is concerned, there may be little to choose between them.

The Advantages of the Fixed Price System

Where bargaining is vigorously carried on by considerable numbers of persons there will be a certain diversity of price for the same goods. *A* buying from *X* will succeed in getting better terms than *B* has obtained. This state of things seems to be rather widely regarded as unfair. At least it is an object of attack in a considerable number of codes. Thus Article 3, paragraph 8, of the code of the National Basket and Fruit Package Manufacturers Association reads: "There shall be one price to all and all methods of rebating to make sales are unethical".[2]

[1] *The New Competition* (Chicago, A. C. McClurg, 4th ed. 1915), p. 180.
[2] Heermance, *op. cit.*, p. 54. *Cf.* 203 and 482.

As a matter of fact the practice demanded by these codes represents the method by which the retail trade of the United States has been conducted for the past two or three generations. It appears to have originated in Great Britain, and in any event was introduced into this country by A. T. Stewart, the famous New York retail dry goods merchant, in the third or fourth decade of the last century. As everyone knows, with but rare exceptions the prices in retail shops are set at the lowest point which the merchant will accept for the goods; and the customer must take them or leave them at this price, and the prices are thus the same to all.

Now the advantages of such a system are almost incalculable, as anyone will realize who has ever shopped in an Oriental bazaar. Here the seller names a price from two to four times as high as he would be willing to accept, and the prospective purchaser from one quarter to one half as much as he—or she—expects to pay. From these somewhat remote points the two parties approach each other by slow and hesitating steps. The operation may perhaps last half an hour, and the bargain be completed a block away from the shop after the customer has retired, "shocked" at the rapacity of the seller, and the seller has made the run because he cannot bear to think of the lady as leaving the city without carrying with her some of his beautiful wares.

Such a performance may be amusing and worth all it costs, conceived as a game played occasionally in the pursuit of the picturesque; but as a steady diet it would be unendurable to the American mind. It is extremely time consuming and thus expensive; it is to many persons somewhat nerve racking; it opens the door to a lot of lying; it is unfriendly. It gives great advantages to the possessor of a plausible manner, a glib tongue, and a poker face. But these qualities have no social value; and a system that confers upon this type of person its largest rewards is not a satisfactory one. It puts a premium, to be sure, upon lynx-eyed vigilance; but the suspiciousness which is the source of such vigilance is something with which we should be only too glad to be able to dispense. Finally the moveable price system, as we may call it, accomplishes little or nothing in the long run. For if I know by experience before I enter the place that the shop keeper will end by selling at about fifty per cent of what he demands at the start, I know about where I stand approximately as well as if he had named his lowest price when I came in. This age-old system is thus a monument to the stupidity of the race, and its complete elimination in the retail trade throughout the English-speaking world is one of the most important advances in business methods achieved in modern history. Accordingly while we can not call such bargaining wrong, we must hope that it will eventually disappear from the wholesale trade as completely as it has from the relations between the retailer and the ultimate consumer. The movement in this direction is doing more to elevate business to the dignity of a profession than any other factor now operating in the field.

Obligations of the Fixed Price System

However this may be, when the fixed price system has once been adopted or has become the custom of the trade, it lays upon the seller a new and definite obligation. For now, either by implication or else in so many words, he is professing to name his ultimate price at the outset. He is therefore bound by every consideration of good faith to do so. In such a system the man who offers a secret rebate, whatever form it may take, is guilty of fraud; and the man who accepts it is guilty of compounding with fraud.

The "fixed price" is of course a price that is the same to all buyers. The code demands for equality of price are thus, as we have suggested, demands for the introduction or the maintenance of the fixed price system. Present day economic society, however, is a very complicated affair, and the demand for complete equality of price under all possible circumstances would, we think, be going too far. Thus it would be absurd to condemn the attempt to induce the customer of a rival to try my goods by offering him a nominal price on a single order, just as it would be absurd to condemn presenting him with a sample of a product of my factory. What may properly be condemned, however, is giving such a person a permanent advantage over the rest of my customers when I pretend to have adopted a fixed price policy.

A more important qualification is the right of the producer to vary his prices in different communities for the purpose of meeting *bona fide* competition. This practice was indeed at one time forbidden by a number of the states. These state laws, for example, explicitly forbade the producer to charge more for his goods in one locality than another. All such laws were declared unconstitutional by the courts. The economic objection to this legislation was that it failed to recognize that the conditions of competition, and with it the level of prices, may properly vary from one place to another; or else it would confine the producer to his own locality. The second alternative is neither fair to the individual nor useful to the excluded community. Both parties may profit by the expansion of an industry; the latter by acquiring one more servant; the former in that, while his range of profits may be lower than he would be willing to accept as a whole, nevertheless he is better off with a small profit than with none. Where the producer sets different prices in different localities to meet varying transportation costs, or different costs of doing business on the part of his competitors, or other differing competitive conditions, whatever they may be, in a *bona fide* attempt to get business for himself, no moral blame can be attached to his conduct. The same is true of the owner of two stores in different localities, who may have to maintain a different scale of prices in each or close one of them.

Finally we shall have to admit that occasionally the absence of fixed price is a needed protection against monopoly price, and is thus the less of two evils. This statement holds especially for the manufacturers of very highly standardized products where practically all competition turns on price.

The Obligation to Accept the First Bid

The employment of a fixed price system whether professedly or by implication creates, as we have seen, an obligation on the part of the seller to state his lowest price at the outset, and then to stick to it. There is a somewhat similar obligation upon the purchaser in certain cases which is often ignored. When a man or an organization calls for bids the implication is first, that the bids are confidential; second, that the first lowest bid will be accepted. This then is an implied agreement—an agreement, therefore, which should be regarded as equally inviolable with any other agreement. Unfortunately, however, there are business men who use the lowest bid received merely as a club to beat down other bidders to lower offers than their original one.

We can not but believe that this habit is as self-defeating as it is vicious—like most other forms of crookedness. Many men are so self-centered that they do not realize that others are sizing them up and "have their number", just as they are constantly sizing up those with whom they deal. In the course of time it becomes known whether a man plays fair with his bids or whether he does not. And if he does not the bids are formulated accordingly. It is therefore not at all surprising that those who are known to refuse invariably to entertain any modification of the first bids actually receive the lowest proposition the bidder is willing to make the first time; and that they declare that even looking at the matter from the point of view of actually getting the most for their money they would not exchange this method for the other. Here, as in so many other cases, we believe, the trickster ends by cheating himself. Having sold his honor he does not even get the poor return in money for which he bargained.

Price Discrimination as a Means to Monopolistic Control

The Clayton Act (Section II) declares

> "It shall be unlawful for any person engaged in commerce, in the course of such commerce, either directly or indirectly to discriminate in price between different purchasers of commodities, which commodities are sold for use, consumption, or resale within the United States or any Territory thereof or the District of Columbia or any insular possession or other place under the jurisdiction of the United States, where the effect of such discrimination may be to substantially lessen competition or tend to create a monopoly in any line of commerce: *Provided,* That nothing herein contained shall prevent discrimination in price between purchasers of commodities on account of differences in the grade, quality, or quantity of the commodity sold, or that makes only due allowance for difference in the cost of selling or transportation, or discrimination in price in the same or different communities made in good faith to meet competition."

This is the law of the land, and as such it ought to be obeyed. But apart from its prohibitions, and in the event that they should be withdrawn, the limitation it places upon discrimination is a thoroughly sound one, and is morally binding quite regardless of whether one professes to employ the fixed price system or not.

We have seen that the attempt to destroy a competitor, not by giving the service that will properly attract his customers away from him, but by blackjacking him in any number of different ways, including undercost selling, is a wrong to him, to those dependent upon him for wages or support, and to the consuming public. But differential prices may be used to the same end. And whether the end is the destruction of some particularly efficient competitor who stands in the way of our domination of the market, or whether it is the destruction of all competitors in our field, that is to say, the creation of a monopoly, the wrong is the same. If competition is the most effective economic system at present available the attempt to create a monopoly is disloyalty alike to the system and to the community. The men who attack Socialistic propaganda as "unAmerican", and attempt to build up, at the same time, a monopolistic structure which, if permanently successful in any considerable number of fields, would assuredly lead to Socialism; the men who talk about business governing itself and complain of government interference, and then do that which is certain to bring—not interference but intervention; these men are either essentially fools or hypocrites.

How to Create a Legitimate Monopoly

Outside of the well-marked fields of transportation and public utilities there is only one legitimate way to create a monopoly. It is by giving service so superior whether in quality or terms or both that competition is impossible. Such monopolies actually exist. In a certain town of about 20,000 inhabitants there is a department store that stands in solitary grandeur without a rival. It is owned and managed by a group of brothers, all able and vigorous men, and with perfect confidence in each other. For many years it has never had a competitor that lasted for any length of time. The reason is that when a newcomer appears the inhabitants of the town, after sampling his goods, invariably go back to the "old stand". To succeed on your merits and then to maintain your position by following the same methods—this is honorable victory. And if it means monopoly it is a kind of monopoly which cannot be too warmly approved.

Fair Prices under Monopolistic Conditions

A combination of circumstances may temporarily, and without complicity on our part, thrust us into a monopolistic position. May we in this case take advantage of the opportunity to exact a price higher than the competitive or market price? To bring the matter before us let us examine an actual situation.

A builder took a contract to complete a power dam by a specified date, agreeing to forfeit $500 for every day he took beyond that period. His operations were somewhat delayed by bad weather, but he was still hoping to be able to complete the work within contract time when his last shipment of 1,000 barrels of Portland cement was destroyed by a bridge giving way. Obtaining new shipments and waiting for the repair of the bridge would have delayed him at least a week. So he applied to a dealer in the vicinity who had a sufficient supply on hand to enable him to continue operations practically without interruption. This dealer, being aware of the circumstances, refused to sell any cement at less than $4.25 per barrel. The market price at the time was slightly over $2.00, and the dealer had been selling it regularly at that rate. The builder, faced with the prospect of having to pay several thousand dollars forfeit if he did not obtain supplies at once, finally consented to buy the stock at the dealer's price.

This, in our opinion, was essentially a holdup. Everyone is entitled to such a rate of return as is necessary to insure a sufficient supply of his "line of goods" for the market. This is what the supplier actually will get in free and open competition. It is thus, according to Chapter XIII, a fair rate; and anything above it is unfair.

In the cement dealer incident, as in Jacob's little deal with Esau, one man has another by the throat and is withheld by no scruples from exploiting his advantage to the utmost. What gives the exploiter his power in such situations is not merely the fact that he is the only supplier available but also the further fact that he is superior to his victim in economic strength. Economic strength is unequal where it makes more difference to one party than it does to the other whether the bargain is struck or not. Such is the position, under many circumstances, of the employer as against his employees, especially the employer of semi-skilled or unskilled labor, when the supply is so much greater than the demand that what has the appearance of free competition is in reality an approach toward monopolistic control. In this relationship the wage agreement has all the characteristics of a forced sale. If the average factory worker has been able to save a few hundred dollars he has done about as well as can be expected of him. This is all that stands between him and starvation, and is his only protection in time of sickness or disability. It is all his family has to fall back on in the event of his death. To him the need for a job is desperate. To his employer, on the other hand, it ordinarily makes little difference whether he hires one man more or less.

Hence the moral justification of the trades union which can do something at least to make the scales even. Hence the moral justification of minimum wage legislation.[3] Hence, furthermore, the obligation upon the employer, where there is neither union nor legislative limitation, to pay something more, if circumstances permit, than the lowest wage which he could obtain by pressure. We are of course aware that the wages an employer can pay are dependent in large part upon what his competitors are paying. We are aware of much else that can be said to the same effect. But after all the good reasons have been given and all the poor excuses have been offered, the fact remains that gross inequalities of income can only be justified by necessity; that wages which do not provide for the food, clothing, shelter, and medical care required for a healthy existence, and for something laid aside for a rainy day, are a disgrace to a civilization; and that the callous bargain hunter who is always running after sweat shop goods, and the employer who squeezes his employees down to the last possible cent, are using their position of strength to take from others that to which they themselves have no moral right, and are making it difficult if not impossible for less greedy employers to treat their employees fairly.

Still worse is it when the strong manoeuver the weak into a position which makes them still weaker and then exploit the resulting weakness. It is said that certain chain store systems make contracts with small factories to take their total output. Then after their former

[3] A brief discussion of this subject will be found in the Notes, p. 302.

customers have made other business connections, the system forces the factory thus reduced to impotence to work at a beggarly return.

The Right to Raise Prices in Time of Scarcity

In view of the preceding discussion what shall we say of the right to raise prices in times of scarcity? At first glance this looks like taking advantage of the necessity of others; and we know of more than one business man who has taken this position and acted in accordance with his convictions. In a delightful and stimulating little book by William M. Salter,[4] there is told the following incident.

> "In the little town of Weymouth, Mass., a few summers ago, there was a great scarcity of ice—almost an ice famine. Strange to say, one dealer did not put up his prices. 'Why?' he was one day asked. 'Why?' he replied, 'Why should I? It hasn't cost me any more'."

Admirable as was the spirit that prompted this reply, it represents too narrow a view of the facts of the situation. There are three counter considerations which our ice dealer apparently ignored, and they appear to be decisive. In the first place, no one is called upon to play the game: Heads I lose, tails you win. In periods of exceptional abundance or of limited demand the market price will go down. In that case the customers can hardly be expected to say: "The price you are asking is really too low; please allow me to add twenty per cent to your charges in order that you may make a reasonable profit". The working men are insisting, properly enough, that it is not what they get by the hour or by the day that counts; but what they get in the course of a year. On the same principle a business man must use a very considerable period of time, a cycle, we should say, of not less than five years, in order to determine whether he is making a reasonable profit. And he must allow for losses to offset his gains.

The second reason for this conclusion is always pointed out by the economists. A decided rise in the price of a commodity at once cuts down the amount of waste. If there were equality of income only those who needed it most would purchase it, and these only to meet their more insistent needs. The existence of great inequalities of

[4] *Anarchy or Government* (New York, Thomas Y. Crowell and Co., 1895), p. 107.

wealth keeps matters from working out this way. Nevertheless the vast majority of people have limited incomes, and so the extravagances of the rich do not greatly affect the general rule.

Finally, price increase normally creates an increased supply; and this, in the end, will lead to a general and relatively permanent reduction in price.

CHAPTER XVI

PROPERTY IN IDEAS

This chapter will be devoted to inquiring whether and how far the possessor of information or the originator of an idea is morally entitled to its exclusive control, so that he is at liberty to set the terms upon which it may be used by others, just as in the case of material objects. The original ideas here considered will be such as can not be protected by patent or copyright. There can be no adequate account of the ethics of price without some attempt to clear up the confusion which reigns in this field.

The subject before us is far from being a simple one. What is plainly wrong has a disconcerting way of passing over into what is plainly justifiable by imperceptible gradations; and in the gray between the black and white will be found some puzzling situations. Here apply the words of Justice Holmes: "In cases of this sort, as in so many others, what ultimately has to be worked out is a point or line between conflicting claims, each of which has meritorious grounds and would be extended farther if it were not for the other".[1] This was said of legal decisions, but it holds equally for many ethical judgments; and nowhere more, perhaps, than in this particular field.

Problems in Intangible Property

In treating this subject we mean to let the reader work out his own conclusions for himself through the examination of a group of typical cases. He is to ask himself in each instance: Is the conduct described right or wrong, and why? After the completion of this piece of mental exercise he may, if he chooses, compare the results of his thinking with the opinions which we ourselves have formed and set forth. The cases follow.

1. A man by the name of Bristol presented by letter to the presi-

[1] Boston Ferrule Co. *v.* Hills, 159 Mass. 147.

dent of the Equitable Life Assurance Society a new system for soliciting life insurance. The company made use of it and found it very profitable, but refused to compensate Bristol in any way whatever.

2. "During the years 1898 and 1899, 1900 and 1901 [Harry C. Haskins] devoted a large part of his time to the study of industrial conditions connected with the output of pig lead in the United States, and conceived a plan of uniting outstanding lead interests, which had not already become a part of the National Lead Company, into one company, and either obtained options thereon or opened negotiations for their purchase. He then laid the plan before [Thomas F. Ryan], a capitalist, seeking his coöperation and aid, himself agreeing to contribute, if necessary, as much as $200,000, if Ryan would join him therein, and also contribute enough to carry the enterprise through. Ryan expressed a willingness to join him therein, provided an examination of the plan and papers by Ryan's attorneys and experts confirmed the statements made by Haskins to Ryan, and such examination confirmed such statements. Ryan, however, availed himself of the information furnished by Haskins, and, independently of him organized a company, and got control of the industries, and made large profits therein."

3. " 'Bud' Fisher had for some time been drawing cartoons for a San Francisco newspaper, centered about the doings of 'Mutt' and 'Jeff', when in May, 1909, he entered into a contract with the Star Company, the publishers of the *New York American,* to draw for them for a period of years. The names 'Mutt' and 'Jeff' were never applied by the cartoonist to his drawings as such, but, with the consent of the Star Company, he published three books under the title 'Mutt and Jeff Cartoons'.

"Until December 11th, 1914, the *American* published the cartoons under titles furnished by Fisher, which usually contained the words, 'Mutt' or 'Jeff', but Fisher never furnished the simple title 'Mutt and Jeff'. On December 5th, 1914, Fisher made a contract with the Wheeler Syndicate, Inc., agreeing to furnish his cartoons exclusively to it as his agent for newspaper publications for a term of three years from the expiration of his contract with the Star Company, on August 8, 1915. On December 9, the [*American*] inserted the words

'Mutt and Jeff' before the title furnished by Fisher for a cartoon, so that it read 'Mutt and Jeff. The Little Fellow Knows Some Law and Proves it. By Bud Fisher.' Against this change Fisher immediately protested without effect. After January 19, 1915, to and including January 29, the [*American*], without Fisher's consent and over his protest removed the titles furnished by him with his cartoons and placed on each of them the title, 'Mutt and Jeff. By Bud Fisher.' Fisher refused to furnish any further cartoons to the [Star Company], which published none by him after January 29, 1915.

"Until this time, neither the [Star Company] nor any of its employees ever published any cartoon characters similar to Mutt and Jeff. Fisher did no work for [it] except to draw these cartoons and was not a general employee of the Star Co. After August 8, 1915, he was under no obligation to furnish any cartoons to [it]. The characters had been exclusively drawn by him and had become generally known to newspaper publishers and to the public as Mutt and Jeff and were generally recognized as such.

"[After August 8, 1915, Fisher was] engaged, through the Wheeler Syndicate, in selling to newspapers throughout the United States and Canada the right to publish new Mutt and Jeff Cartoons which [appeared] from day to day, and [were] generally of the same kind as those previously drawn by him.

"After Fisher ceased furnishing his cartoons to the Star Co. it caused certain of its employees to draw cartoons in the form of comic strips consisting of characters drawn in imitation of Mutt and Jeff, which were so like Fisher's cartoons as to be likely to deceive the public into thinking they were in fact Fisher's genuine Mutt and Jeff cartoons, advertised its cartoons as 'the original Mutt and Jeff cartoons', and prepared to publish them in the *New York American* and to sell them to the newspapers throughout the United States."

Had Fisher a property right in the names of "Mutt and Jeff" after giving up his connection with the *American,* so that, except with his consent, no one else might use the names together with the style of drawing which he had been using in connection with them? In considering this problem eliminate the issue of deception by supposing that the Star Publishing Company had either (1) used new names instead of "Mutt and Jeff", or (2) had said plainly: "By our own artist", or, "By William Jones".

4. Timothy Dorman was a salesman for Daniel Boosing, a wholesale butter and eggs merchant in the city of Buffalo. After some years of service he went into business for himself and solicited the customers of his former employer. The facts of the situation are thus summarized by the referee who reported the case to the court.

"Of the 107 customers whom Dorman was serving for plaintiff at the time his employment terminated, it appears that about 32 were new customers whom Dorman had secured for plaintiff during the course of his employment, and it is fair to infer that the remaining 75 were customers of the plaintiff at the time Dorman entered his employ and that their names appeared on the route book which plaintiff turned over to Dorman when the latter began his employment. There is no substantial dispute as to the proposition that the entire 107 persons or firms were listed in the city directory as retail dealers in butter, eggs, *etc.;* that they conducted business places and publicly displayed the character of business in which they were engaged; that with the exception of two or three they were not exclusive customers of the plaintiff, but dealt more or less constantly with the plaintiff's competitors in the butter and egg business; that 18 of said persons or firms were located on Washington Market, a public market in the city of Buffalo; and that substantially one-half in volume of the sales made by the defendant Dorman for the plaintiff while in his employ was to these dealers on Washington Market."

The significance of the facts is thus stated by the same referee. "A salesman . . . learns the names and addresses of his master's customers, and the individual preferences, traits, and characteristics of such customers, and the dates at which they are accustomed to buy, the kind and grade of goods which they are in the habit of purchasing, the promptitude with which they pay their bills, and generally their financial credit and standing; and he also gains an influence with them."

5. Eldridge Boyce was a driver employed by the Witkop and Holmes Company of Buffalo, retail dealers in tea, coffee, dry groceries, *etc.*, in active competition with the stores of the Great Atlantic and Pacific Tea Company, located in the same city. When Boyce's

term of employment began he was assigned a certain district in which to deliver goods and trading stamps to customers and to solicit new trade. With this end in view he was provided with a list of 400 customers of the company. This was his portion of a total list of about ten thousand, created not merely by its salesmen (about twenty in number), but also by special canvassers, and brought up to and kept at this high figure to a very considerable extent by the use of trading stamps. After a year of service Boyce withdrew, turning back a list of about 450 customers, and retaining no written memorandum of their names or addresses. He thereupon entered the service of the Great Atlantic and Pacific Tea Company. He proceeded at once to visit the customers of his former employer, and induced them to transfer their trade to his present employer, taking up the trading stamp books of the old employer, and issuing to the customers like books, of the same value, of the new employer. He thus made use of his knowledge of customers gained under one employer for the benefit of another. Does the answer as to the justification of these actions differ if the initiative in the change of employers came from the Tea Company?

6. The Westminster Laundry Company of St. Louis circulated through the city by means of sign boards and other devices a "blind" advertisement consisting of the word "stopurkicken", intending, when public curiosity had been sufficiently aroused, to follow it up with another campaign connecting the word with the name of its business. But before it had taken this second step the Hesse Envelope Company flooded the city with cards bearing the word "stopurkicken", followed by its own name. Was this an infringement upon a property right? Is the situation changed by the fact that the word was invented by the D'Arcy Advertising Company and purchased from them by the laundry company?

7. During the World War the International News Service was in the habit of copying news from bulletin boards and from early editions of certain New York papers, and telegraphing it either as it stood, or after rewriting it, to other newspapers, its customers, in western cities. The news in question was gathered by the Associated Press and could not be protected by copyright. Was the International News Service justified in using Associated Press news in this way?

Would it have been justified if it had required its newspapers to credit the news to the Associated Press? What this question really asks is: In what sense, and on what grounds, if any, can the news collected by the Associated Press be called its property?

8. The Flagg Manufacturing Company manufactured a zither of somewhat peculiar construction which was their own invention, but which did not differ sufficiently from the standard zither to make possible the obtaining of a patent. The instrument was intended for the use of music strips for which the company held a patent, and its originality consisted in its adaptation to this purpose. After a considerable market had been established, a man by the name of Holway put on the market a zither in exact imitation of the Flagg Company's zither as far as essentials were concerned, marking it, however, plainly with his own name so that no deception as to the maker was practiced upon the purchaser.

9. At considerable expense a company called Meccano Limited placed upon the market an ingenious toy, consisting of strips of metal of various shapes, with perforated holes at regular intervals, with which it was possible to build in miniature some of the more common mechanical contrivances. The toy was sold in outfits, seven in number, each outfit fitting in with the previous ones purchased, thus creating more and more possibilities in the way of new constructions. After this toy had been on the market for some time the American Mechanical Toy Company was formed for the purpose of manufacturing and placing upon the market a toy identical with the other in every respect, so that its products could be used along with the Meccano outfits and could supplement the latter at any point. These it sold at a lower price than the Meccano goods, in consequence of which it was able to cut heavily into that company's business.

In discussing this problem ignore the following issues: (1) Deception through passing off one's goods as the goods of another. (2) Infringements of patents. The Mechanical Toy Company could have put its wares on the market without deception had it so desired; and the Meccano devices were in large part unpatentable, and may, for the sake of illustration, be conceived of as entirely so.

10. A certain drug firm originated and placed upon the market a

drug called Bismuth Emetine Iodide which proved to be of very great value in the treatment of amoebic dysentery. The method of preparation they kept secret. After it had been on the market for a short time many physicians wrote to E. R. Squibb and Son, well known drug manufactures, asking them to prepare this new drug; at the same time the research department of the firm discovered the method by which it was made. The proposal to manufacture and market this drug, thereupon, came before the board of directors of the company. By vote they refused to do so, inserting in the minutes of the meeting the statement: "We do not like to pirate our competitors' discoveries".

The Foundation of the Right to Property in Ideas

The general principle upon which the moral right to intangible—and to tangible—property rests is the proposition that a man is entitled to a return for his industry provided this industry is directed with reasonable efficiency to the supply of human wants; and if this right is anywhere limited—as by patent or copyright—or abolished the reason must normally be found in the claims of some plainly preponderant public good. Guided by this standard, we have reached the following conclusions about the cases we have invited the reader to study. In the following we have divided the problems into groups, according to their subject matter.

The Right to the Exclusive Control over Original Plans and Methods. Whatever obligations *A* may have to society as a whole he has no such obligations to *B* in the ordinary course of business affairs as would justify the latter solely in his own interest in taking the products of *A's* industry away from him without his consent. This is theft, whether the property is tangible or intangible. An inventor brings to a manufacturer some new mechanical device for his judgment upon it. If the latter appropriates it and refuses to pay for it, this is as truly an act of theft as if he had picked the inventor's pocket. This is exactly what Thomas Fortune Ryan did to Haskins, and appears to be what the president of the Equitable Life Assurance Society did to Bristol. They appropriated plans which had been worked out by someone else, made money out of them, and then refused to pay for them. Haskins could hardly have protected himself, but Bristol was unwary. He should have made some ironclad contract before he broached the scheme. But as we have seen this makes no difference in the morality of the act; and the chances are he thought that in approaching the President of the Equitable Life Assurance Society he would be dealing with an honorable man.

The same situation meets us when we turn from larger transactions to smaller ones, and from original ideas, involving presumably much mental labor, to information. "*A* wishes to sell his house and lot. *B* tells him in confidence that *C* desires to buy it, and solicits employment to negotiate the sale. *A* declines; but acting upon *B*'s communication meets *C* and himself negotiates and closes the contract of sale."[2] Notwithstanding the opinion of the learned judge to the contrary we believe that here *A* clearly cheated *B* out of at least part of the commission. Like Bristol, *B* was careless about protecting himself. But it is not commonly held that if I am careless about leaving my front door unlocked when I go out for the evening this exonerates the thief who utilizes the opportunity to help himself to my silverware.

This group of cases seems at first sight to be quite elementary. In all of them information or ideas having cash value are offered, accepted, used, and not paid for. It is difficult to see how this differs from "blowing" a safe and running off with the securities.

Nevertheless the matter is by no means a simple one. In the first place when one person makes use of somebody else's ideas, the situation may be quite different from that in which he helps himself to another person's silverware or securities. For my ideas can frequently be used by others without depriving me of their use, while material possessions can not. In the second place public policy demands in general that ideas should circulate as freely as possible. Accordingly only those limitations should be placed upon their adoption which are necessary in order that their production may be encouraged. For this reason it seems proper that improvements in such things as business methods should be at the disposal of the

[2] Bristol *v.* Equitable Life Assurance Society, 132 N.Y. 268.

public. This holds all the more because such ideas are usually taken from the common intellectual stock of the race, and owe more to this source than to the labor of him who calls himself their creator.

Thus some near-genius conceives of a clean towel service for offices. Another goes this one better, and establishes a clean diaper service. A third starts a cab company with cabs painted in a distinctive way, the local organizations in different cities being affiliated at least so far as to afford a fair guarantee of a similar scale of prices and grade of service throughout. Mr. Campbell works out a method of canning soups in concentrated form.[3] The Ford Company devises a system of assembling the parts of a car. A. T. Stewart introduces the one-price policy into the American retail trade. Is no one else to be allowed to use these ideas? If so, how long is this prohibition to last? A monopoly here would place an intolerable bar to social progress. The originator therefore must be content with whatever extra returns he gets from being first in the field. Apart from this, he has proved himself a public benefactor; and if this fact gives him no satisfaction that is just his hard luck.

How, then, are we to deal with the conflicting considerations here set forth? Subject always to the claims of the whole as against the individual, the proper solution seems to turn on whether the use of the idea can be shared or not. When a manufacturing concern helps itself to the inventor's ideas, patents them, and puts the profits into its own pocket, this is clearly theft. One man is here diverting to himself the results of another man's labor, and there is no counteracting social good involved to serve as a justification. It is on this basis that we condemn vigorously Ryan's appropriation of Haskins' proposals. On the other hand, when someone copies the ideas embodied in a clean towel service, the conditions are reversed. If the imitator operates in another city, the originator suffers no loss whatever. If the imitator starts a rival route in the same territory, we shall have to judge that the social interest involved and the difficulty of drawing a hard and fast line (which is a *desideratum* in ethics just as it is in law) clears the transaction of wrong. The use of Bristol's

[3] *Current Opinion,* LVII (1914), 440.

selling plan by the Equitable Society is perhaps in the gray, because there was no way by which it could permanently retain exclusive possession of the plan, but is nearer, in our opinion, to the black than to the white.

The Rights of an Employee as against a Former Employer. The next group of incidents concerns *A's* rights when he changes employers. In 3, the Star Company of course paid Fisher for his cartoons as he delivered them. But they attempted to retain for their own use the reputation which his creations had acquired while their creator was in their employment. Even if it had been true that up to the termination of their contract he had drawn for no one else, it would also remain true that what he had been selling them was services, not reputation. Their attempt to appropriate the latter was on a par with the attempt of the United States Watch Company to steal the reputation of the American Waltham Watch Company. It happens that both of these cases are alike in another respect. The Star Company, like the United States Watch Company, was attempting to make its customers believe that its wares came from another source than the actual one. In other words each added fraud to theft.

In 3, we are dealing with original ideas, and again the problem seems a simple one. In 4 and 5, however, we deal with information acquired during the course of one's employment; and some variants of this theme, at any rate, are extremely perplexing. The general principles upon which the solution of such problems as these must rest appear to be the following.

In so far as the special information used by a business organization in the conduct of its business is the creation of its owners or of employees paid to obtain it, such information would appear to be its property, and thus not properly available for use in any way on the part of an employee after he leaves its service. But if this proposition were allowed to stand without limitation, it would condemn employees to a kind of slavery. For to require them, on leaving their employer, to divest themselves of all knowledge acquired during the course of their engagement would be, in effect, to compel them to go into some entirely different line of business, concerning which they know nothing. Imagine this principle, for example, applied to young men who have studied for four years in a college of pharmacy, and spent two or three years more in a drug store learning the business. Are they to be forbidden the use of the knowledge gained as employees, or are they to be forced to go into the butcher business? Or if they are at liberty to start a drug store somewhere, must they be banished to some other town than that in which they have learned their trade? This would be an intolerable infringement upon personal liberty.

Here, accordingly, is a conflict of interests which can only be met by some kind of a compromise. This, it would seem, ought to run along some such lines as the following. A former, like a present employee, may not sell his employer's business secrets to a rival, just as the rival would have no right to try to purchase them. He may not make and take away with him copies of papers representing business transactions or other materials which are essentially of the nature of secret documents and which can only be regarded as the employer's property. Again he may not disclose to others secret inventions or discoveries which his employer has employed him to make, and thus, in effect, purchased from him; and with regard to such a matter as this there should be a clear understanding in advance. Apart from this, in the absence of a specific agreement to the contrary, he may use any information acquired in the course of his past employment as an aid in his present business activities, whether as himself employer or employee.

These principles, in our opinion, clear Dorman of all wrongdoing. The case of Boyce is more difficult. His employers had, at great expense, worked up a list of customers who could be counted upon as more or less permanent because of the hold which the trading stamp secures, once a new book has been started. It can be very plausibly argued that this list was their property, and that whatever additions were made by their agent were theirs, just as much as the material goods produced by a factory employee. This conclusion is made more appealing by the fact that apparently the Great Atlantic and Pacific Tea Company took the initiative in the change of employers.

Here is certainly a conflict of claims, each of which can urge much for itself by way of justification. Our decision would be that in this case, at any rate, the claims of freedom to advance oneself in one's vocation are of more weight than the possible loss of customers; and therefore, provided this was not part of a raid planned by the Tea Company, Boyce could change his employer and use his knowledge of possible customers with a good conscience.

Many milk companies, as well as others which face the same problem, now require their employees who distribute their products to sign a contract that on leaving their employer they will not engage in the same occupation for the two following years. This requirement seems to us so harsh that we think it should be used only when conditions have become intolerable, and even then as a last resort.

Certain phases of the larger problem seem to have been dealt with very effectively in the Code of the American Institute of Chemical Engineers, as follows.

"When a chemical engineer undertakes for others work in connection with which he may make improvements, inventions, plans, designs, or other records, he shall preferably enter into a written agreement regarding their ownership. In a case where an agreement is not made or does not cover a point at issue, the following rules shall apply:

"a. If a chemical engineer uses information which is not common knowledge or public property, but which he obtains from a client or employer, any results in the form of plans, designs, or other records shall not be regarded as his property, but the property of his client or employer.

"b. If a chemical engineer uses only his own knowledge or information, or data which by prior publication or otherwise are public property, and obtains no chemical engineering data from a client or employer except performance specifications or routine information, then the results in the form of inventions, plans, designs, or other records should be regarded as the property of the engineer and the client or employer should be entitled to their use only in the case for which the engineer was retained.

"c. All work and results accomplished by the chemical engineer in the form of inventions, plans, designs, or other records, outside of the field for which a client or employer has retained him, should be regarded as the chemical engineer's property.

"d. When a chemical engineer participates in the building of apparatus from designs supplied him by a client, the designs remain the property of the client and should not be duplicated by the engineer nor anyone representing him for others without express permission.

"e. Chemical engineering data or information which a chemical engineer obtains from his client or employer or which he creates as a result of such information must be considered confidential by the engineer; and while he is justified in using such data or information in his own practice as forming part of his professional experience, its publication without express permission is improper.

"f. Designs, data, records and notes made by an employee, and referring to his employer's work, should be regarded as his employer's property.

"g. A client does not acquire any exclusive right to plans or apparatus made or constructed by a consulting chemical engineer except for the specific case for which they were made." [4]

The Right to "Detached Ideas". The next group of problems concerns what we shall venture to call "detached ideas". They are, negatively, not ideas looking to forms of service or coöperation, or representing plans for business activities of any kind; nor are they ideas for the shaping of material things, such as we shall study below. The best explanation of the term is the incidents themselves to which the phrase points.

"Stopurkicken" was an original idea, the result of the working of an ingenious mind. The Hesse Envelope Company appropriated a value which had cost the Westminster Company good money. In most cases ideas, as we have seen, can be shared, so that all that is ever lost to their originator is the privilege of exclusive enjoyment. But the Hesse Company destroyed all possibility of use for those who had paid for this idea.

In the case of the Associated Press against the International News Service we are dealing with information rather than original ideas; but it is information that was gathered at a great expenditure of money, time, and labor. In return those who sowed were entitled to the harvest, and the rival organization had no claim to it whatever. It is mere confusion of thought to say, with the apologists for the International Company, that when news has been placed on a bulletin board it then becomes the property of anyone who reads it, who may then make what use of it he pleases. As we have already pointed out there is no such thing as an absolute right to do what we will with our own. The reader of a bulletin is at liberty to make certain uses of it, including telling his neighbor about its contents, if he wishes. But from this fact it by no means follows that he may make any and every use of it. And when he uses it to divert into his own pockets the money which would otherwise go to those whose

[4] Heermance, *op. cit.*, p. 80.

industry and capital created the value, he is depriving the latter of justly earned compensation.

The Right to the Exclusive Use of Original Designs. Our last group of cases deals with the imitation of material goods embodying an original idea. If mental work ought to receive a return, just as physical work does, this is preëminently true of the original contributions of the creative mind. But the puzzle often is to discover what is original, and to what extent. This, of course, it is the function of the patent office and the courts to determine. And since the line must be drawn somewhere, and the standards used in drawing it inevitably possess a certain element of arbitrariness, —like the legal age of voting,—apparently the best rule we can lay down is that patents ought to be respected as a matter of morals as well as of force, and that ideas for which a patent would be refused may be freely appropriated.

On this basis we ourselves conclude the Flagg Company suffered no wrong when Holway put on the market a zither exactly like their own. He protected the purchaser against deception, as will be remembered, by plainly marking his instruments with his own name. The Meccano case, however, seems to us a somewhat different one. Its originators also were unable to obtain patents for most of the features of their toy. It is doubtless true, as the courts asserted, that each idea incorporated into the units that constituted the toy was merely a slight modification of some well known device or mechanical principle. On the other hand the whole may be something more than the sum of its parts. And whoever has seen a vigorous boy and a set of Meccano in a state of interaction will feel there is something in the idea as a whole which is highly original and which is deserving of a reward. So much so, that, as it seems to us, a man of sensitive honor would hesitate to appropriate it for his own profit.

But whatever may be said of our patent office and our courts as supplying standards of originality, the unfortunate fact is that in this country at least they do not even attempt to cover more than half of the ground. In particular they leave untouched the great field of imitation of patterns. This includes models in clothing, and patterns in the ordinary sense of the term; as those for laces, wallpaper, upholstery and gowns. These could be—not patented, indeed,—but copyrighted, and at a very reasonable cost and a very small expenditure of red tape, as is done in some European countries. This system would give us a judge with no personal interests to obscure the vision, who, before granting a monopoly to a pattern, would be in a position to determine whether it exhibited a significant element of invention. We ought to have some such tribunal in the United States, and its decisions ought to be obeyed not merely as law, but as a matter of justice. As conditions are today, however, a man working in this field must be a law to himself, except where his disputes can be referred to a trade association. He ought therefore to be a *law* to himself, and to act as if he were an impartial judge in his own court. For ideas in patterns are just as much entitled to protection as ideas in pumps; and if for whatever reason the government refrains from affording such protection the honorable man will protect himself against his own love of gain. The only reason that can be suggested for doing otherwise is the fact that a copyright runs for a limited period of time only, whereas a right acknowledged as a matter of honor would seem to be in essence eternal. But this reason is not decisive. For in the first place such acknowledgment might be granted subject to conditions to be suggested below for the respect for trade secrets. What is more to the point, in matters of taste, demand changes so quickly and is so completely dominated by novelty, that the money value of a new idea in this field invariably evaporates in the course of a short span of time.

In view of the preceding discussion the attitude to be taken toward the trade secrets of our competitors can be stated in a few words. Trade secrets in such matters as chemical formulae should be respected for a period equal to the duration of a patented invention, free from all attempts at discovery. To ferret them out is no more in the permanent interest of the public than to abrogate our patent laws. It is on a par with the publication in the United States without compensation of British books before the days of international copyright,—something which certain highminded firms refused to do. They should not, however, be allowed a longer immunity than a patent. Why should they be favored over patented ideas? The state has adopted patent laws for certain good ends and the substantial justification of the time limit which they carry with them is generally admitted, even by those who talk loudest about having an absolute right to the fruits of one's labor. Inventors should not be allowed to beat the government by secret processes with an immortality morally guaranteed. There is nothing wrong, however, in choosing secrecy as a means of guarding one's rights. For this reason these secrets should be treated as if they were covered by a patent.

Legal Rights to Ideas

The problems of this chapter, with the exception of the last, were obtained from the records of the courts. The following are the decisions rendered in each instance. We have not the knowledge requisite for a discussion of the underlying principles involved in these decisions, but we believe they can be formulated as follows:—(1) Property rights in ideas will be protected where this can be done effectively; but effective protection is difficult and often impossible. (2) The interests of the public call for free circulation of ideas. Between these two objectives, partly in conflict, partly not, the decisions swing, apparently determined, to a considerable extent, by the personal equation of the judge.

(1) Bristol *v.* Equitable Life Assurance Society, 132 N.Y. 264 (1892). Action against the Equitable Life Assurance Society was denied. The essence of the argument for this decision seems to be the following.

> "Without denying that there may be property in an idea or a trade secret or system, it is obvious that its originator or proprietor must himself protect it from escape or disclosure. If it cannot be sold or negotiated or used without a disclosure, it would seem proper that some contract should guard or regulate the disclosure, otherwise it must follow the law of ideas and become the acquisition of whoever receives it."

This conclusion the court seems to think is buttressed by its illustration of the man who informs *A* that *C* desires to buy his house (see above p. 224).

(2) Haskins *v.* Ryan, 71 N.J. Equity, 575 (1906). The court re-

fused to recognize Haskins' claim, asserting that "it has never, in the absence of contract or statute been held . . . that mere ideas are capable of legal ownership and protection".

(3) Fisher *v.* Star Co., 231 N.Y. 414 (1921). The court found in favor of Fisher. The grounds on which the decision was based were two in number. (1) The misrepresentation involved in attempting to deceive the public into believing that the cartoons drawn by another were the work of Fisher. This consideration does not concern us here. (2) "The plaintiff is the owner of a proprietary right existing in the characters represented in such figures and names", and consequently the action of the Star Company resulted in "an unfair appropriation of [the cartoonist's] skill and the celebrity acquired by him in originating, producing and maintaining the characters and figures". Among precedents, the decision in Associated Press *v.* International News Service (see below) was appealed to.

(4) Boosing *v.* Dorman *et al.,* 133 N.Y. Suppl. 910 (1912). The court dismissed the complaint. The opinion of the referee, which the court accepted, reads in part as follows:

"Secret processes of manufacture have been protected when they were the property of the master, and the servant had acquired knowledge of them purely by reason of his employment. In this case we are asked to go further than any reported case, and to say that a salesman calling upon well-known dealers and soliciting orders and delivering goods for his master, and thereby acquiring a personal knowledge and influence with his customers, shall be forever, after the termination of his employment, debarred from dealing with the same customers for his own benefit. In other words, according as he is successful as a salesman in his master's employ, just so far is his sphere of usefulness limited should he embark on a business venture on his own account in the same line. I know of no principle of law which sustains such a theory."

(5) Witkop & Holmes Co. *v.* Boyce, 118 N.Y. Suppl. 461 (1909).

"There can be no escape from the conclusion that the names and addresses of this large list of customers of plaintiff residing in a well-defined accessible territory were placed in defendant's possession for the sole and only purpose of being used for plaintiff's benefit. They were part of plaintiff's assets in business. These names and addresses were plaintiff's property. The plaintiff originated, made up, and secured these lists of names, and the trade naturally to follow the continuation of the business relations established by the intercourse of months and years between plaintiff and these customers was the property of the plaintiff. . . . The defendant had no right to use such information thus imparted to him in a confidential manner for the benefit of plaintiff's competitor and to the plaintiff's damage."

This opinion was adopted by another division of the same court in People's Coat, Apron & Towel Supply Co., *v.* Light *et al.,* 157 N.Y. Suppl. 15 (1916). But in what was practically an identical situation a Maryland Court reached an opposite conclusion. In Fulton Grand Laundry Co. *v.* Johnson, 140 Md. 359 (1922), it was held that

"It is a settled principle of law that trade secrets are to be protected, but the divergence [in opinion] begins when the question to be determined in particular cases is whether the things sought to be protected should be classed as a trade secret. And this is the real question presented in this case. A thing can hardly be said to be a secret, in the sense that it should be guarded by a court of equity, which is susceptible of discovery by observation and which is open to the observation of anyone who thinks it worth while to observe. . . . We are not willing to hold that in any ordinary business an employee, going into business for himself or into the employment of another, should be enjoined from seeking to do business with friends he has made in the course of the previous employment merely because he became acquainted with them while so engaged and as a result of such previous employment. . . . Such a rule would tend to destroy the freedom of employees and to reduce them to a condition of industrial servitude."

(6) Westminster Laundry Company *v.* Hesse Envelope Company, 174 Mo. Ap. 238 (1913). This case was decided in favor of the defendant. In the opinion of the court since the word "stopurkicken" was not a trade mark, it was not property. Furthermore there was no unfair competition because "unfair competition consists in passing off or in attempting to pass off upon the public the goods or business of one person as and for the goods or business of another".

On this decision 27 *Harvard Law Review* (1913) 99 makes the following pertinent editorial comment:—

"The mere lack of a familiar classification does not excuse the court from denying recovery. True, the interest to be safeguarded is intangible, but so is good will. The plaintiff here has at heavy cost created a thing of undoubted value in the business world and his loss is plainly demonstrable; much more so, for example, than damage to a man's reputation. It is novel situations like these that challenge the power of our law to expand, and the failure to do this in the principal case has permitted the defendant to escape liability though he has without justification inflicted serious practical loss."

We may add that the ancient definition of unfair competition employed by the judge would be accepted by no court today as an adequate representation of what the term involves.

(7) International News Service *v.* Associated Press, 248 U.S. 215 (1918). The Supreme Court of the United States declared that the news gathered by the Associated Press was property that would be protected by law as against any competing news service which attempted to make use of it for purposes of gain. The official summary of the essential part of the decision reads as follows:—

> "As against the public, any special interest of the producer of uncopyrighted news matter is lost upon the first publication. But one who gathers news, at pains and expense, for the purpose of lucrative publication, may be said to have a *quasi* property in the results of his enterprise, as against a rival in the same business, and the appropriation of those results at the expense and to the damage of the one and for the profit of the other is unfair competition against which equity will afford relief."

This conception of a property right as holding against one party but not others, is thoroughly sound and has a great many very significant consequences.

Alexander Woollcott's delightful book *While Rome Burns* contributes an interesting parallel to the above division and limitation of legal property rights. Mr. Bernard Shaw, it seems, "poured out" upon Mrs. Patrick Campbell, the distinguished actress, "a torrent of love letters for several years". The public of course would have been delighted to participate in this glorious feast. Mrs. Campbell, who was a practical person as well as an artist, was very anxious to meet these wishes in full. However when she attempted to act upon this laudable ambition to serve humanity she found herself

> "Thwarted by the law which, in both England and America, protects the writer of such heady correspondence. . . . If I write you a letter, it belongs to you. That is, the document itself belongs to you and it would be your privilege to sell it as a holograph rarity to some presumably feeble-minded collector. But as a piece of literature, good or bad, it belongs to me. The right to publish it remains with me and passes to my heirs." [5]

(8) Flagg Mfg. Co. *v.* Holway, 178 Mass. 83 (1901). "In the absence of a patent, the freedom of manufacture can not be cut down un-

[5] Alexander Woollcott, *While Rome Burns* (New York, The Viking Press, 1934), p. 137.

der the name of preventing unfair competition. All that can be asked is that precautions be taken, so far as are consistent with the defendant's fundamental right to make and sell what he chooses, to prevent the deception which no doubt he desired to prevent."

(9) Meccano Limited *v.* Wagner, 234 Fed. 920 (1916).

> "Unfair competition exists . . . in that the complainant has established a business system which is peculiarly his own. This was done at the expense of time, thought, labor, and much money. . . . [In this system the Meccano Co.] has acquired a proprietary right of which its competitor can not deprive it by introducing his goods into and as a part of complainant's business and business system. In this respect the case strongly resembles Prest-O-Lite Co. *v.* Davis, 209 Fed. 917, . . . [and] 215 Fed. 349."

This case and others involving the same principle, and equally perplexing in character, will be found in Nims, *The Law of Unfair Business Competition,* 3rd Ed., Sec. 289a.

MORAL PROGRESS IN THE BUSINESS WORLD

CHAPTER XVII

GROUNDS FOR OPTIMISM

Every intelligent person is interested in the possibility of moral progress, if for no other than egoistic reasons. Equally as a producer and as a consumer, he can fare best in a community where business is conducted efficiently, honestly, and with fairness.

The Outlook for Higher Moral Standards

In certain respects the prospects in this direction seem somewhat discouraging. Many forms of temptation are becoming stronger and more wide-spread everyday, particularly the temptation to get wealth at any cost. The demands for comforts and luxuries are steadily becoming more insistent, partly because self-indulgence grows by what it feeds on, partly because of the craze to be in the class with those who have such things, partly because there are more kinds of wares to buy than there were a generation ago, and partly because more time and skill are spent in advertising and displaying them. Where these influences do not affect a business man directly, they affect him through the demands made upon him by his family.

If each succeeding decade thus witnesses an increase in the force and variety of temptations, many of the old barriers are being weakened or swept away. The most serious of our losses is the old-fashioned home, together with—in the more favorable instances—its social and material environment. Two or three generations ago most Americans lived in a small community, and they lived for the greater part of their lives in the same community. This supplied the soil in which personal interest in neighbors could develop and flourish, provided there was reasonably good native endowment to begin with. If not, there was always the stern face of public opinion. What has happened since, we all know. Taking these and all the other relevant factors into consideration, it is not strange that the outlook for moral progress appears somewhat bleak.

The Existence of Latent Capacities for Good

There would be some gleams of sunshine in the picture if we could believe that there exist in all men latent capacities for good which need only be cultivated wisely to spring into vigorous life. If the material is there to work with, the past triumphs of the human mind justify almost any expectations of ultimate success. Consider for a moment what has happened in the struggle to control nature. For a million years or more countless numbers of the human race lived where Marco Polo's "black stones" were lying but a few feet below the surface, hidden from view by a thin layer of soil. Finally came the discovery of coal and its application through Watts' engine to the work of the world. There followed in its train a long list of inventions which within a hundred and fifty years have transformed the material side of our civilization so completely that our manner of life today is farther removed from that of our ancestors in 1776 than was that of the latter from the life of the Pyramid Age, three thousand years before Christ. Man has remade his world by discovering latent resources and learning how to use them.

There is no reason why what has happened in the realm of matter should not happen sooner or later in the realm of mind, provided always that the necessary latent capacities exist there also. That they do exist is proved by the way in which most people meet a crisis. Here, where the stakes are perhaps life and death, the scales fall from our eyes, we see the issues for the moment as they really are, and respond, at whatever cost, to the demands of the situation. For this reason "there is always a supply of [physical] courage when needed".

In 1929 a hospital in Cleveland was destroyed by fire. The disaster was aggravated by the fact that the heat converted the X-ray films stored in the basement into great clouds of poison gas.

"Among the heroines of the disaster was Gladys Gibson, telephone operator at the clinic who died [the same] night in a hospital. The telephone girl saw the cloud of yellow poison gas coming and knew it carried death, but she stayed at her switchboard, making heroic efforts to warn everyone in the clinic of their danger and to rally police, firemen, and ambulances. Finally she collapsed. Someone carried her out, dying." [1]

Gladys, it may be argued, must have been a very exceptional young person. As a matter of fact she may have had, on the whole, a commonplace character. For equivalent strength and devotion have been displayed under certain conditions by the most abandoned criminals.

Thomas Mott Osborne, as warden at Sing Sing, was apparently the first official in that institution to recognize that criminals might still be human beings and to treat them as such. As a result, he was the object of a measureless admiration and gratitude on the part of the unfortunate men committed to his charge. His program brought him into conflict with the interests of a lot of dirty politicians, and in order to get him out of the way, they planned a frame-up. He was accused, among other things, of winking at sexual perversion. Twenty-one of the prisoners were indicted for such perversion, with penalties hanging over their heads, if found guilty, running as high as forty years. Each of them was offered immunity from prosecution and liberation from prison if he would agree to perjure himself by testifying against the warden. All flatly refused. One of them, when approached, replied: "Nothing doing; I ain't no skunk. I'm not going to commit dirty work for anybody".

After his vindication as a result of this magnificent display of loyalty, Mr. Osborne said: "Of all my prison experiences, I hold this as the most amazing; that there could not be found among that score of 'hardened criminals' a single man willing to perjure himself in order to escape indictment and conviction, and to secure release from prison".[2]

There is some stuff of this sort in every one of us. Soon after the sinking of the Titanic with its exhibitions of heroic self-control, George Kennan, the famous traveler, wrote to the *Outlook* as follows:

"The courage and unselfishness shown by an overwhelming majority of the passengers on the ill-fated steamship Titanic have recalled to my mind

[1] Associated Press despatch.

[2] *The Survey-Graphic,* LXV (1931), 378.

the remarkable exhibition of the same heroic and generous characteristics by the citizens of San Francisco during the great earthquake and fire of 1906. I did not myself reach the city until some weeks after the disaster, but the remembrance of the events of that period of strain and suffering was still fresh in the mind of every observer or participant, and I was greatly impressed by the enthusiasm and deep feeling shown by everybody in speaking of the behavior of the population. One friend of mine in Oakland—a man not at all inclined to be 'gushing' or 'effusive' in speech—said to me: 'I am glad that I lived to see the things that happened in the first ten days after that great catastrophe. Those days were the best and most inspiriting part of my life. Religious people talk about the kingdom of heaven, but few of them expect to live long enough to see it realized on earth. I saw something that very nearly approached it in San Francisco, Berkeley, and Oakland in the week that followed the fire. Cowardice, selfishness, greed, and all the baser emotions and impulses of human character practically disappeared in the tremendous strain of that experience, and courage, fortitude, sympathy, generosity, and unbounded self-sacrifice took their place. Men became, and for a short time continued to be, all that we may suppose their Creator intended them to be, and it was a splendid and inspiriting thing to witness. We imagine that we live in a selfish and materialistic age, and perhaps we do; but I know now of what human nature is capable, and I can never again take a pessimistic view of the world's future.' " [3]

Such things are in men. The crisis passes, and then all too often these same strange beings are cutting each other's throats in business deals, or refusing to testify in an investigation of racketeering because they are *afraid*. For a moment they awoke to a realization of what suffering, loss, or impending death meant to the other fellow. But now it is all over, and the men about them are again for them mere lumps of matter to be kicked out of the way or crushed, as before. All this time the potentialities for something better are there. The problem before the world is to arouse and strengthen this power to put oneself in the other man's place, and the allied power to care deeply for the good of the whole; in particular, to wish to leave the world a better place for our having lived in it. Solve this problem and you have the good life and a society fit to live in.

No such solution is at hand as yet. Important contributions have indeed been made in many homes for thousands of years; and this is indispensable. Other contributions have been made in certain schools; and they have proved very valuable. Some things have been

[3] *The Outlook*, CI (1912), 84.

accomplished in the business world, and of these we mean to speak later. But we believe the great conquests in this field lie in the future, perhaps at a time when biology, psychology, and the social sciences are as far advanced beyond their present status as physics and chemistry are beyond what they were two hundred years ago. The problem will be solved ultimately, for the age of science and its application to the needs of human life has just begun. In the meantime, we of this generation must live and do the best we can.

The Sense of Craftsmanship as an Ally of Morality

Two changes in contemporary society which are not beyond the possibilities now open to us, would help a great deal. We need a more wide-spread sense of craftsmanship—joy in producing the best and pride in its production; and we need a living and vivid sense of the values which the world has to offer apart from a heap of gold.

The joys of craftsmanship are due to success in the solution of problems. They are thus an unknown world to the drudge who, like the worker in a Ford factory, mechanically performs the same monotonous operation all day long, day after day. The exercise of a vocation under such conditions can be little more than a mere means to the pay check at the end of the weary week. A man thus circumstanced is little better than a slave; and this is true whether he earns a dollar or a thousand dollars a day. The free man does not watch the clock. His heart, as we say, is in his work because it is enjoyable for its own sake.

The opportunities for living such a life are far more wide-spread than some people seem to suppose. We ourselves, at any rate, are convinced from what the men most vitally concerned have themselves told us that a vigorous mind, more eager to get the best out of life than to pose as a martyr, can find something of interest in most forms of work, provided he possesses the powers requisite for the attainment of a fair amount of success.

One of the writers of this book once rode for a few hours on a train in company with a locomotive fireman. Although forty-five years of age, he had never attained the dignity of "sitting on the right-hand side of the cab". It might therefore be supposed that he would be indifferent and soured. Quite the contrary; he exhibited great enthusiasm about the workings of the mighty machine which he served, and the skill involved in keeping the fire just hot enough and not too hot to make the steam gauge register the proper pressure in the boiler. "You enjoy your work then", said the writer. We had both been slouching upon rather uncomfortable seats. At this question the fireman straightened up, raised his head, and looking his companion squarely in the eye, replied: "Ah, when I put my foot on the 'gangway' I am a new man".

The significance of these facts for morals is that pride and joy in craftsmanship are among the most powerful of all motives for the production of genuine work. Where present as a living force, they are the relentless foe of all misrepresentation and sham. Ruled by them, the craftsman can no more bring himself to substitute the flashy imitation for the reality than could a lover of precious stones wear paste diamonds. Since such men do not have to be watched, the successful employer, other things being anywhere near equal, will be he who can succeed in infusing this spirit into his employees. The opposite is also true. The most certain penalty of dishonesty is that it destroys the sense for craftsmanship. And where a dishonest employer communicates the infection of his character to his employees, instead of doing as much as they can they now do as little, and that little they will do as badly as they dare.

Varied Interests as an Ally of Morality

There are several reasons for that frenzied pursuit of wealth which may properly be called "money madness". An important one is poverty of inner resources. A man who really cares for nothing but money has nothing with which to occupy his mind besides schemes for getting money. Furthermore his one chance of happiness lies in the attainment of wealth. He may find when it comes, *if it comes,* that like the late Frank Munsey, he has bought a gold brick. "Success," said this multi-millionaire near the close of his life, "is like piling up a big fortune in front of cattle." [4] But of this

[4] Geo. Britt, *Forty Years—Forty Millions; the Career of Frank A. Munsey* (New York, Farrar and Rinehart, 1935), p. 287.

fact he can not be persuaded in advance; and in any event, the pursuit of the dollar is his only chance. He has put all his money on one horse. On the other hand, a man rich in interests has spread his investments, and when he has obtained a reasonable competence, has something more interesting to do with his time than to think out means of ruining others.

In brief:—Any social forces which tend to create and maintain the healthy satisfactions of craftsmanship and cultural interests are powerful allies of that spirit of service which constitutes the core of the moral life.

What the Individual Business Man Can Do for Moral Progress

Such agencies of progress are somewhat impersonal. What can an individual business man do, in the course of his daily work, to raise the moral tone of that part of the business world with which he is in contact? For one thing, if he has the requisite time and strength, he can join with others in the work of some one or more of the organizations which exist for this purpose. This involves cooperation with like-minded men. But apart from this, he can do certain things by himself.

In the first place he can see to it that his employees are straight. We have spoken of this before. One of the most terrible effects of dishonesty on the part of the employer is that it either demoralizes the employees or takes from them all zest in their day's work.

Here as in so many other cases the dishonorable man may easily overreach himself. A certain manufacturing firm, for example, was taking order after order which it knew, and its employees knew, it could not fill by the time agreed. Asked concerning the effects of this form of lying upon the morale of the men, the foreman said: "I am confident it has a tendency to breed distrust and contempt, to make the men careless in regard to the sacredness of contracts. They grow lax and drift into the habit of doing things indifferently or imperfectly. I know it affects me that way".[5] No one can afford to have crooked employees, or even employees who take no interest in their work. Theodore Roosevelt once had a cow-boy in his em-

[5] *The Outlook*, CXXIV (1920), 612.

ployment who offered to brand the cattle of a neighbor with his employer's brand. Mr. Roosevelt at once discharged him on the ground that a man who was willing to swindle others in his employer's interest would not hesitate to swindle his employer in his own interest.[6] This obvious fact is frequently ignored. In other words some otherwise intelligent men are such hogs that they can not see even their own permanent interests.

In the second place, whether buying to sell or buying for personal consumption, we can all make it a principle not to buy from anyone who has once cheated us. This is a desirable policy even where we have ample means for protecting ourselves against further deception. To be sure, we can not make a man inwardly honest by helping to cut his profits, because honesty that is practiced only because it is the best policy is not genuine honesty. But, as has already been said, external honesty is very important, because successful dishonesty, if at all wide-spread, and even if only temporarily successful, tends to undermine the resolution of weak-spined men who would be honest enough if they had happened to live among honest people. And the demoralization may spread until no one but a man of very exceptional ability and heroic courage can conduct his business honorably. Accordingly, whenever we use our purchasing power to help the honest succeed, and prevent the dishonest from prospering, we are promoting the cause of morality in the community.

We might call the preceding a proposal for a business boycott. Even more effective in the case of notorious and demonstrable malefactors of wealth, and perhaps of lesser men, too, would be the social boycott. Most men want great riches not primarily for what they bring in the way of creature comforts or luxuries, but for their prestige value. Their millions show that they have played the game and *won*. To whom do they exhibit themselves but to those about them, especially those with whom they come into personal contact. If such persons show that they are not impressed by success in a fight won by hitting below the belt; better still, if they show they despise the creatures who will do anything to win, the wreath of victory will shrivel and fade. If it is well known beforehand that this will be the

[6] Theodore Roosevelt, "Citizenship in a Republic", *The Outlook,* XCIV (1910), 992.

result of violence, treachery, and trickery, the unprincipled contender for victory will think twice before he will risk cheating himself out of his prize. Toadying to the crooked rich on the part of otherwise honorable men is probably responsible for as much of the deviltry that goes on, at least in the world of big business, as any one factor in our national life.

In the fourth place, we could produce a veritable revolution in business practice if we would take the pains to learn our business so well that suppliers would be unable to cheat us. Here is where the housewives of this country have their chance. They hold the retail trade—and trader—in the hollow of their hands. If they would learn their business, which is to buy intelligently, they could mould trade and trader alike to their standards, and usher in a new epoch in business history.

Finally the best thing any man can give to the world is himself. But enough was said about this subject when discussing imitation in Chapter III.

To do our part to make the world a better place to live in is a duty because we owe practically everything we have and are to those who have gone before us. And the only way we can repay this debt is to play our part as our past benefactors played theirs.

This, indeed, is not so much a duty as a privilege. We need some goal larger than the petty interests of the self, some task which we can share with others, some cause which will give meaning and purpose to what would otherwise be the aimless passage of the years. "I was born of a pioneer family, but I have no frontier", complains a member of our younger generation. This young man lacks vision. For almost anywhere in the business world he can, if he chooses, find numberless problems even more significant and far more difficult than those which faced the men who first brought civilization to the wilderness. If he can do nothing else, he can learn to see his job as one part of that marvellous organism, the creation of ten thousand years of thought and labor, by which the many and complicated wants of the inhabitants of this planet are provided with at least a measure of satisfaction; a measure of satisfaction almost infinitely beyond what even the ablest among them could have attained by his own unaided efforts.

Even the commonplace motives of economic self-interest are served by devotion to these impersonal ends. The higher the standards of conduct in our business community, the less likely are we to be swindled, or pushed to the wall by brute force. The higher the standards the more easy it is to conduct an honest business ourselves. The higher the standards the nearer the approach to a friendly world, in which people can trust and rely upon each other, and, whenever desirable, work together for common ends. A friendly world is a pleasanter and more attractive place in which to work than is a den of snakes, with its suspicions, its hatreds, its bitterness, and its essential loneliness.

More than this, the present generation is not at all inclined to bear the ills it has; on the contrary, it is quite in the mood to fly to others that it knows not of. Every serious financial or other business scandal that reaches the public ear, every would-be monopoly that kills off its competitors right and left and flaunts its greed and violence in the face of decent people, is one more blow to the existing business order. The flood of criticism may fall as the depression wanes—to return on the appearance of the next depression. But it is to be as stupid as were those who surrounded the late Czar Nicholas to take it for granted that the thing which has been is that which shall be, and there is no new thing under the sun. Most of Europe is either Fascist or Communist. What goes on there can never permanently leave us untroubled. It was certainly the American Revolution that supplied the spark which touched off the French Revolution—that tremendous cataclysm which all the wise men knew could never happen. And sparks can blow across the Atlantic both ways. Those therefore who really care for the preservation of our economic and political institutions will recognize that they must do their part to make them worthy of preservation.

CHAPTER XVIII

ORGANIZATIONS FOR THE IMPROVEMENT OF BUSINESS PRACTICE

A characteristic and important feature of present-day American business life is the group of voluntary organizations created and operated entirely or in part for the purpose of raising the standards of conduct in the business world. The present chapter attempts to give a brief account of some of these activities.

Trade Associations

Industry's attempt to regulate itself is in certain respects best represented in the work of the Trade Associations. "A Trade Association is an organization of producers or distributors of a commodity or service upon a mutual basis for the purpose of promoting the business of their branch of industry and improving their service to the public through the compilation and distribution of information, the establishment of trade standards, and the coöperative handling of problems common to the production or distribution of the commodity or service with which they are concerned." [1] Mr. Herbert Hoover, while he was Secretary of Commerce, suggested an extensive list of activities which were proper functions of Trade Associations. His list included, among other things, the following:—(1) Statistical activities; (2) Legislative activities; (3) Studies leading toward the simplification and standardization of production and distribution processes; 4) The establishment of adequate and uniform cost accounting systems; (5) The study of credit and collection systems and the interchange of credit information; (6) The settlement of trade disputes and the establishment of standards of fair practice and standards of ethics for the industry; (7) The establishment of more effective employee relations; (8) The standardization and simplification of insurance procedure; (9) The study and simplification

[1] *Handbook, American Trade Association Executives*. Chicago, 1924.

of traffic and transportation problems; (10) Commercial research in markets and methods of distribution; (11) Industrial research in technical and production problems; (12) The improvement of relations with the government; (13) The interchange of patent rights; (14) The working out of coöperative purchasing plans for the joint negotiation of purchases; (15) The regulation of output to existing or prospective demands; and (16) The control of pricing policies, including price fixing.[2]

Trade associations are direct recognitions of the fact that business needs to be controlled by something a little more rational than the pure unvarnished laws of competition. For competition, however attractive it may appear in the text books, has a trick of getting out of hand and becoming destructive, and this entirely without aid or intention on the part of the great majority of the members of a trade. The real problem has always been, not "Shall there be any control?" but "Who is to do the controlling?" There have been three answers, capable of amalgamation in varying degrees. First, Let nobody control—let the "natural laws" of economics take care of the situation; Second, Let the business men work out a system of controlling their own fields, with a minimum of government policing to see things through; Third, Let the government do the controlling.

American business men, of course, have always insisted that the second answer is the correct one; which means that business ought to be permitted to regulate itself. This is exactly what the trade associations have been trying to do for three decades; but, except for the notable success of some associations in their educational activities, they have not got very far because the very things which they have felt it necessary to do are forbidden them by law.

A portion of the activity of every trade association has been devoted to Mr. Hoover's sixth class of objectives, the establishment of standards of fair practice for the industry. The results of the Association's discussions in this field were usually expressed in a formal "Code of Ethics" or "Code of Fair Practice" which was adopted by and distributed to the membership, and occasionally followed up by a considerable amount of educational work.[3] But since the associa-

[2] *Trade Association Activities,* Bureau of Foreign and Domestic Commerce, pp. 3–7.

[3] A collection of early codes of this sort will be found in the book frequently

tions usually had no power to enforce the regulations thus set forth, the result was that the responsible and reputable members of the industry obeyed them when they could, while the less reputable members tended to obey them only when there seemed to be no reason for not doing so. The codes were not entirely ineffective, however, because in most associations some public spirited individual or some socially minded committee carried on a vigorous campaign on their behalf. The result was that thousands of business men for the first time learned not only that certain business practices were not acceptable among gentlemen, but began to get an inkling as to *why* they were not acceptable. Since it is perhaps true that with most business men a genuine insight into the nature of an unfair practice is at least as powerful a deterrent as the prohibition of the practice, it is probable that the codes of the trade associations, together with the educational work which supported them, should be given credit for much real improvement in business standards.

But while the trade associations met with measurable success in the elimination of many types of unfair trade practices, they found their efforts balked when they came to grips with the two processes the malfunctioning of which gave rise to most of the other evils which bothered their members. Since the associations had been organized for the purpose of mutual benefit to the members of the industry, and since intelligent business men recognized that a major part of their troubles came from ill-advised, ignorant, or consciously predatory price competition, or from ignorant and bungling attempts to adjust production to demand, it is natural that they should have desired to exert associated effort toward the control of prices and, to some extent, the control of production. But this field of endeavor was denied them under the anti-trust laws, and every attempt at price control met with rigorous repression at the hands of the regulatory bodies and the courts. Under the anti-trust laws, any formally organized trade association or any other organized group which made any attempt at (1) unification in selling, (2) exclusion of objectionable individuals from the markets, (3) curtailment of

---

referred to in earlier chapters, above, *Codes of Ethics,* collected by Edgar L. Heermance.

production, or (4) control or manipulation of prices, found itself very quickly in hot water.[4]

This is not to say that there was anything essentially immoral about attempts on the part of business men to lessen the ravages of unlimited competition which, as has been said, under many circumstances become destructive not only to the interests of the business men but to the interests of consumers as well. But apparently the American public has felt that if the door of price control were opened for certain reasonable cases, it might prove difficult to keep it closed for others less reasonable; and so the restrictions on all associated activities which dealt with pricing policies have been continued.

In the meantime the associations have had at their disposal another resource in connection with pricing policies, which, however, has been of little use to them. Nothing has ever prevented the members from forming "gentlemen's agreements" with respect to prices. This has been tried frequently enough, but usually without success. The failure must be laid to the fact that most business men fail to act like gentlemen in the presence of a mere agreement, and require an organization with a considerable equipment of teeth to enforce arrangements of this sort. This tendency should not be interpreted as a general reflection upon the character of such men under other conditions; for thousands of men whose word in all other types of agreement is as good as a written contract fail to abide by "gentlemen's agreements" dealing with pricing and production policies. A chain is no stronger than its weakest link; and where some spineless member of a group succumbs to the temptation offered by the prospect of a temporary gain, the others are apt to feel themselves justified or even compelled to follow his example. Perhaps it is in recognition of this fact that the attacks of the law upon the price control activities of the Trade Associations has always been directed to the specific devices and techniques which were designed to give teeth to these organizations.

Under the National Industrial Recovery Act which, among other things, was designed to gather practically all American business men

[4] For cases see *Trade Associations, Their Economic Significance and Legal Status,* National Industrial Conference Board, Inc. (New York, 1925.)

into some formally organized trade association under the belief that this regimentation would make the problem of control much simpler, the restrictions placed by the anti-trust laws upon the control of prices and production were temporarily relaxed, and, as a result, trade association activities suddenly took a new turn. Under the National Industrial Recovery Administration the old codes were replaced by new ones. New codes were written by the hundreds. These, however, proved to contain essentially the old familiar lists of unfair practices, plus a new set of regulations dealing with now permissible control of prices and production, plus such wage and labor regulations as the government succeeded in getting the associations to adopt. It is fair to say that, beyond the recognition of the fact that pricing policies may be unfair and that it is possible to go too far in limiting the business man's freedom to control prices, nothing new was contributed by this entire movement to our knowledge of the requirements of fair competition. Even this one novelty was not so much a contribution to knowledge as it was a simple legal recognition of a new standard which business men had been adopting progressively for the past two decades.

To the association members who had been attempting futilely for twenty years to win the right to use price control devices, this suddenly acquired freedom, however, was by far the most welcome element in the new situation, and it accordingly received the chief emphasis in most of the NRA codes. This was to be expected since, apart from the unfair methods which involve coercion, misrepresentation, or direct destruction of a competitor's plant, market, personnel or reputation, most forms of unfair competition express themselves through pricing policies. Given a control over such policies which will prevent undercost selling, it is theoretically possible to force competition to proceed on the basis of true productive efficiency; so that in one sense it may be said that what the country needs is a moral standard which will prevent a business man from selling at less than cost—except under unusual and socially desirable circumstances.

Unfortunately, it can not be recorded that the trade associations, acting under the NRA, met the problems presented by pricing policies with any great success. When they faced the problem of defining the cost below which it should not be permissible to sell, they discovered that they were confronting an extraordinarily difficult problem. What cost? Still more important, Whose cost? One's own cost? The costs of one's competitors? The average costs for an industry? The costs of "representative" concerns? The costs of the best units in the industry or of the worst? Any particular cost was likely to seem unfair, and in practice did seem unfair, to some members of the industry. What actually happened was that a number of varying definitions of "cost" were used in the several codes, and every adoption had to be forced upon substantial and vocal minorities, with protests arising from the representatives of the public interests in many cases as well.

Whatever the trade associations may have hoped for from the National Industrial Recovery Act, the unconstitutionality of the act has for the time being made the movement one of historical interest only, and it will not be discussed in greater detail here. For the moment, trade associations are back approximately where they were in 1932, with the possibility that they will be given somewhat greater freedom in the exercise of price and production control. Accordingly our problem becomes: What can the trade associations under these conditions do to improve trading and competitive standards in their industries?

Opportunities for real service by the associations will be apparent to anyone who will revert to Mr. Hoover's classification of functions. Much work has already been done in connection with trade statistics, cost accounting, interchange of credit information, and research in common industrial and marketing problems. These activities are designed to make each individual in the industry better fitted to meet the problems which he must face. We have held, in a preceding chapter, that it is the duty of every business man to know his own business, partly because the public requires and deserves only capable service, and partly because ignorance is the source of a good many unfair conditions which even the most efficient competition can not master. Where prices in an industry are driven far below cost this may be the result of conscious predatory attempts on the part of certain individuals who present one problem to the industry; or it may be the result of ignorance on the part of a large and miscellaneous group who present quite another problem. Obviously if costs are the most important single element in commercial processes and, in one sense at least, one of the most important elements in any form of fair competition, it is essential for all members of an industry to know just what their costs are. In standardizing the approach to this problem through the study of costs and through the design and installation of uniform systems of cost accounting, the Trade Associations have done work of inestimable value to their own groups and to the cause of fair competition as well. The approach of the associations has varied from simple work by committees in disseminating accurate information on costs, to elaborate studies conducted by great universities for the national associations.[5] The United Typothetae of America has maintained an elaborate staff of accountants whose sole function was to install an adequate and uniform cost accounting system in the plants of members and to instruct the members in its use. The result of such activities multiplied hundreds of times in hundreds of associations has been to put business men on a basis where they could make really accurate comparisons of costs and prices with those of competitors. By stigmatizing certain practices as ill-advised and censurable it has eliminated an enormous amount of cutthroat competition which had formerly resulted from inaccurate knowledge of costs and from the failure of business men to realize just how far they could go in the reduction of prices without getting themselves or others into trouble.

Statistical reporting and research in market conditions have likewise served to give the membership of the trade associations a better grasp on the facts of their own business. The coöperative statistical reports covering stocks of goods on hand and in production, the marketing studies on a national scale designed to show prospective demands for products, and weekly or monthly reports on the conditions of the markets, are designed to make it possible for all members to compete on the basis of an equal knowledge of the situation which they are attempting to meet. Thereby the amount of unwise dumping of products on the market, and of other demoralizing practices, has been much reduced.

[5] See studies for the National Wholesalers' Association, the American Retail Jewelers' Association and others, by the Bureau of Business Research of Harvard University.

But while we can not but compliment the trade associations on their work in this field, we can not assert that it has been finished. Only a few of the leading associations have substantially completed their task of education, and this field will remain open for profitable service for decades to come.

They still have plenty of opportunity also to expand their codes of fair practice and to conduct more effective educational work in getting them observed. Too many of the old codes were mere paraphrases of other associational codes, in many cases apparently patched together by a harried secretary who was working against time to get something to present to his governing board at its next meeting.[6] Those associations which have vexing problems which do not respond to such pressure as code committees can bring to bear are at liberty to call for assistance upon the Federal Trade Commission under the Trade Practice Conference plan. But in general it may be said that the success of the associations in ridding themselves of recognized bad practices will depend upon their power to educate their members to higher standards of conduct. Police powers have never proved effective against a resistant group which failed to recognize the real significance of the evils caused by commercial anarchism. For this reason the authors feel that the essentially educational activities of the trade associations, if pursued consistently, patiently, and intelligently, will be more fruitful in the long run than any policing functions which they may undertake to discharge, either by themselves or through coöperation with the government.

The trade associations have been closely identified in the public mind with lobbying activities before state legislatures and before Congress. For these activities they have perhaps received more censure than they deserve. When legislation concerning a given industry or industrial group is being considered, the representation of individual members is impracticable, and the trade association would seem to be the ideal organization to undertake coöperative representation for the lot; since if the association has performed its task it has at hand complete statistical and historical information

[6] Note the similarity in phraseology between many of the codes in Heermance, *Codes of Ethics.*

concerning the industry. The right of the industry to representation would be denied by few; and the fact that some trade associations occasionally adopt methods which will be frowned upon by reasonable citizens is no argument against the general principle. The lobbying activity of the associations is, in itself, perfectly defensible and may therefore be regarded as one of their normal functions.

Better Business Bureaus

A group of organizations which work in a much narrower field than the trade associations, but which have performed a very effective service along their own lines is the Better Business Bureaus. Their aims are stated in their own words as follows:

"To further and promote honesty, truthfulness, and reliability in the sale of merchandise, securities and services, discourage fraudulent and deceptive methods in business, and thereby to increase public confidence in advertising, salesmanship and business generally." [7]

The organization created and maintained for the realization of these ends is:

"A national agency maintained by business to facilitate self-regulation of business and to promote public confidence in advertising and selling.

"A non-profit corporation, supervised by a Board of Directors elected by the membership and serving without compensation.

"Operated by a staff of experienced executives who have no other business connections.

"Affiliated through coöperation (although operating independently) with 54 Better Business Bureaus in the United States and Canada.

"An organization representing all phases of business and all sections of the country.

"A recognized agency of publishers and national advertisers to coöperate in maintaining high standards of business practice." [8]

The National Better Business Bureau is primarily interested in enforcing high standards of reliability in national advertising in both periodicals and newspapers, and in policing other national selling activities. The local bureaus, dealing intensively with the problems of a given city or trade area, concern themselves with unfair practices in their own communities only. The parallel between this distribu-

[7] *Annual Report, National Better Business Bureau, Inc.*, 1935, p. 1.

[8] *Protecting Public Confidence in Periodical Advertising* (New York, National Better Business Bureau, Inc., 1935), p. 3.

tion of responsibility and the distinction between interstate and intrastate commerce as found in our business legislation is close. All of the bureaus are purely voluntary organizations established and supported by business men without any public support whatever. In larger cities special offices and investigation staffs may be maintained, while in smaller places the Bureau frequently operates in conjunction with the local Chamber of Commerce.

The Better Business Bureau of New York City maintains two separate organizations, the Advisory Council of the Merchandise Section, which deals with every sort of unfair practice resorted to by merchants and advertisers in New York City, and the Advisory Council of the Investor's Section, which deals with questionable practices connected with the sale of securities and other investments. The control which this powerful organization exercises depends for the most part upon the following factors:

"(1) Facts developed by its own investigations, revealing practices which business men themselves feel to be wrong and which they have corrected voluntarily upon request by the Bureau.

"(2) Recommendation of sound standards for advertising and selling, both as to fundamental principles and as to particular situations in principal trades.

" (3) The weight of public opinion invoked when and if necessary against persistent violators of truth and fair dealing.

"(4) The control exercised by newspapers for the protection of their readers and advertisers, wherein they decline to publish advertising which is found to mislead the public and/or is reasonably held to be unfair to competitors.

"(5) Tested State and Federal laws and regulatory ordinances of the city." [9]

Complaints as to questionable treatment by New York City business men may be lodged directly with the Better Business Bureau by customers or by competitors who feel that they have been unfairly treated. The Bureau maintains an extensive staff of investigators who proceed with dispatch to check up on the merits of the complaint. When an investigation, which may include such practical methods as the photographing of a show window with objectionable advertising material on display, unearths evidence of unfair practice, the Bureau descends upon the offending merchant with

[9] *The Voluntary Work of New York City Business in Developing Fair Advertising and Selling Practices*, pp. 4–5.

its evidence and brings pressure to bear to have the practice eliminated, corrections made, and in many instances, restitution effected.

Using these methods, the Bureau has been conspicuously successful in handling many types of cases. It deals impartially with the small and with the large offenders, and has upon occasion carried on a lengthy and vigorous offensive against the largest department store in the world.[10]

Fake sales, fake reductions in prices, the misrepresentation or misdescription of fabrics, furs and the like, have been eliminated in hundreds of cases through the activities of the Bureau. Frauds of all kinds are investigated and checked either by pressure brought by the Bureau, by merciless publicity, or, where these measures fail, by an appeal to the law.

The following extract from *Members' News Bulletin No. 103* of The Better Business Bureau of New York City, dated September 22, 1936, will indicate how the work of the bureau is conducted:

> "Continuing his campaign against false and misleading advertising, under Section 421 of the Penal Law (The Printers' Ink Model Statute), William C. Dodge, District Attorney of New York County, through his assistant, James J. Wilson, has achieved another conviction.
>
> "This was against Erwin S. Dayan, proprietor of The Fifth Avenue Linen Corner, 417 Fifth Avenue, at 38th Street, who was charged with falsely advertising cotton handkerchiefs as linen. The Better Business Bureau made numerous purchases at the store. The specific ones on which the prosecution was based, were the purchase of men's handkerchiefs at 19¢ each, represented by a window card as linen, which were actually cotton; and men's handkerchiefs at 16¢ each, advertised as 'French Linen,' which were cotton.
>
> "Dayan was found guilty in the Court of Special Sessions, following trial on September 14th and 15th, 1936, . . . [and] was sentenced to pay a fine of $500.00 or be committed to the City Prison for sixty days.

The Indianapolis Better Business Bureau will serve as an illustration of what is being done in some of our smaller cities. This Bureau consists of approximately 400 business concerns, representing some fifty lines of business, which finance the work through private subscriptions. Twenty-one directors from eighteen different lines of business serve without compensation in controlling the operations of

[10] See the records of the Bureau's campaign against the "6% less" claim of R. H. Macy & Co.

the Bureau in the fields of advertising-merchandising, consumers' complaints, financial inquiry, and consumer information.

Among its more specific functions the Indianapolis Bureau reports the checking of questionable advertising statements upon complaint from competitors, from customers, or upon its own initiative; the testing of fabrics and the careful identification of fabrics, furs and other commodities of whose character and qualities the consuming public is likely to be ignorant; the investigation and control of trick merchandizing schemes, such as lotteries; education in regard to the laws which apply to particular types of retailing; the issuance of warnings to the public against new "rackets" or dangerous or fake drug products; thorough investigation of and publication of information on fraudulent investment schemes and other financial "rackets", and many other services as well. Among other activities the Bureau in 1935 listed 99 investment or selling "rackets" which had been used in Indianapolis over a short period of time, and which had been either destroyed or at least curbed by the quick attack and merciless publicity to which they were subjected by the Bureau.

In the course of an interpretation of its aims this Bureau says:

> "The Better Business Bureau is founded, and its operations are based, upon the premise that such practices destroy public confidence; that they cause definite monetary loss to business by increasing the sales expense; that they build up sales resistance which is costly to overcome; that they damage and sometimes destroy investments in advertising; that they divert business inequitably and unfairly to those who through their use of such practices do not deserve it; that business is stagnated in proportion as the business dollar is diverted into crooked business or fraudulent schemes which are uneconomic and non-productive; that business has a right to act in self-defense through its agent, the Better Business Bureau, when faced with the possibility of such damage." [11]

The frank recognition of the fact that the operations of the Better Business Bureaus are largely dictated by considerations of self-interest does not in any way invalidate the sincerity of the movement or warrant the suggestion that the Bureaus have a tendency to move in a case only when that course appears to be temporarily profitable to their members. It supplies rather an intense and a continuing moti-

[11] *The Indianapolis Better Business Bureau.* Published by the Bureau, 1935, p. 3.

vation to "clean house", and offers the public considerable assurance that honest business men will continue to do what they can to rid their fields of unscrupulous competitors. If this process, while defending the public interests, at the same time makes business easier and more profitable for the worthy survivors, this is in any case no more than the ideal result of all methods of fair competition, which tend, as we have shown elsewhere, continually to shift the business of society, together with its rewards, into the hands of those who are best fitted to perform it. It is one of the natural characteristics of perfectly free competition that enlightened self-interest normally proceeds towards social betterment. If business men have advanced far enough in the scale of social and moral evolution to discover the fact that fair treatment of the consumers upon whom they depend for business is essential to continued success, a greater and a more permanent benefit has been won than can ever be gained by attempts to dictate to them courses of action which they do not understand and cannot appreciate, and which, as often as not, the reigning reform politician of the moment, with the hurried and experimental draft of a new bill in his hand, understands no better than they.

It is the power of the Bureau to act with extreme dispatch and its willingness to shoulder responsibility for an attack, even under threat of suits for fabulous damages, that make the Better Business Bureau a far more efficient contributor to the destruction of illegitimate business methods than the direct appeal to the law itself. While the law may be available to the citizen in one sense, it is not available in another. The amounts involved are frequently too small to justify a law suit, the court action would in any case be extremely slow, and innumerable new victims might be caught during the progress of the trial; while any concerted attempt on the part of the numerous victims to appeal to the courts would bury the latter under an avalanche of business. The Bureau, on the other hand, can descend upon the issuer of an unfair or an untrue advertisement with such rapidity that the objectionable copy can be withdrawn from the next issue of the newspaper or periodical which had been carrying it. Furthermore it has the advantage of a long period of experience in investigation and in the handling of such court cases as it finds it necessary to undertake. Moreover, the proceedings are carried on entirely at the expense of the business men or of the public prosecutor of the community. Because the actual and prospective victims of the frauds are never asked to contribute anything more than the record of their own experience with the grafter in question they are not able to complain that "justice would be all right if it didn't cost so much".

It is true that the Better Business Bureau movement still exists in a somewhat rudimentary form, though many of the local units are well articulated, exceedingly active, and far beyond the experimental stage. But there are only fifty-four local bureaus in a country which has ninety-eight cities with over 100,000 population, and many more cities with a sufficient volume of business to support at least a part time committee devoting its energies to this service. Such a group might contribute more to their communities and more to the standing of their business or profession in the community than they can contribute through many of the other social activities which they so zealously pursue. With the growing realization of this opportunity for usefulness it is to be hoped that business men will continue to organize new units of this type until the country is adequately served.

The Luncheon Clubs

Conspicuous among the organizations which business men have developed for the purpose of establishing high standards in the commercial world are the semi-fraternal limited membership luncheon clubs. Some of these have inaugurated notable educational programs which have had a marked effect upon certain parts of the business world.

Crawford McCullough, after his election as President of the International Association of Rotary Clubs in 1921, said,

> "I feel that it is high time that Rotary should get back to first principles and assert itself in terms of a continuing program of individual and group service, through the medium of vocation. If Rotary can develop a program which will encourage and foster high ethical standards in business and professions through a long continuing program, it will provide the medium for a great service to the business world." [12]

[12] *Codes of Standards of Correct Practice.* Rotary International, 1931.

At that time a campaign was inaugurated, the aim of which was a written code of standards of correct practices for each state, provincial, or national craft association. Various trade associations had had "codes" at earlier periods, but Rotary aimed at "complete coverage". An adequate code was described as one dealing with the principal business relationships: (a) That between employer and employee; (b) That between the craftsman and those from whom he purchases; (c) That with fellow craftsmen; (d) That with the general public and with the government; and (e) That with patrons and prospective customers. Fairness has thus been conceived of in its broadest possible aspects. The campaign was a practical one, with five definite stages of development. (1) A development among business men of interest in higher ethical standards, leading to a desire for standardization of business conduct on a high plane; (2) The actual writing and adoption of written codes; (3) Educational campaigns conducted by the craft associations for the purpose of inducing conformity to the craft standards on the part of the membership; (4) The establishment of some type of coercive measures to compel the observance of craft standards by those engaged in the vocation concerned; and (5) International standardization of business practices made by combining two or more provincial or national codes into one composite whole. The close parallel between these early aims and those which were developed under the NIRA will be noticed. Rotary International claims to have had a part in the adoption of more than two hundred separate codes of fair practice, and both directly and indirectly to have exercised a strong influence in the preparation of the codes which were finally completed under NIRA. Educational work on business standards has been more or less generally carried on by all local clubs for many years, a suggested minimum of time to be devoted to this particular type of work having been set at four meetings per year. Because Rotary is a purely voluntary and private organization the establishment of coercive measures to compel the observance of the standards which it favors proved to lie beyond its power; so that its influence remains almost exclusively educational.

Other major luncheon clubs have similar aims. The statement of objects of the Lions Clubs contains the following: "To encourage efficiency and promote high ethical standards in business and professions; provided that no club shall hold out as one of its objects financial benefits to its members". The Constitution of Kiwanis International describes as one of the objects of the association, "To promote the adoption and the application of higher social, business, and professional standards". The program presented by its Committee on Business Standards in 1935 contained the following five recommendations:

(1) That each club educate its members in regard to the officially approved statement of Kiwanis Business Standards.

(2) That each club during the year devote some program to the subject of business and professional standards and related topics.

(3) That each club urge its members to study existing business and professional codes and to use their leadership in trade and professional groups to improve existing statements of standards or codes or to assist in the drafting and adoption of such where none exist.

(4) That each club promote on the part of its members or in coöperation with other organizations round table discussions of unfair trade practices.

(5) That each club urge the schools of its community to provide addresses on business standards and practices and that each club offer its members as speakers on such topics.

Most of the other service clubs have similar statements in their literature which show that they regard the improvement of current business standards as an integral part of their program of action.

The extent to which the Service Clubs attain these objectives varies no doubt with the character of the membership in the individual clubs and with the interest and vigor of their leaders. In general, these organizations have undoubtedly made a significant contribution to the improvement of business morals, and have done much to bring "business" nearer the status of a profession. When it is recalled that there are in excess of 7,500 regularly organized service clubs with a membership exceeding 300,000 in the United States alone,[13] and

[13] A letter from Chesley Perry, Secretary of Rotary International, November 29, 1935, placed the number of Rotary Clubs in the United States at 2,503, with an aggregate membership of 109,350. The world membership was placed at 163,000 in 3,883 clubs.

A letter from Melvin Jones, Secretary-General of Lions International, November

that the membership is for the most part made up of the leaders in their respective fields, it will be obvious that this remarkable movement can accomplish, if it will, an enormous amount of good.

Moreover, there seems to be no question but that the members of a given organization tend to divest themselves of questionable practices, in dealing with each other, whether they happen to be interested individually in the club's codes of conduct or not. The strong pressure brought to bear to force the development of good fellowship certainly serves as a powerful deterrent to unfraternal business dealings and so quite justifies itself.

In the earlier days of these organizations there was some evidence that the brotherly spirit did not extend much beyond the confines of the club itself. There existed, in fact, a definite tendency for members to trade only with other members wherever possible (a custom which it would be impossible to work into any theory of fair competition). But with maturity and increasing size and dignity these adolescent habits seem to have been largely outgrown; so that today the Service Clubs must be described as influential groups of business men who are a real force in maintaining decent standards among business men.

While the only coercion which the Service Clubs can bring to bear to enforce their standards is that of social pressure, it must be observed that this pressure can be very effective upon occasion. In a Midwestern city of about 60,000 people several consumers protested to a member of one of the service clubs that one of his fellow members was following the practice of displaying a different quality of merchandise in his windows from that which he actually offered for sale in his shop, and was trying to utilize the old trick of "switching". The member with whom the protests had been lodged took with him two other members of the Club for a private conversation with the offending member. The protests having been found justified, the offending

---

26, 1935, placed the number of Lions Clubs at 2,723, with an aggregate membership in excess of 80,000.

At the end of 1935 the number of Kiwanis Clubs exceeded 1,900, with membership in excess of 90,000.

Other membership figures are Gyro, 3,000; Optimists, 6,000; and American Business Clubs, 1,500.

Local groups with no national affiliations swell the total considerably.

merchant was informed that unless he stopped the practice immediately his activities would be brought up for discussion and consideration before his fellows in the organization. This warning carried such weight to a merchant who was proud of his association with a group of the most reputable business men in the city that he mended his ways immediately, and the objectionable practice was thus eliminated without any legal or public action of any kind.

Consumers' Leagues

Consumers' Leagues are organizations, not of business men, but of the consumers who are served by them. They represent quite a different angle of approach to the problem of raising business standards from any that we have examined thus far. It has been pointed out elsewhere in this volume that competition can normally be fair only when it is enlightened competition; that is to say, when both parties to the transaction understand all of the conditions surrounding it. Where prices or terms of sale or conditions of employment have been the result of the most vicious kinds of exploitation many citizens might revolt against taking advantage of them, if aware of the facts. But in a complex marketing system such as ours, where the source of goods is seldom known and where goods produced by exploitation can not be differentiated on the shelves or on the display counters from those produced under proper conditions, customers buy without the knowledge which might temper strictly economic judgments with moral considerations. Some states require that special labels be attached to all prison made goods, to enable customers to distinguish between them and the products of free labor; but no state is likely to require a manufacturer to mark his products in such a way as to show whether he has treated his employees or his competitors fairly or not.

The principle upon which the Consumers' Leagues were founded is perfectly clear. If it is wrong for a business man to create a bargain by unfair means, it is wrong for the informed consumer to take advantage of such a bargain and to encourage the continuance of such practices by lending financial support through purchases. The organizers of the movement appreciated the fact that it was impossible for most consumers to know anything about the conditions under which goods or services were supplied to them; and understanding that the consumers *must* know these things, if they are to exercise the simplest moral judgments in these fields, they set about to organize agencies for supplying the necessary information.

The Consumers' Leagues, both local and national, have been almost exclusively organizations of women interested in the problems of women in industry; and they have consequently confined their activities largely to the trades in which women are particularly interested either as buyers or as employees, notably the department stores, the needle trades generally, and, to some extent, the manufacture of food and the operation of hotels and restaurants. Their first attack was upon conditions in the department stores in New York City. Their investigations convinced them that in many of these stores the women employees were being treated unfairly, with low pay, long hours, inadequate hygienic and rest facilities, and inhuman rules concerning conduct when on duty. Legal restrictions prevented them from publishing uncomplimentary data or from actively organizing a boycott; so they adopted the procedure of publishing a so-called "White List", which included the names of all those stores which had been investigated and which had been found to come up to a standard of employee treatment which they considered to be a reasonable minimum. The effect of the movement in immediately changing conditions in many large stores and eventually improving them in all was enormous. The work of the Consumers' Leagues gave the first impetus to the development which has brought personnel work in most of the large department stores in the United States to a very high level indeed.

But the beneficial effects of this enlightening movement were not limited to the employees alone. More far reaching, perhaps, was the training which the movement gave to thousands of women in the recognition of the fact that the customer has his share of responsibility for the maintenance of fair competitive practices, and that this responsibility can be adequately discharged only by complete and unvarying refusal to deal with an unfair or crooked business man, even when refusal to deal with him means the loss of a bargain. To the person of normal moral perceptions who is aware of what he is doing, the decision to forego a bargain which he knows is the product of another's partial or complete destruction represents no great sacrifice. Just how great a reservoir of moral earnestness lies waiting to be tapped by this process of education in the actual facts of the market we do not know. But we have some evidence of the pressure at which it will flow when it is released and properly directed in the response which thousands of women made to the early "White Lists" of the New York Consumers' League, and in the voluntary boycotts which women and other buyers have effected, entirely without formal organization, against the products of foreign nations which have indulged in what they consider to be unfair and unreasonable racial discrimination. Without question, when adequate agencies for distributing information are available, we may expect that the reasonable citizen will exercise his moral judgments as well as his arithmetical judgments as to price, and by so doing clear the ground of much bad business through the destruction of its markets.

The Consumers' Leagues are, of course, only a start in this direction. Other social agencies contribute something to the movement, but not much. A broader development, enlisting the interests of women in every city and leading to a keener appreciation by average consumers of the conditions and forces which lie behind the things which they so casually buy at the counters or order over their telephones would be a long step forward toward the moral millennium in American business.

CHAPTER XIX

SOCIAL CONTROL THROUGH GOVERNMENTAL AGENCIES

Governmental agencies for the repression of crime, the enforcement of contracts, and the protection of the community against certain kinds of fraud, have existed for so many centuries that they are now taken for granted. But over and above the traditional services of the criminal and civil courts and their organs, the government of the United States has in comparatively recent years created certain agencies and introduced certain devices intended to protect business men and consumers against business wrongs.

The most important and otherwise significant of these newer agencies is undoubtedly the Federal Trade Commission. The principles which underlie its activities, and the methods by which its results are obtained seem worthy of a brief description. Our account of its work will be supplemented by a sketch of the legislation adopted by the State of Wisconsin with a view to initiating a still more comprehensive program along the same lines.

The Federal Trade Commission

The Jurisdiction and Powers of the Commission. The Federal Trade Commission was created by the Federal Trade Commission Act in September, 1914. Under this act the Commission was apparently given rather broad powers. Section 5 reads:

> "Unfair methods of competition in commerce are hereby declared unlawful.
>
> "The Commission is hereby empowered and directed to prevent persons, partnerships, or corporations, except banks and common carriers subject to the acts to regulate commerce, from using unfair methods of competition in commerce."

In addition, the Commission was entrusted with the enforcement of four provisions of the Clayton Act, which was also passed in 1914.

These provisions prohibit the following practices:—(1) Any discrimination in prices which substantially lessens competition or tends to create a monopoly in any line of commerce; (2) The refusal to sell goods to one who deals in the products of a competitor or the granting of special rebates on condition that a customer refuse to deal with a competitor, where the effects may be to substantially lessen competition; (3) The acquisition of the stock of one corporation by another where the effect of the acquisition may be to substantially lessen competition; and (4) The holding of simultaneous directorships in two or more directly competing corporations by one person.[1]

The procedure of the Commission is marked by the greatest flexibility. Only the most informal notice of the existence of questionable practices is necessary to start an investigation. If the Commission is able to determine that the practice complained of is carried on in interstate commerce, if it is satisfied that it comes under the jurisdiction of Section 5 of the Federal Trade Commission Act or the appropriate sections of the Clayton Act, and if it believes that the prosecution of a complaint would be in the public interest, it can investigate the facts and, by a well standardized method of procedure, go on to make a report and issue an order requiring the respondent to cease and desist from the practices in question.

The Commission has no power to assess penalties for failure to observe its orders, but if they are not obeyed it may apply to a United States circuit court of appeals for a review of the order, after which, if it is sustained, the respondent is subject to the jurisdiction of the court and can be disciplined by it.

The power of the Commission to eliminate what it considers to be unfair methods of competition is thus measured by the extent to which the courts agree with it in its interpretation of the term. The broad and vague powers granted under Section 5 of the Federal Trade Commission Act have offered the Commission a free hand in selecting fields for its investigations; and its history may be described as one of experiment in which it has ventured into field after field in an effort to determine just where it would be permitted to operate.

The Senate Committee which reported on the Act apparently wished to allow the Commission considerable latitude in this respect.

[1] Sections, 2, 3, 7, and 8.

"The Committee gave careful consideration to the question as to whether it would attempt to define the many and variable unfair practices which prevail in commerce and to forbid their continuance or whether it would, by a general declaration condemning unfair practices, leave it to the commission to determine what practices were unfair. It concluded that the latter course would be the better, for the reason, as stated by one of the representatives of the Illinois Manufacturers' Association, that there were too many unfair practices to define, and after writing 20 of them into the law it would be quite possible to invent others." [2]

The Commission, however, was not left to roam over the field of business conduct and select for slaughter whatever appealed to it as wrong. Since its decisions are subject to review by the federal courts, it can accomplish nothing in the way of repression except within limits imposed by these courts. As a matter of fact those of its decisions which have been allowed to stand cover only such transactions as the courts had already placed under their ban.[3] The hope which many persons at one time entertained that the establishment of the Commission would lead to the elimination of objectionable business practices which the courts had never made any attempt to suppress, was thus doomed from the outset to disappointment. Furthermore, as provided in the Federal Trade Commission Act itself, all proceedings must be in the public interest. This enactment "prevents the Commission from becoming a clearing house to settle the everyday quarrels of competitors, free from detriment to the public, which should be adjusted through the ordinary processes of the courts".[4]

Finally an injury to some competitor or competitors must be shown. What this means is illustrated by the action of the courts in Raladam Co. *v.* the Commission. This company markets an obesity cure called Marmola. The active agency in this drug is a thyroid extract. Much evidence was offered to show that the use of this preparation was likely to be dangerous to health except as taken under the direction of a competent physician. As usual the experts differed. But regardless of this fact, the Circuit Court of Appeals and the United States Supreme Court dismissed the case on the ground that

2 *Senate Report* No. 597, 63rd Cong., second session, p. 13 (June 13, 1914).

3 Federal Trade Commission *v.* Gratz, 253 U.S. 427 (1920), reprinted in *Federal Trade Commission Decisions,* II (1920), 564.

4 L. B. Silver Co. *v.* Federal Trade Commission, 289 Fed. 985 (1923), reprinted in *Federal Trade Commission Decisions*, VI (1925), 559.

the Commission had failed to show that the business of any competitor had been injured by its advertisements or by its sale.[5]

However this decision is not so far reaching in its effects as might appear at first sight. For in Federal Trade Commission *v.* Winsted Hosiery Co. the Supreme Court of the United States declared that misrepresentation of goods which deceived customers was a wrong committed not merely against them as consumers but also against honest competitors.

> "For when misbranded goods attract customers by means of the fraud which they perpetrate, trade is diverted from the producer of truthfully marked goods. That these honest manufacturers might protect their trade by also resorting to deceptive labels is no defense to this proceeding brought against the Winsted Co. in the public interest."[6]

The chief function of the Commission is thus the suppression of the more generally recognized forms of unfair competition. It is at liberty to make any investigations into the facts which it may consider desirable, and to avail itself of any information which may come into its hands from whatever source. When it finds a case of what it regards as unfair competition, it may order the delinquent organization to cease and desist from the practice in question. If this order is not complied with, the matter is then turned over to the courts, as described above, p. 270.

The Trade Practice Conference. Early in the history of the Commission it became apparent that an unfair method of competition was seldom the unique possession of one business man, and that certain unfair practices tended to become more or less standard throughout an industry. The prosecution of individual cases against each of the many operators in such a field was a needlessly laborious and expensive method of control. Moreover, it was soon discovered that the nature of the unfair practices was sufficiently understood and appreciated by practically all of the members of the group, and that

[5] *Federal Trade Commission Decisions,* XII (1930), 363; Fed. Ct. of Appeals, 42 Fed., new series, 430 (1930), reprinted in *Federal Trade Commission Decisions,* XIV (1931), 683; 283 U.S. 648 (1930), reprinted in *Federal Trade Commission Decisions,* XV (1933), 598.

[6] Federal Trade Commission *v.* Winsted Hosiery Co., 258 U.S. 483 (1922), reprinted in *Federal Trade Commission Decisions,* IV (1923), 610. Cf. Federal Trade Commission *v.* Keppel & Bro., 291 U.S. 304 (1933), reprinted in *Federal Trade Commission Decisions,* XVIII (1935), 684.

they were resorted to by most business men simply as a measure of self-defense which they believed they could not well abandon unless they could be given some assurance that their competitors would do likewise. Frequently a relatively small proportion of the membership in the industry was insistent upon the perpetuation of the practice in question; and so, on the principle that "one rotten apple can spoil a barrel" they were able to contaminate the entire field.

The invention of the particular procedure which the Commission calls the Trade Practice Conference offered a method by which industries could be cleaned up at wholesale rather than at retail.

The Trade Practice Conference is a purely voluntary assembly, meeting on the initiative of either an industrial group or of the Commission, at which questionable practices are discussed in open meeting. Where the vote shows substantial unanimity of opinion as to the undesirability of any of these practices, a formal report, embodying these conclusions, is drawn up for submission to the Commission. This report is subject to modification by the Commission, and reaches its final form only when so worded as to be acceptable to both parties. A copy is thereupon presented to each member of the industry and he is expected to sign an agreement to observe its provisions. Such agreements are kept on file with the Commission.

There is no compulsion in the process, but an overwhelming majority of the members of an industry usually submit without reservation to the rulings of the conference. They become a pledge to each member that, if he will conduct his business in a fair and honorable way, his associates will do likewise. This is sufficient to keep most business men in line, and the signed agreements and the exercise of the normal powers of the Commission take care of the rest.

Upon occasion the rulings of a conference are given the authority of law. In California, for instance, where a Trade Practice Conference dealing with certain evils in the dairy business was held, the director of agriculture of the state is given power to revoke the license of any dairy produce exchange which is guilty of "violation of any . . . rules of the Federal Trade Commission governing unfair trade practices in the handling of butter, cheese, and/or eggs".

The success of the conference method and the nature of the discussions leading up to the adoption of the rules enable us to draw several very interesting conclusions with respect to American business men in general. They have made it apparent that business men understand the unfair nature of many of their practices as well as or better than the public bodies appointed to control them. Moreover, the majority everywhere are sincerely desirous of eliminating them from their part of the business world. Honest individuals, merely as individuals, however, can not purge an industry; and in many cases can not, or at any rate believe they can not refuse to take advantage of the prevailing practices if they wish to remain in the field. While a rigorous application of the principles of morality might require them to desert an occupation in which unfair methods of competition were necessary, they find it difficult to see what public interest could be served by leaving the field entirely in the hands of the wolves. As a result they have been unwillingly continuing in the old ways, feeling it essential to the preservation of their business, but looking constantly for a means of escape.

The necessity for coöperation on the part of the honest and public-spirited business men in ridding their fields of the relatively few individuals who devise unfair practices and insist upon maintaining the conditions which perpetuate them has always been obvious. Something more than coöperation, however, seems to have been necessary; and it was not until the government lent the weight of its authority to back up the honest men that the movement was conspicuously successful. The Trade Practice Conference, as a kind of partnership between government and business, performs the double duty of protecting the honest competitor against the dishonest, and of protecting the public interests. The success of this method of control offers some hope that the business man's cry of "Keep the government out of business" and "Let business clean its own house" may yet come to have some meaning in America. The Conferences have been successful to an extent which the Trade Association activities directed toward the same end have never approached, and the part played by the government has been so inoffensive and unobtrusive that industry itself has been glad to accept its help.

Up to the end of June, 1935, more than 150 industries had adopted codes of fair competition at Trade Practice Conferences of the type just described; and for the fiscal year ending June 30, 1935, but 34 complaints of alleged violations of rules came through.[7] It should be understood that these codes have been taken far more seriously by the members of the industry than had similar earlier codes drawn up by the Trade Associations themselves. The small number of violations is explained by this fact.

A reading of the rules contained in many of the codes will reveal that a larger number of them deal with prohibitions of illegal acts. Thus the Annual Report of the Federal Trade Commission for the fiscal year ending June 30, 1934 says:

> "Among trade practices which have been discontinued as a result of trade-practice conferences are the following: False and misleading advertising, commercial bribery, use of marked-up or fictitious prices, imitation of trade-marks or other identifying marks of competitors, deviation from established standards of an industry by deceptive means or devices, selling of goods below cost with the intent and effect of injuring a competitor, price discrimination where the effect may be to substantially lessen competition or tend to create a monopoly, false marking or branding of products, secret payment or allowance of rebates, defamation of competitors, and shipping or delivering products which do not conform to samples submitted."

In this brief recital acts prohibited by the Clayton Act will be recognized, as well as various others for which an injured party would appear to have adequate remedy at law. Nevertheless, the inclusion of these prohibitions in a well recognized code which has been publicized throughout the industry is by no means waste motion. It vastly increases the probability that the prohibition will be effective, and at the same time frequently releases the honest man from the expense, labor, and uncertainties involved in protecting himself and society through an appeal to the courts.

Settlement of Cases by Stipulation. Another semi-formal procedure adopted by the Federal Trade Commission in its attempt to protect consumers and honest competitors from a wide variety of unfair practices has been the settlement of cases through stipulations. The business organization against which complaints have been rendered, when confronted by the evidence collected by the Commission, is given the opportunity of voluntarily agreeing to abandon the practices in question in preference to facing a formal trial by a court. If

[7] *Annual Report, Federal Trade Commission,* 1935, p. 93.

the organization decides to do so it signs an agreement to "cease and desist", and the Commission retains this agreement with the understanding that should the organization resume the practices, the facts as agreed in the stipulation may be used against it in legal proceedings. This has proved to be an extraordinarily economical method of handling complaints, and has undoubtedly made it possible for the Commission to dispose satisfactorily of a much larger amount of work than it could otherwise have done.

Since the function of the Commission is regulatory and prohibitive rather than punitive, and since the public interest and the interest of competitors are suitably served by the abandonment of unfair methods, this particular procedure may be looked upon as in all respects as useful as that involving formal trial. The efficiency of the Commission is greatly increased by confining this procedure to the less important types of cases and leaving the more formal procedure to the more serious offences where the incidental publicity is in itself one of the important deterrents from future misconduct.

The stipulation system, on June 30, 1935, had been in effect for nine and one half years, during which period 2,257 stipulations had been approved and accepted by the Commission. Of this group 37.2% related to false and misleading advertising, while the remainder covered a wide and varied field.[8]

Special Board of Investigation. While the general run of complaints dealing with unfair practices is handled by the Commission through its Chief Trial Examiner, a tremendous increase in the volume of complaints in the field of advertising led, in 1929, to the establishment of a Special Board of Investigation to deal with this particular evil. This Board gives special attention to newspaper, magazine, and radio advertising. While these cases are not regarded as distinct from the rest of the work of the Commission, this special method of handling them has been adopted in order that the Commission might take advantage of the increased efficiency which comes with specialization in this troublesome field. Suspected misrepresentation is carefully investigated and where actual misrepresentation is found orders to cease and desist are issued, unless the case can be settled by stipulation. In a majority of instances the stipulation

[8] *Annual Report,* 1935; p. 51.

method is sufficient. While certain publications must be continually scrutinized with great care "it is found unnecessary to review all the issues of publications of high ethical standard where the publishers carefully censor all copy before acceptance".[9]

In the scrutiny of radio broadcasting, national and regional networks weekly submit copies of all commercial continuities for programs wherein linked hook-ups involving two or more affiliated or member stations are used. Other stations and electrical transcriptions are checked or sampled by other methods. This service was started July 1, 1934 and up to June 30, 1935, 459,253 continuities had been received by the Commission. Of these, 376,539 had been reviewed, and 38,873, or 10.5 per cent of the whole, were referred for investigation as being possibly false or misleading. Wherever possible, cases in this field are settled by stipulation, the orders of the commission being invariably directed towards telling the advertisers what they may *not* say, and in no case making any suggestions as to what they *should* say.

Other Duties of the Federal Trade Commission. In great measure the Federal Trade Commission has taken over the regulation of anti-trust developments which had been previously vested in the old Bureau of Corporations. In addition to these duties and to its duty to prevent unfair practices in interstate commerce, it is required under the act to investigate alleged violations of the anti-trust laws, upon the request of either branch of Congress, the President, or the Attorney General, in addition to such inquiries as it may make upon its own initiative, and to report its findings to the proper authorities. It is also saddled with the administration of the Export Trade Act, usually known as the "Webb-Pomerene law", which grants exemption from the anti-trust laws to export combines or associations under certain conditions. Finally it has been entrusted with the administration of the Securities Act, and from 1933 to 1935 was required to make such investigations as might be necessary to enable the President to carry out the provisions of the National Industrial Recovery Act.

To a considerable extent all of these duties lead the Commission to a broad consideration of the whole field of fair competition. The various investigations, of which eighty-seven are listed in the Annual

[9] *Annual Report*, 1935; p. 102.

Report for 1935, have been very closely associated, for the most part, with problems of fair competition, or they have helped to establish a background of information against which the Commission could proceed with more confidence in preventing unfair practices. But the loading of so many responsibilities upon the Commission could not fail to have the effect of dissipating its energies and limiting its power to prevent specific evils. The duties confided to it are all of the highest degree of importance, and it is entirely appropriate that they should be undertaken by experts; but if the energies of the Commission are gradually led away from the direct attack upon unfair methods of competition by the pressure of these other duties, a great opportunity for good will have been lost.

Important as have been the direct effects of the Commission's activities, the indirect effects have doubtless been even greater. It has wakened the thoughtless, provided guidance for the perplexed, strengthened the hands of the honorable, and educated thousands of business men to a more complete recognition of their obligations to their fellows.

The Wisconsin Plan

Once the Federal Trade Commission had demonstrated its effectiveness, a number of states adopted legislation which, under their Departments of Markets, granted powers over intrastate commerce substantially equivalent to those of the Federal Trade Commission over interstate commerce. Wisconsin has carried this type of legislation farther than any other state. Today it is attacking the problem of the elimination of unfair trade practices with a new plan and with a new commission to administer it.

The failure of the NRA in a field where improvement was so obviously needed doubtless had some influence on this development, but it was by no means the only force at work. The Wisconsin Marketing Law of 1927 contained the following provisions:

"99.14 Methods of Competition and Trade Practices. (1) Methods of competition in business and trade practices in business shall be fair. Unfair methods of competition in business and unfair trade practices in business are hereby prohibited.

"(2) The Department [of Markets], after public hearing, may issue general orders forbidding methods of competition in business or trade practices in business which are determined by the department to be unfair. The Department, after public hearing, may issue general orders prescribing methods of competition in business or trade practices in business which are determined by the department to be unfair.

"(3) The department, after public hearing, may issue a special order against any person, enjoining such person from employing any method of competition in business or trade practice in business which is determined by the department to be unfair. The department, after public hearing, may issue a special order against any person, requiring such person to employ the method of competition in business or trade practice in business which is determined by the department to be fair.

"99.15 Damage for Violation. Any person who shall suffer pecuniary loss because of a violation by any other person of any order issued under section 99.14 may sue such person for damages thereof in any court of competent jurisdiction and shall recover twice the amount of such pecuniary loss, together with costs, including a reasonable attorney's fee.

"99.16 Distribution Methods and Practices. (1) The methods of distribution and practices in the distribution of food products and fuel shall be free from needless waste and needless duplication which tend to increase the cost of such products to the consuming public. Methods of distribution and practices in the distribution of food products and fuel, wherever such waste or duplication tends to increase the costs of such products to the consuming public, are hereby prohibited.

"(2) The department, after public hearing, may issue general orders forbidding methods of distribution or practices in distribution which are found by the department to cause waste or duplication as defined herein. The department, after public hearing, may issue general orders prescribing methods of distribution or practices in distribution which are found by the department to avoid waste or duplication as defined herein.

"(3) The department, after public hearing, may issue a special order against any person, enjoining such person from employing any method of distribution or practice in distribution which is found by the department to cause waste or duplication as defined herein. The department, after public hearing, may issue a special order against any person requiring such person to employ the method of distribution or practice in distribution which is found by the department to avoid waste or duplication as defined herein."

It will be observed that the powers granted to the Department of Markets in Wisconsin are somewhat broader than those granted to the Federal Trade Commission. Where the Federal Trade Commission is limited to the consideration of unfair methods of competition, the Department of Markets of Wisconsin is permitted to define both unfair and fair methods and to enforce the employment of the latter. In practice, however, the work of the Wisconsin Department has been largely prohibitory. It has believed that such advantages as we may hope to achieve from our system of competitive business would result largely from the freedom of the individual to experiment with new methods of production, distribution, and exchange; and that, within very broad limits, a business organization, individual or corporate in form, ought to be allowed to attempt such new methods as it wishes. Social interests, it was convinced, would be adequately served by the prohibition of all methods which were definitely known to be detrimental.

The cases dealt with under this legislation since 1927 have been similar to those dealt with by the Federal Trade Commission. The Biennial Reports of the Department of Markets disclose a large number of typical evils, such as misrepresentation in advertising special sales, false disparagement of competitors, unfair price discrimination, inducing breach of contract, conspiracies to injure competitors, exclusive dealing devices, and the like.

Despite reasonable success in administering these laws the disappearance of the NRA was the signal for improved legislation specifically designed to avoid the errors and legal pitfalls into which the federal administration had fallen. The Wisconsin Recovery Act of 1935 contains among others the following provisions:

"110.04 Codes of Fair Competition and Trade Practices. (1) (a) Methods of competition in business and trade practices shall be fair. Unfair methods of competition in business and unfair trade practices in business are hereby prohibited. The governor is hereby vested with the power and jurisdiction and it shall be his duty to investigate, ascertain, declare and prescribe reasonable codes or standards of fair competition and trade practices for the various trades and industries in the state in which the competition is essentially and preponderantly intrastate or for certain trade areas within the state, and to make reasonable classifications of persons, employments and standards of fair competition and trade practices in such business. In determining trade areas the proximity thereof to state lines shall be taken into consideration. Such codes or standards of fair competition and trade practices shall be prescribed and approved by the governor after such reasonable public notice and hearing as he shall specify, and if he finds (1) that such code or codes are not designed to promote monopolies or to eliminate or oppress small enterprises and will not operate to discriminate against them and will tend to effectuate the policy of this chapter, and (2) that such code or codes are not inequitable and that the interests of the consumers and the general public will be protected, and (3) that such code is necessary for the stabilization of the intrastate business of such trade or industry. The governor may, as a condition of approval of any such code, impose such conditions (including the requirement for the making of reports and the keeping of accounts) for the protection of consumers, competitors, employees and others, and in the furtherance of the public interest, and may provide such exceptions to and exemptions from the provisions of such code as the governor in his discretion deems necessary to effectuate the policy declared in this chapter. In case of a conflict between a provision of this chapter or a code approved hereunder and a statute administered by the public service commission of Wisconsin, or a lawful order thereunder, the latter shall prevail, provided, however, that the provisions of this chapter shall not apply to owners and operators of trucks in the hauling of farm products, produce or supplies to or from the farm. Licensed hotels and the trades or businesses operated in connection therewith, and trades or industries selling, installing or servicing more than one line of merchandise or service shall for the purpose of this chapter be considered as one trade or industry, and be subject to the code approved for said hotel or industry, provided, however, that barber shops wherever operated shall be subject to the code for the barber industry.

"(b) Upon the approval of any such code covering any trade or industry or subdivision thereof, all persons, firms or corporations engaged in such trade or industry or subdivision thereof, shall, as to the intrastate trade or business carried on by them, be bound by such code and by any standards adopted and approved by the governor, subject only to such exemptions to the application thereof as may be provided in the approved code or imposed by the governor as a condition of the approval of the code.

"(2) Among other things, codes of fair competition and business practices shall establish standards of maximum hours of labor, minimum rates of pay and working conditions. If any code shall provide that it shall constitute unfair competition to sell below cost of production, or reasonable cost, the governor may, upon approval of any such code containing such provision, provide a method for determining said cost of production or reasonable cost and make such provisions in relation to the enforcement thereof as he may from time to time determine. Any farmer or dairyman who elects to come under this code shall be entitled to the cost of production plus a reasonable profit. Every code of fair competition or agreement, approved, prescribed, or issued under this title shall contain the following conditions:

"(a) That employees shall have the right to organize and bargain collectively through representatives of their own choosing, and shall be free from the interference, restraint, or coercion of employers of labor, or their agents, in the designation of such representatives or in self-organization or in other concerted activities for the purpose of collective bargaining or other mutual aid or protection:

"(b) That no employee and no one seeking employment shall be required, as a condition of employment, to join any company union or to refrain from joining, organizing, or assisting a labor organization of his own choosing."

In administering these and other sections of the 1935 law the governor is authorized to delegate any of his functions and powers, except the power to prescribe, approve, modify, amend or terminate codes, to such officers or employees as he may designate, and this power to delegate has been tested in the Wisconsin Courts and has been found to be constitutional.[14]

In April, 1936, in accordance with the above legislation, there was created under special executive order,[15] the Wisconsin Trade Practice Commission to be composed of two commissioners, and the Wisconsin Trade Practice Review Board to be composed of ten citizens. The Commissioners are to administer the Act, and the Review Board is to act as a court of appeals in all matters concerning the definition of unfair practices and the enforcement of regulations concerning them.

The Wisconsin plan, then, calls for the organization of various industrial or trade groups with common interests, each to have a code containing the rules of fair competition in their application to the industry in question. The administration of codes is to be in the hands of the Wisconsin Trade Practice Commission, the expenses of administration being distributed among the membership of the trade. Any of the decisions of the Commission may be appealed to the group of citizens comprising the Review Board, which will at the same time examine all protests and complaints from citizens and consumers. Each industrial or trade group will have a code committee which will have wide advisory powers and which will keep a check on obedience to its provisions; but the enforcement of all codes will be centered in the hands of the Commission. Clause 110.04 (5) of the Act provides such teeth as the regulations are permitted to have:

"The several circuit courts of the state are hereby vested with jurisdiction to prevent and restrain violation of any code of fair competition and business practices approved under this section and it shall be the duty of the several district attorneys in their respective districts, under the direction of the attorney-general, to institute proceedings in equity to prevent and

[14] State No. 39, January Term, 1936, State of Wisconsin: in Supreme Court. *In re* petition of the State of Wisconsin on relation of the Attorney General and the Tavern Code Authority and Hart Phelps *et al.*

[15] *Executive Order* No. 6.

restrain such violations. Any trade or industrial association or group or any person who is a member thereof who is damaged by a violation of a code may petition the circuit court having jurisdiction to restrain such violations."

As yet the system has been applied only to those badly organized groups of small units which dispense personal services or which are engaged in activities in which labor is the prevailing cost. Such are the cleaning and dyeing industry, the barbers, tavern keepers, painters, paperhangers and decorators, window cleaners, highway construction workers, shoe rebuilders, bowling alley proprietors, crushed stone, sand and gravel producers, mason, concrete, and carpenter contractors, and the bottled soft drink makers. Codes will be promulgated for other industries as needed.

It is probable that, with wise direction, the new organization may yet set the standard for similar development in many other states of the union. This state by state growth of legislation dealing with the morals of business is nothing new. In past years, when repeated attempts had failed to obtain federal legislation to control untruthful advertising, this method of attack was eventually abandoned and the Printer's Ink Model Statute was adopted by most of the individual states. After manufacturers had failed for twenty years to get resale price maintenance bills through Congress they turned to the state legislatures for protection, and are meeting with a very considerable degree of success in this movement. It is probable that the method of working through state laws up to an eventual federal act may prove more successful in the long run than the attempt to force the development in the opposite direction.

CHAPTER XX

A SUMMARY

Now that we have reached the last stage of our journey, we may find it profitable to look back for a few moments upon the road which we have been traveling.

One of the fundamental purposes of ethics is to enable us to make reasoned judgments of right and wrong; that is to say, to form opinions concerning the rightness of our actions and those of other persons which do not depend upon "hunches" and private prejudices, nor upon the ideas prevailing in the community in which we happen to have been born and to live. Public opinion in matters of morals is indeed worthy of great respect, for it represents the experience and insight of the race as it has come down to us after thousands upon thousands of years of struggle and toil, failure and success. Nevertheless while its standards are often, perhaps usually sound at the core, they are not infrequently either inadequate or even positively misleading. Hence they must be subjected to a critical testing if they are not to fail us in some of the most important concerns of life. We have accordingly been attempting to work our way through to a consistent view of our rights and duties as business men, and have proceeded by seeking the answers to two intimately related questions: (1) What is the nature of fair competition and in what respects does it differ from unfair competition? (2) What mistakes do we most frequently make when passing moral judgments upon human conduct?

The Characteristics of a Fair Exchange

Competition, as we have seen, is in many respects a crude piece of machinery. Why then is it tolerated? Because of the belief that, given the present imperfect state of intelligence and character in the world, it is better adapted for supplying the economic needs of mankind than any other practicable alternative. But the justification thus urged does not extend indiscriminately to any and every transaction that may take place in the business world. It covers only those which are in harmony with the end which the system exists to secure. This end is the completest attainable satisfaction of man's economic wants. Hence our definition of fair competition as that which attempts to succeed on the merits of its goods or services.

Such a system is fundamentally fair, whatever its incidental imperfections, because it is based on an exchange of goods, necessitated by the division of labor; and the exchange will usually be in the interest of both parties, and may always be if they are willing to have it so.

The fundamental characteristic of a fair exchange is that both parties know precisely what they are giving and what they are getting. This excludes conscious misrepresentation of every kind, both active and passive. It likewise excludes unconscious misrepresentation due to carelessness or laziness. For the primary effects of such misrepresentation, at any rate, are ordinarily identical with those of lying.

The second characteristic of a fair exchange is that both parties are glad on reflection that it took place. This excludes over-persuasion as described in Chapter VII. Over-persuasion takes places when one person, *A,* without misrepresentation, plays upon *B's* weakness of will, and talks him into an agreement which *A* believes *B* will later repent.

These two considerations, as they stand, are inadequate. For a man who pays the earnings of a life-time to a surgeon who, by performing an emergency operation, saves his life, knows what he is getting and giving, and will be glad the operation was performed even under such unfortunate financial conditions, provided there was no other surgeon within reach at the time. "All that a man hath will he give for his life." But if the operation was a relatively simple one and the fee charged was $5,000, people would very properly call this robbery. At the other end of the scale are the sweat-shop workers who sell their labor for a pittance because if they are to live they can not do otherwise. No one calls this fair. If, then, an exchange is to be fair, the price or wage demanded and accepted must be not merely what one party or the other is willing to give or take; it must be such a price as would result from genuine and vigorous competition between buyers and buyers, on the one hand, and sellers and sellers on the other.

The significance of the competitive price is that it represents what must be paid on the average in order to get the particular service or commodity which the community desires. Any given supplier is entitled to get what proves to be necessary, in general, to induce men to perform this particular kind of service; and he is entitled to no more. This represents his share of the world's goods, as far as this particular transaction is concerned. For the same reason it is what the purchaser ought to pay, according to the principle stated in Ch. XIV, p. 201.

In some respects the most revolting form of unfair competition is that which is described in Chapter II under the name of coercion. Whatever the details, its essence consists in threatening a man with ruin or serious financial loss unless he conforms his buying or selling policy to the aggressor's will. To accomplish this end, the latter must have superior economic strength and be the kind of person who is willing to use it ruthlessly. As such he is an offender against the third condition of fair business dealing. The difference between such a man and the surgeon of whom we have been talking is that the latter *finds* the situation of which he takes advantage, while the coercer *creates* it. To be sure the latter does not ordinarily take *all* his victim's property; what he usually demands is that the normal profits derived from his victim's purchases be sluiced into his till. The result may or may not be an unfair price. But in any event it is an unfair use of economic power, because it is an attempt to gain at the expense of another without the excuse of counter-balancing social advantage.

The coercive methods of Chapter II represent unfair treatment not merely of one's customers but also of one's competitors. In fact the harm suffered by each of these parties represents two sides of the same transaction. This is true, in the last resort, of all forms of unfair competition. The typical situation in the business world, when reduced to its simplest possible terms, consists in two competitors making a proposition to a possible customer. This relationship, as may be remembered, can be represented thus:—

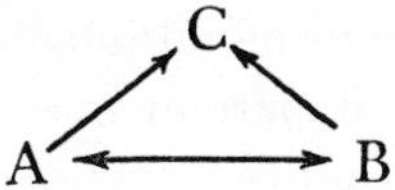

Here *A* and *B* are offering goods or services to *C*. If *A* and *B* are treating *C* with complete fairness, it follows necessarily that they are treating each other fairly. For example, *A* is doing nothing directly to drive *B* from the market or to prevent *B* from having access to *C*.

Full knowledge of all essentials, satisfaction, upon reflection, at the terms of the exchange, the terms themselves the product of an agreement reached in the course of open and vigorous competition—these are the three fundamental conditions of a fair business transaction. The word "terms" includes, of course, not merely money but all the factors entering into the agreement. Where these conditions exist fair treatment as between competitors will be found also. Hence they include, in principle, all forms of fairness in the relations of business men to each other. They are far from representing perfection. But they do represent the nearest approach to it which the competitive system and the limits of human intelligence and character permit.

The Principal Mistakes in Moral Judgments

If a conclusion is sound, it can usually be reached by several different routes. This is emphatically true of the principles emerging from this study. We may start from a definition of fair competition based upon the ends for the sake of which competition is permitted to exist. On the other hand, we may start from our ordinary, everyday notions of right and wrong and attempt to render them more intelligent and more consistent than they sometimes are. If we succeed in our program, we shall find ourselves in possession of the same definitions of fair service, fair treatment of competitors, and fair price which we obtained by following the other route.

We here begin with the fact that everyone draws the line somewhere; that is to say, every man has his code. This, as we have seen, holds for even the "hardened criminals" in a penitentiary. With this fact as a starting point we attempt to draw up a list of the principal mistakes that we make in our moral judgments. If we can succeed in eliminating all the more important ones, we shall have a code of business ethics which will prove to be identical in nature with that which we have just been formulating. The most serious of these mistakes are due to a failure to observe the following rules.

(1) In passing judgments of right and wrong upon either ourselves or other persons, we must look to the intended results rather than the actual ones. However where the failure of the actual results to be identical with those which were expected is due to the carelessness or laziness of the actor, in other words, to his own fault, he is morally responsible also.

(2) We must take into account the interests of *all* the parties affected by the conduct. We tend to content ourselves with a spotlight view of the consequences of actions. The genuine moral standard demands a floodlight view. It may be true that only an omniscient being could discover all the interests affected by an act. But just in so far as we omit any from our picture, we do so at the risk of error; just as when we ignore any relevant fact about a corporation in deciding whether or not to buy its stock.

One of the most serious sources of this form of error is failure to observe the secondary effects of conduct; for these effects, in their total extent, are often far more important than the primary. A somewhat different, but equally mischievous form of the same mistake is the trick we all have of putting self with its interests in the center of the stage, and turning all the light on it, to the obscuring of all competing considerations. This explains why we constantly judge self and others by entirely different standards, as was shown above, on page 3.

(3) In so far as the nature and extent of the effects of actions are dependent upon circumstances, these circumstances must be taken into account in determining right and wrong. A number of illustrations of this fact were supplied in the chapters on contract.

(4) In passing moral judgments, we must ignore our private likes and dislikes, admirations and disadmirations, for the persons con-

cerned. To deny this is to say that while it is wrong for a sneak thief to steal umbrellas, it is all right for a forger to forge checks or a burglar to "blow" a safe. We are to look in every case at the magnitude of the interests involved, and where choice is necessary, select the greater good instead of the less; or where some harm is inevitable, the less harm rather than the greater.

(5) A fifth and last principle will call for a somewhat more detailed discussion.

The Claims of Positive Service

Through our examination of the attitude assumed by William of Orange toward the lynching of the DeWitt brothers, we have learned that for ethics there is no fundamental difference between the intention that issues in action and one that reaches its goal through inaction. We must now proceed a step farther and point out that the intention to injure and the refusal positively to help others in the attainment of their ends are frequently indistinguishable. When, for example, a man lies or breaks a contract, he may with equal truth be said to be injuring his victim or refusing to give him aid. This fact opens up a new field which we have not attempted to explore systematically. It calls upon us to watch our step, for we can not give others either our time or our money indiscriminately. The reasons are those which make us dread the secondary effects of the dole. Even too much liberality in releasing people from their contracts is likely to tempt them to take their responsibilities too lightly when forming them.

The underlying principle, however, is clear, whatever may be the difficulties in applying it. If we owe it to others not to injure them, then, for the same reasons, we owe them such positive service as it lies in our power to give, in so far as, in so doing we do not do more harm than good on the whole to those affected, including self.

At least two forms of such service are open to everyone in business or professional life. One is the practice of our vocation. We may call a failure to give proper service to our customers a positive harm, or we may with equal accuracy call it a refusal to give them due help. Since every adult, and not merely every child, is dependent upon others for his very existence, to say nothing of those things which make existence worth having, it is perhaps immaterial, at bottom, which way we look at the matter. But a clear recognition of the fact that our duties extend beyond being inoffensive will give us the clearest and most adequate position from which to view those obligations of fair service which we have tried to set forth in this book. Such a position will show us at a glance that we are bound to give our customers, our clients, our patients, or our pupils, the best services within our power, in return, of course, for a fair compensation.

The second obligation which rests upon everyone of us, according to the measure of our ability and our opportunity, is that of making the world a better place for human beings to live and work in. Every advance achieved by civilization from the Stone Age to the present moment is the fruit of struggle and sacrifice. All these riches have been poured into our lap without a turn of our hand. The least we can do is to pass on this heritage undiminished. But this course alone, important as it is, would have got the race nowhere. Our recognition of past services can be genuine and complete only as we continue the work which our predecessors began. Such work may take many forms, for the term "civilization" covers a multitude of things. But the foundation of all civilized life is character, and the effort to raise standards of conduct in the world about us is therefore more important and, when successful, more fruitful, than any other course of action open to us. And the issues involved are not merely a continuation of past progress. Left to themselves morals will grow worse rather than better. Upon the ability of the race to produce men who, whether in some small sphere or on the great stage, will respond to this call, depends the very existence of civilized life on this planet.

If the man who fell overboard had been able to swim, he could have been saved. The same thing may be said of the human race. No one can assert with certainty that the "civilized peoples" of the world are civilized enough to save their civilization. If war, the product of national pride, selfishness, and folly, continues to be chronic, all that is best in life will be destroyed, perhaps for centuries to come. If business should degenerate into a ruthless and brutal war of each against all, life for every one of us, great and small, good and bad, would cease to be worth possessing, even though the outer trappings of civilization happened to survive. If civilization is to endure, however, one thing appears to be certain. It will not be saved solely or primarily by passing new laws or devising new institutions. Not that these things are unimportant. But laws and institutions can be made to work only where there are men of high principles to operate, maintain, and conform to them. There is no substitute for character. And only in a society where there exists a very high level of character can there be any near approach to adequate standards of production whether in quantity or quality, faithful and loyal service, genuine satisfaction in work, and an equitable distribution of wealth.

NOTES

NOTES

CHAPTER V

Can the Competitive System Exist without Some Compromise with the Principle of Caveat Emptor?

In the period immediately following the world war a bond salesman complained that the X Company was marketing a bond with ordinary security, bearing 6½% interest, when there were available Victory Loan Bonds not subject to taxation and yielding 6¾%. He raised the question whether this was not unfair to the uninformed purchaser. Stated in general terms, the problem before the inquirer's mind was whether a seller is bound to inform prospective purchasers of better bargains attainable elsewhere than he himself is able or willing to offer. To those readers of Chapter V who have really understood its drift this inquiry will suggest an even more searching problem, namely, whether our doctrine of the duty to tell the whole truth can be carried through to the end in our competitive world without destroying those who practice it; and in case the majority of business men actually did practice it, without destroying the competitive system itself.

A partial answer has already been given in the text. It was there held, for reasons duly assigned, that (1) I am not bound to disclose what I propose to do with that which I buy, after I have bought it; and (2) I am not bound to disclose my opinion—as distinct from knowledge—about values; as for example how much gain might be expected from the purchase of a given phosphate deposit or from certain stocks or bonds. But these replies do not end our difficulties. Let us suppose that I am selling a certain grade of silk and price it at $2.00 per yard. I then learn that a competitor is selling silk of exactly the same grade at a price 10% lower than mine. Am I then reduced to the alternatives of dropping my price to his level, or informing my prospective customers that they can go farther and fare better? By no means; for to sell at my competitor's price might be to sell at a price which would be unfair to me. He may have been caught in some kind of a financial jam and be compelled to sell at a price less than that to which he is fairly entitled; or he may not know his own costs; or he may have had the good luck to pick up a stray bargain. My duty as supplier is to sell my goods at a fair price—whatever this term may turn out to mean. And a price fair to me, as will be shown later,[1] represents a price which it is right or just for the purchaser to pay.

Turning from price to quality, suppose I am a grocer and know that my rival in the next block has on sale today better strawberries than mine. Am

[1] Ch. XIV, p. 201.

I bound to drop my price below his and tell my customers who prefer quality to economy that they can get better fruit at his store? But why has he better strawberries than mine? The fundamental reason is that the supply is limited: there is not enough of the best to go around. If then I send my customers to him and they should buy him out then his customers would have to come to me and purchase my inferior wares. What is true of strawberries is true of stocks and bonds and indeed of practically all commodities of whatever kind. And what holds for material things holds equally for personal services, as those of the automobile repairer, the contractor, the manager, the lawyer, and the physician.

From the above it follows that the purchaser, broadly speaking, must not expect always to be able to obtain the best, but must be satisfied with the "mine run". There is another reason for this conclusion. A manufacturer, call him *A,* puts on the market, at great expense to himself, a vacuum cleaner. A rival, *B,* then devises one which is decidedly better. Is *A* under obligation to drop his price below *B's,* because at equal price he would be bound to tell his prospective customers that they could do better by buying from *B?* Again the answer is No. If men are to expend labor, time, and money in putting legitimate goods on the market, and in addition are to accept all the risks involved, they are entitled to compensation for their services, even if the resultant product is not the very best, provided it is the best they are able to furnish. And their compensation must come from the sale of their goods.

There are indeed exceptional cases in which an honorable man will inform his prospective customer that he can do better elsewhere. Furthermore this actually happens throughout this land over and over again. A physician who is not a charlatan will send certain difficult cases to the appropriate specialist; a lawyer who is not a shyster will treat his clients in the same way under parallel conditions; some manufacturers will refuse orders which they know they can not fill satisfactorily, even though they know they might "get away with" inferior products of their own make; and there are—a few—building contractors who will not undertake construction work unless they are reasonably certain that they can complete their contract by the date when it is absolutely necessary for you to take possession. A neighbor contributes the following. A carpenter was putting double windows on his new house. The masons had left a gap between the masonry and the sills. In answer to an inquiry the carpenter said he could make the necessary repairs, but that there was a firm in the city which had certain equipment which he himself did not have, and which would make it possible for them to do a better job at a lower price than he could.

The proper limitations upon frankness in selling discussed in this Note thus turn upon considerations drawn from (1) the requirements of fairness to the seller (price); (2) what may be called the material necessities of the case (scarcity of the best); and (3) the fundamental requirements of any economic system that labor and risk must and ought to be paid for when devoted to socially useful ends.

The point of these reflections, which certainly do not run in the ordinary grooves of thought, is this: Certain practices which lie at the foundation of our competitive system and which are taken for granted by "everybody" can, as a matter of fact, demonstrate their right to exist when submitted to the critical scrutiny of ethics.

CHAPTER XII

Legal Limitations on Property Rights in the United States

The law governing the use of property in the United States has developed along lines largely determined by Chief Justice Shaw of the Massachusetts Supreme Court in the famous case of Commonwealth *v.* Alger.[2]

Alger owned land on Boston harbor and according to an ancient statute his boundary line extended to the edge of the water at low tide. Within this territory he built a wharf which did not obstruct navigation but which he was ordered to destroy, without compensation, because in building it he violated a series of laws passed by the Massachusetts legislature forbidding wharves in certain parts of Boston harbor. He appealed to the courts for protection. The case finally went to the state supreme court where his plea was denied.

The opinion of the court was based upon the following principle. "We think it is a settled principle, growing out of the nature of well ordered civil society, that every holder of property, however absolute and unqualified may be his title, holds it under the implied liability that his use of it may be so regulated that it shall not be injurious to the equal enjoyment of others having an equal right to the enjoyment of their property, nor injurious to the rights of the community. All property in this commonwealth, as well that in the interior as that bordering on tide-waters, is derived, directly or indirectly, from the government and held subject to those general regulations which are necessary to the common good and general welfare. Rights of property, like all other social and conventional rights, are subject to such reasonable limitations in their enjoyment as shall prevent them from being injurious and to such reasonable restraints and regulations established by law as the legislature, under the governing and controlling power vested in them by the constitution, may think necessary and expedient."

CHAPTER XIII

1. A Momentous Supreme Court Decision

The state exercises its power to determine rates chiefly in the field of public service corporations, including railroads. But according to the opinion of the United States Supreme Court in Munn *v.* Illinois [3] it has a moral and a legal right to intervene and set prices wherever this is clearly desirable in the public interest. The nature and significance of this momentous de-

[2] 61 Mass. 53 (1851).
[3] 94 U.S. 113 (1876).

cision is well stated in the following quotation from Professor John R. Commons.[4]

"The legislature of Illinois had fixed the maximum charges permitted to be made by grain elevator and warehouse companies for the handling and storage of grain. This business of a warehouse had always been a private business, and had never been granted any special privilege or franchise by the sovereign either in England or America. The majority and the minority in the Supreme Court agreed that in the case of a special grant of sovereign power, the power of the sovereign to regulate the charges went along with the grant. The charges must be reasonable, and this was the common law rule applying to all special grants or licenses, whether express, implied, or claimed by prescription through long usage and consent, such as public ferries, bridges, turnpikes, wharfingers, or hackmen and draymen who made use of the King's highways. The judges disagreed as to whether this sovereign power could lawfully be extended to a grain elevator and warehouse which did not need and did not have a special grant of sovereign power to carry on its business.

"The majority introduced a new principle of law, as charged by the minority, in order to sustain the power of the Illinois legislature to fix the prices for the handling and storage of grain, and to compel the owners to furnish service at those prices. This was, in effect, the principle that it was *economic conditions* and *not a special grant of sovereignty* that determined the right of the sovereign to regulate prices. The Munn Case was not the case of a railway depending on a public franchise, but of a private business. These warehouses, without a special grant of sovereign power, had become strategic centers for control of the prices of grain shipped from the Northwest, by the mere fact of location, character of the business, and power to withhold service. The majority, recognizing this economic fact, held that property lost its strictly private character and became 'clothed with a public interest when used in a manner to make it of public consequence and affect the community at large'. Thus the *fact* of economic power over the public in withholding service and thus fixing prices need not proceed from a sovereign grant of a privilege, but proceeds, in this case, from the circumstance that the public had come to depend on the use of the owner's private property. Therefore the owner had employed his property not merely to his own use and enjoyment, but had devoted it to use by the public. To that extent he must submit to be controlled by the public."

2. Industry, or Effort, as a Product of Chance

The rewards of economic service, we have said, are divided between chance and industry, or effort. Payment according to chance we object to, and call for its elimination in so far as this would not result in more harm than good. Payment according to industry, however, we approve. To this conclusion some readers may object that, after all, the amount of a man's industry is also a matter of chance. Either he was born with a bias toward hard work, or was "conditioned" to it in his childhood or youth by parental

[4] *Legal Foundations of Capitalism* (New York, The Macmillan Co., 1924), p. 32.

command or example, or by the necessities imposed by external circumstances. Payment according to industry thus turns out after all to be a surrender to chance.

The answer is that the fundamental ideal of the writers of this book is payment according to need. In our opinion, however, a distribution of economic goods solely on the basis of need would be self-defeating because it would leave little to distribute. Therefore, we conclude, men must be paid to work, regardless of any puzzles concerning the agencies to which their habits of industry may in the last resort be due. Furthermore in so far as work is disagreeable we think it fair that they should be compensated for it, for the reasons stated in the text.

3. One Step toward Payment According to Needs

As long as the family remains the economic unit, the needs of different units can be compared roughly by counting the number of persons in a family, noting their age (for the economic needs of young children are not so great as those of adults), and making due allowance for the economies which result when several persons share the same menage. However since the world's resources are not unlimited, this system would require some control by the distributing agency (for example, the government) over the size of families. This could be accomplished by making no extra allowance when the number of children exceeded a specified maximum.

4. The Meaning of the Term "Maximum Desirable"

Most adults are at once economic producers and consumers. As consumers their interests lie in the direction of large scale production. As producers, however, they object and ought to object to long hours or excessive speeding up which give them no time for relaxation or self culture; or else leave them too exhausted at the end of the working day to profit by such leisure as they have. Fortunately there is no such conflict between these aims as was once believed to exist. Almost any man in whatever field will in the long run do more work in an eight hour day than in ten hours, to say nothing of twelve. However there is a limit to this progression. Few or none will accomplish more in a four hour day than in six hours. The term "maximum desirable", on page 190, is intended merely to point to the above facts. An economic system must produce in order to supply human wants; but it must not devote so much time to production that none is left for living. This holds particularly for those engaged in soulless and monotonous occupations. The term "maximum desirable", of course, does not solve this problem, but merely calls attention to its existence.

5. More Material on the Role of Chance in Business Affairs

In the interests of clarity and brevity the picture of the role of chance in modern economic society has been greatly oversimplified in the text. We do not intend to go to the bottom of the subject in this note, but must try to convey some notion of the part played by at least one unmentioned factor.

The rewards resulting from ability are at the mercy of chance, not merely because the amount and nature of our native ability is outside our power to control, and not merely because the amount and intensity of the demand for our particular brand of ability is also out of our control, but, in addition, for a third reason, equally significant. This is the large role played by scarcity of intellectual endowment in proportion to the economic demand for such gifts. Apart from favoritism and intrigue the reason why the president of a great corporation can command a salary of one hundred thousand dollars a year is the rarity of the qualities requisite properly to fill such a position. If in his generation three or four times as many men of equal administrative ability had happened to be born he might not have been able to command an income of one tenth of that amount, and yet have been compelled to work just as hard as he does now in order to attain and maintain his position.

The unskilled laborers at the bottom of the scale are subject to the same law as their managers at the top. Let us suppose that at a given time their wage is two dollars per day. Then suppose that in the course of a year a million immigrants rush in to the United States from the south of Europe. The day's wage may thereupon drop to a dollar fifty, though exactly the same amount of work is demanded as before.

One more fact is perhaps worth noting. Equal increments of ability—if this term means anything—do not result in equal increments of compensation. The big prizes are reserved for the few top-notchers. In the great days before 1929 musical performers such as Paderewski and Kreisler could get from five to six thousand dollars per performance. Those who were regarded by the experts as in the class just below these giants were paid about twelve hundred dollars. Those in the next class received from two to three hundred; and those in the fourth class—many of them genuine artists—whatever they could pick up. If the reader will study the incomes of lawyers and physicians in his own town he will find something of the same large and abrupt transitions as he passes down the scale of intellectual ability.

6. The Evils of Economic Inequality

The fundamental excellences of the present economic system lie in the field of production; its most serious defects in the field of distribution. The outstanding feature of the distribution of wealth today is great inequalities of income. The more serious evils of this situation are here briefly enumerated.

In the first place inequality in the distribution of income is very wasteful of the material conditions of human happiness. This is due to what may be called the law of diminishing returns as applied to money:—The more dollars you have the less the value of each as a means of happiness. If, for example, you divide an annual income of $100,000 between ten families in such a way that eight get $1,500, one gets $8,000, and one gets $80,000, you will have thrown away most of the possibilities of comfort and happiness which the money was capable of affording. If, then, you add another $1,500 to the incomes of the first eight, subtracting this amount from the income of the last, you will have revolutionized their whole mode of living without affecting his in an appreciable degree. A family of five with an annual income of $1,500 does not even have all the necessities, and can do no saving for a rainy day or old age. At $3,000 it has all the necessities, some of the comforts, and an occasional taste of the luxuries. At $8,000, or certainly at $10,000, all the necessities and comforts and as many luxuries as are good for anyone. Thus the more unequally a given sum of money is divided, the less it can accomplish in relieving its recipients from want and suffering, and providing them with the good things of life.

In the second place, while the primary if not the sole justification for inequality is its effect in promoting industry, even from this point of view there is an offset. The sons of the rich, many of whom may be expected to inherit their fathers' business ability, are tempted to degenerate into mere loafers, or worse. The very poor, on the other hand, do not have sufficient food, clothing, shelter, and medical care to be physically vigorous and thus capable of doing their best work.

A more important evil resulting from great inequalities of income is the danger with which they threaten the state. For, as the history of every wealthy nation shows only too clearly, the state cannot afford to have extremely powerful subjects. They are apt to get control of the government and use it for their own ends, instead of the government controlling them. The existence of a large class of discontented poor is also likely to be almost as dangerous as the concentration of enormous wealth in few hands, because it is likely to lead to the rule of the demagogue, and sometimes to violence or fear of violence. In the United States, however, perhaps the most serious effects which it has upon government is the widespread bribery from which we as a people seem to be unable to free ourselves.

Of all the evils which are due to the unequal distribution of wealth the most serious are the effects upon morals. Extremes of wealth and poverty are about equally inimical to health of character. This is especially true of the children in the family. In the one case they are apt to be spoiled by the excessive self-indulgence which is permitted them, so that they become selfish, lazy, and weak of will. In the other, they too often suffer from the lack of those moral influences that flow from a healthy and happy home life. This holds particularly for the inhabitants of the slums of our great cities.

To this arraignment it is often replied that prizes are the spice of life. And that were financial inequalities to disappear much of the interest of business life, and perhaps of life outside, would be annihilated. There is an important element of truth in this contention. Business is, among other things, a game; and the lure of competitive games is so deeply ingrained in human nature that many men spend the major part of their leisure hours in trying to beat an opponent on the golf links or at the card table, or in watching or "listening to" the contests of the baseball and the football field.

The reference to games supplies the solution to this very genuine difficulty. The Greek contestants at Olympia subjected themselves to years of grueling training in order that they might win—a crown of wild olives.

So today, after a certain amount of income has been secured, business men struggle primarily for the athlete's reward,—standing among their fellows, and, in addition, power. But in some form or other these prizes will always be available in any society in which inequalities of endowment exist and in which there is need of leadership and authority.

CHAPTER XV

The Justice of the Legal Minimum Wage

A just economic system is one that operates in such a way as to make for the best interests of society as a whole. The very best may be unattainable at the present time because of the selfishness and stupidity of many of its members, and because, when new methods of production are introduced, thereby increasing the total wealth of the community, population immediately jumps, thus producing a ratio of national income to the number of those who share it which may be little or no more favorable than that of the pre-existing situation. This tendency, of which Malthus quite properly made so much, may be overcome in the course of a few generations. But the other factors will prove more difficult to deal with. Nevertheless society is bound at any given time to approach as nearly as is then practicable to the goal of universal well-being.

We have expressed our belief that in the present phase of human history the competitive system is better adapted than any rival to the attainment of the ends which the economic system is intended to secure. But business competition, it turns out, breaks down at this point and that. In such cases society not merely may but ought to enter the arena, and, through government, assume control of those processes and practices which escape the limitations that competition sets. Ever since the beginnings of democracy the English race has not hesitated to do so where the interests of consumers were involved, notably in the field of monopoly. In consequence, public utilities and those quasi-monopolies, the railroads and other transportation systems, are compelled and justly compelled to submit to the determination of rates and standards of service by the state.

Today we are aware, as perhaps never before, of the existence of a second extensive and important field where conditions are extremely unsatisfactory because—somewhat as in the case of the railroads—competition has partly broken down. In the labor world, particularly at the lower levels, the supply of employees is ordinarily in excess of the demand. This creates an inequality of bargaining power which is further accentuated by lack of financial resources. The result is a condition of things which ought never to be tolerated unless it is absolutely beyond remedy. That in times of general prosperity—to put the matter as conservatively as possible—large numbers of human beings should receive a wage which makes it impossible for them to get sufficient food, protection from the weather, and medical care, to enable them to live in health and vigor, and to make some provision against sickness, incapacity, and old age, is a blot on our civilization. Twenty-one foreign nations, including Great Britain and its four commonwealths, have attempted to deal with this situation through the institution of the legal minimum wage. In this country about one-third of our states have made modest beginnings in the same direction. But any real solution of the problem has been made impossible in the United States, for the present at least, by the decision of the United States Supreme Court in Adkins *v.* The Children's Hospital in 1922, reaffirmed in a decision on a partially similar case in Morehead *v.* People of the State of New York, in June 1936.[5]

There are certain limitations and defects inherent in minimum wage laws, and experience may show in the end that they do not accomplish satisfactorily the purposes for which they were instituted. But the decisions of the Court do not turn on this eventuality. They assert that the plan itself is fundamentally unjust, and thus in conflict with the provisions of the United States constitution according to which neither Congress nor the individual states may deprive any person of life, liberty or property without due process of law. Into the question of the legal interpretation of this somewhat vague phrase we do not enter. But the question whether a minimum wage is inherently unjust so that no community ought so much as even to experiment with it—this question is an ethical one. As such we mean to examine it in its place.

The gist of the decision of the Court, in Adkins *v.* The Children's Hospital, as read by Justice Sutherland, is, as he himself points out, as follows:

"The feature of this statute, which perhaps more than any other, puts upon it the stamp of invalidity, is that it exacts from the employer an arbitrary payment for a purpose and upon a basis having no causal connection with his business, or the contract or the work the employee engages to do. The declared basis is not the value of the service rendered, but the extraneous circumstance that the employee needs to get a prescribed sum of money to insure her subsistence, health, and morals. The ethical right of every worker, man or woman, to a living wage may be conceded. One of the declared and important purposes of trade organizations is to secure it. And with that principle and with every legitimate effort to realize it in fact, no one can quarrel; but the fallacy of the proposed method of attaining it is that it assumes that every employer is bound at all events to furnish it.

"The moral requirement implicit in every contract of employment, viz., that the amount to be paid and the service to be rendered shall bear to each other some relation of just equivalence, is completely ignored. The necessities of the employee are alone considered, and these arise outside of the employment, are the same when there is no employment, and as great in one occupation as in another. Certainly the employer, by paying a fair equivalent for the service rendered, though not sufficient to support the employee, has neither caused nor contributed to her poverty. On the contrary, to the extent of what he pays, he has relieved it." [6]

The law is thus declared unjust in that its requirements may compel

[5] For the first of these decisions see 261 U.S. 525; for the second, 56 Supreme Court Reporter 918 is alone available as this book goes to press.

[6] *Loc. cit.* 558

certain employers to pay their employees more than the equivalent of the value of their services.

Now the proposition that a fair wage can be measured by the value of the service to the consumer is one to which, as we have tried to show, no real meaning can be attached. However the term "equality of value" may have a fairly definite meaning when applied to the employer of labor who sells the product of that labor. A man's services may be said to be "worth" a given amount to such an employer when the income of the latter is increased by that amount or more as the result of such employment. The employer pays out twenty dollars per week to his employee and get back twenty dollars, plus, ordinarily, an indeterminate amount as a return for his own labor of management and his assumption of risks. This he would lose if he dismissed the wage earner and did not replace him.

If all employers paid their men on this basis much of the agitation for the legal minimum wage would disappear. But do they?

In the first place, except in the somewhat rare cases where piece work rates can be introduced, the employer pays all men doing the same class of work the same wage. But the ratio of efficiency among any considerable number of employees engaged in exactly the same kind of work may run as high as four to one.[7] The employer pays the least efficient, let us say, what he is worth to him; the extra earnings of the remaining workers he puts into his pocket.

In addition to this he may take advantage of his superior economic strength to push down the wages of his employees to a point where the man who is worth twenty dollars a week to him gets no more than twelve or fifteen. And where he does not push them down of his own volition his more ruthless competitors may compel him to do so, because the "worth" of his employees is not absolute but depends, among other factors, on the selling prices of his products.

Now minimum wage laws attempt to remedy this situation in those cases where it is most harmful. They seek to protect at least those whose pay is forced down to a point where they are unable to supply themselves and their families with what we may call the biological necessities of existence. This means the conditions essential to health and vigor. It is difficult to see how an aim of this sort can be condemned.

But Justice Sutherland has his eye fixed on another situation. He thinks the minimum wage law might under certain circumstances force an employer to pay a man twenty dollars whose services were worth only fifteen. And this, he says, would be unjust. "To the extent that the sum fixed exceeds the fair value of the services rendered it amounts to a compulsory exaction from the employer for the support of a partially indigent person, for whose condition there rests upon him no peculiar responsibility, and

[7] This information was given the authors by a friend who is at once a thoroughly trained man of science and an efficient and successful manufacturer; and who has made a very careful study of this subject in his own factory. This ratio checks exactly with those discovered in extensive studies of the rate of accomplishment by large groups of students in statistical work at the University of Wisconsin.

therefore in effect arbitrarily shifts to his shoulders a burden which, if it belongs to anybody, belongs to society as a whole." [8]

To this contention it may be replied that the law does not compel him to pay anyone a cent. He may dismiss his employees who are not "worth" to him the cost of their wage.[9] To this suggestion it may be objected that such a course might result in the employer's bankruptcy. To this, in turn, there are two answers. One is that the extra wage will in the end be absorbed through the advancement of the price to the ultimate consumer; and this is as it should be, for no body of consumers is justified in profiting by the misery of their fellow men. There is also a second and more decisive answer. An employer, like every other worker, is simply a servant of society. No one has a moral right to perform a function for which he is unfitted, whether he is a plumber's assistant, a factory owner, or a physician.[10] Accordingly, where his unfitness is demonstrable beyond reasonable doubt the state has the right to deny him the opportunity to continue his muddling. If an employer is unable to serve his customers satisfactorily they will turn their backs upon him and he will go into bankruptcy. And every rugged individualist will say that his fate was entirely just. But if he is unable to play fair with his employees they may not be able to turn their backs upon him except at the risk of starvation. Here then the state has at once the right and the duty to enter upon the scene and protect its citizens who—unlike the customers—are unable to protect themselves.

The problem of the minimum wage is something more than a matter between certain employers and certain of their employees. Its solution is a matter of moment, even from the most selfish point of view, to every citizen of the United States. In his dissenting opinion in Morehead *v.* People of the State of New York, Justice Stone writes as follows: "In the years which have intervened since the Adkins Case . . . we have had opportunity to perceive more clearly that a wage insufficient to support the worker does not visit its consequences upon him alone; that it may affect profoundly the entire economic structure of society and, in any case, that it casts on every taxpayer, and on government itself, the burden of solving the problems of poverty, subsistence, health, and morals of large numbers in the community. Because of their nature and extent these are public problems. A generation ago they were for the individual to solve; to-day they are the burden of the nation."

[8] *Loc. cit.* 557.

[9] It will be remembered that in the United States the legal minimum wage is of practical importance only to the unorganized laborers, that is to say, to those whose positions are not protected by unions.

[10] Compare what was said above in Chapter VII on the duty of knowing your own business. The same principle applies to ability. No one has a right to take upon himself responsibilities of any sort, economic or otherwise, which he is clearly incapable of meeting.

BIBLIOGRAPHY

The Collegium, *Competition, A Study in Human Motive.*

Dennison, Henry S., *Ethics and Modern Business,* 1932.

Eddy, Arthur J., *The New Competition,* 4th ed., 1915.

Ethical Problems of Modern Accountancy (Vawter Lectures), 1933.

Ethical Problems of Modern Advertising (Vawter Lectures), 1931.

Ethical Problems of Modern Finance (Vawter Lectures), 1930.

Everyday Ethics (Page Lectures), 1910.

Heermance, Edgar L., *Codes of Ethics, A Handbook,* 1924.

———, *The Ethics of Business, A Study of Current Standards,* 1926.

Hobhouse, L. T., *Elements of Social Justice,* 1922.

Hobson, John A., *Economics and Ethics,* 1929.

Knight, Frank H., *The Ethics of Competition and Other Essays,* 1935. (First three papers.)

Lee, James M., *Business Ethics,* 1926.

Lord, Everett W., *The Fundamentals of Business Ethics,* 1926.

Morals in Modern Business (Page Lectures), 1909.

Stevens, W. H. S., *Unfair Competition,* 1917.

Taeusch, Carl F., *Policy and Ethics in Business,* 1931.

———, *Professional and Business Ethics,* 1926.

Tufts, James H., *America's Social Morality,* 1933. (Chapters VII–X.)

Wigmore, John H., and Kocourek, Albert, *The Rational Basis of Legal Institutions.*

Federal Trade Commission Decisions, Vols. I–XIX, 1920–1936.

Federal Trade Commission Trade Practice Conferences, 1929.

Henderson, Gerard C., *The Federal Trade Commission,* 1924.

National Industrial Conference Board, *Public Regulation of Competitive Practices,* 1929.

Nims, Harry D., *The Law of Unfair Competition and Trade Marks,* 3rd ed., 1929.

Radin, Max, *The Lawful Pursuit of Gain,* 1931.

Statutes and Decisions Pertaining to the Federal Trade Commission, 1914–1929.

INDEX

(including law cases cited or otherwise referred to)